# THE SITUATIONIST CITY

# THE SITUATIONIST CITY

*SIMON SADLER*

The MIT Press
Cambridge, Massachusetts
London, England

This book was set in Trade Gothic by The MIT Press
and was printed and bound in the United States of
America.

Library of Congress Cataloging-in-Publication Data

Sadler, Simon.
  The situationist city / Simon Sadler.
      p.    cm.
  Includes bibliographical references and index.
  ISBN 0-262-19392-2 (alk. paper)
  1. Architecture—Philosophy. 2. Avant-garde (Aesthetics)—Europe—History—20th century. 3.Internationale
situationniste—Influence. I. Title.
NA2500.S124   1998
720′.1—dc21                      97–31783
                                      CIP

*TO MY FAMILY AND FRIENDS*

# CONTENTS

## Acknowledgments

I have shamelessly invested the time, energy, and wealth of almost everyone I know (and many I don't) in the making of this book. The least I can do is thank some of them here:

Mum and Dad, for years of tea and sympathy;

Rebecca Gadd, for being fabulous;

Alexis Lachèze-Beer and Benjamin Franks, mind motivators;

Tim Benton and everyone at the Faculty of Arts at the Open University, Milton Keynes, whose patronage has enabled me to finish this book;

Everyone at The School of Theoretical and Historical Studies at the University of Central England in Birmingham, in particular my first supervisor Pauline Madge and former boss Kenneth Quickenden;

My wonderful hosts in France, Henri and Marie Lachèze, and in the Netherlands, Sabrina Dey and Harold Vreeburg;

The staff of the MIT Press, for making this book a possibility;

Those who helped me to get started— Alastair Bonnett, Andy Lowe, Sadie Plant, and David Stoker;

Lucy Forsyth, for taking an interest in my work, and likewise Jonathan Hughes;

Staff of the National Art Library at the Victoria and Albert Museum, London, in particular Simon Ford; of the Gemeentemuseum, The Hague, in particular John van der Ree, Mariette H. Josephus Jitta, Pier Terwen, and Tineke Griffiaen; of the Stedelijk Museum, Amsterdam, in particular Paul Kempers; of the Rijksbureau voor Kunsthistorische Documentatie, The Hague, in particular Marcia Zaaijer; of the Huntington Museum and Library, San Marino, in particular Alan Jutzi; of the Bibliothèque Nationale, Paris; of the Pavillon de l'Arsenal, Paris; of the British Architectural Library, RIBA, London; and of the Library at the Architectural Association, London;

Michael Webb, Peter Cook, Cedric Price, Yona Friedman, Alex Moulton, Tim Benton, Roberto Ohrt, the Louvre (Paris), Presses Universitaires de France (Paris), the Brazilian Embassy (London), and especially Constant, for their generous permission to reproduce illustrations for this book;

All at VMC Photo in Hackney, London, for their photographic wizardry;

Robert Grose, for legal advice;

R.K. and T.A., for the loan of materials;

And to anyone whom I have inadvertently omitted.

Any errors and oversights in the book are, of course, entirely my own.

### A Note on Translations

Wherever possible I have drawn upon the excellent translations of French situationist documents in Ken Knabb, ed., *Situationist International Anthology* (Berkeley: Bureau of Public Secrets, 1981), and by Thomas Y. Levin in Elisabeth Sussman, ed., *On the Passage of a Few People through a Rather Brief Moment in Time: The Situationist International, 1957–1972* (Cambridge, Mass.: MIT Press, 1989). Where no source for a translation from French is given, it is by Alexis Lachèze-Beer and myself. Harold Vreeburg interpreted documents in Dutch, and Bogislav Winner interpreted documents in German and Italian.

Any emphasis contained within a quotation is integral to the original.

### Frontispiece

*Guy Debord, "Life continues to be free and easy," c. 1959, collage of text, postage stamp, and hand-colored figures of soldiers pasted over a portion of Guy Debord and Asger Jorn's screenprint* The Naked City *(1957), Rijksbureau voor Kunsthistorische Documentatie, The Hague. Made as part of Debord's correspondence with his situationist colleague Constant, the piece was a tiny gem of situationist potlatch (art created as a gift) and détournement (art composed from "diverted" aesthetic elements). Its layering of allusions—to colonialism, war, urbanism, situationist "psychogeography" and playfulness—was dizzying.*

*THE SITUATIONIST CITY*

be
ssarily
r effec-
le have to

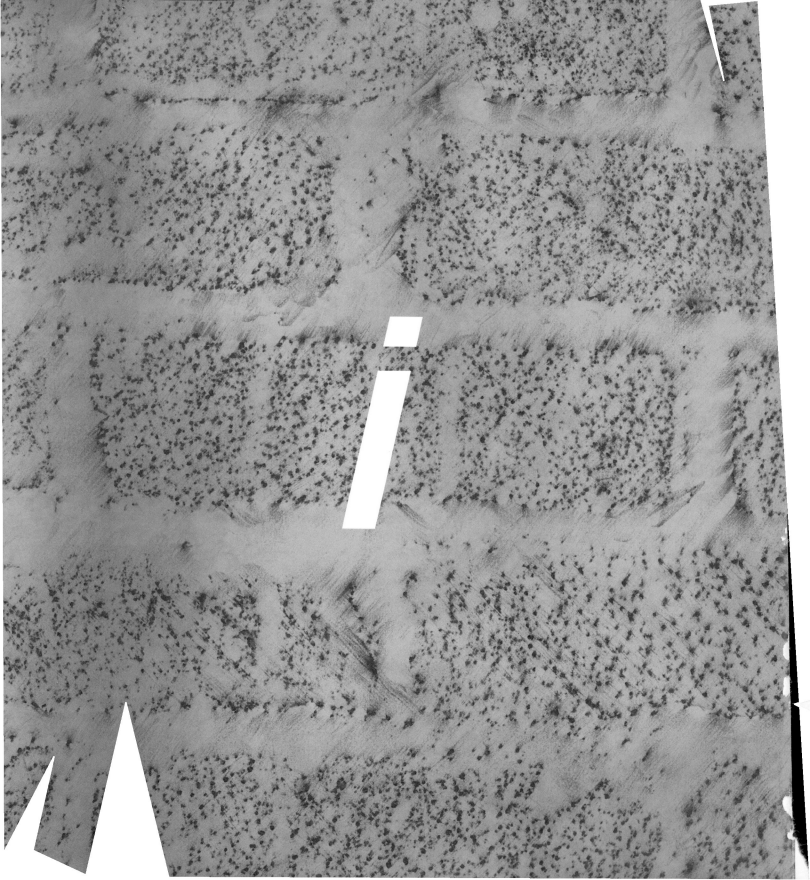

*THE SITUATIONIST CITY*

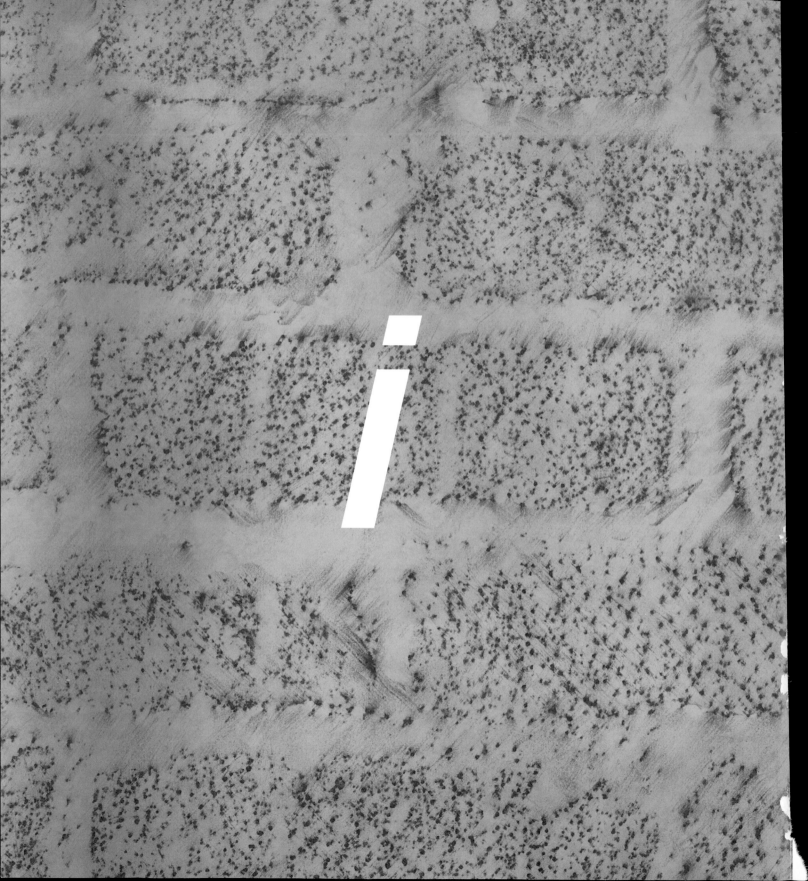

take what they can from where they can in constructing their interpretation of the world: that, surely, was one lesson of situationism.

Yes, situationism has become the subject of academic study. As Simon Ford has noted in his bibliography of *The Realization and Suppression of the Situationist International*, "The explosion of interest that erupted in 1988–1989 [in the wake of the Institute of Contemporary Arts/Centre Pompidou exhibitions on situationism] is in abeyance, but this is being replaced by a much more deeply rooted academic project; books will appear which say more and more about less and less."[4] This, frankly, is just such a book. Whereas studies so far have tended to discuss situationism within broad political and cultural contexts, this book takes perverse care in extracting situationist architectural theory from a revolutionary program that attempted to confront the ideological totality of the Western world. Situationism's broadside attack left its mark upon the libertarian left, the counterculture, the revolutionary events of 1968, and more recent phenomena from punk to postmodernism. But over time it sidelined the art theory that had been the springboard of the entire endeavor.

And so, paradoxically, the focus of this book upon issues of art and design may serve to deepen and widen understanding of situationism. That is its unashamed aim. I have tried to keep it concise in the hope that readers may reach the end. I have tried to locate situationism in history, where it belongs: the sooner that historians have completed the autopsy and preservation of situationism, the sooner others can make something new from its corpus. The air of mystique about situationism, now the reek of decay, has outlived its purpose, to the extent that it ever had one. One is not even meant to use the word "situationism": "There is no such thing as situationism, which would mean a doctrine of interpretation of existing facts," the situationist journal *Internationale situationniste* declared in its first edition. "The notion of situationism is obviously devised by antisituationists."[5]

Of course, situationists knew full well that there was such a thing as situationism, just as anyone with a critical hold on their practice realizes that it is subject to certain parameters, ideologies, and methodologies. There has to be some way of verbally demarcating whatever it was that the situationists thought they were doing by being situationists. The situationists' caution about a "situationism" was a clever way of reminding themselves of the dangers of becoming "academic" in their procedures, a fate that had befallen their avant-garde predecessors, the surrealists, "policed" as they were by their spokesman André Breton. But as a way of throwing academics off the scent forty years later—well, no tactic could be more misguided than denying the existence of situationism. Academics are precisely the people with the time and inclination to unravel such riddles.

I reserve for academics my apology for the reductionist tactics of this book. I have concentrated on the earlier phase of situationism, when art, architecture, design, and urbanism were still primary concerns for the movement. I have suppressed the considerable differences among the avant-garde groups that contributed to situationism, instead drawing out their common ground. And I have claimed this common ground for situationism because the nexus of ideas that I want to explore in this book was almost completely formulated in the decade before the Situationist International finally inaugurated it as a program. Subsequently I have chosen to identify the people who formulated these ideas as "situationists." To find another name for people whose ideas were clearly so important to the formation of the Situationist International seems unnecessarily cumbersome, though readers should constantly bear in mind that officially there was no such thing as a fully fledged "situationist" before 1957 (fig. 0.1).

### The poverty of modernism

The inauguration of the Situationist International was rather inauspicious. In July 1957 eight delegates, "in a state of semi-drunkenness," met in a remote bar in Italy.[6] The delegates represented two key groups: the International Movement for an Imaginist Bauhaus, and the Lettrist International. A third "group," the London Psychogeographical Association, was represented by its only known member, Ralph Rumney.[7]

This was a fruitful conjugation of rather odd bedfellows. The Lettrist International (1952–1957), dominated by Guy Debord, was inclined toward the minimal and conceptual rather than the visual.[8] In contrast, the founder of the Imaginist Bauhaus (1954–1957), Asger Jorn, preferred a hands-on, expressionist approach to the production of art. The Lettrist International was specifically urban, grounded in Paris, while Imaginist Bauhaus activity, located in the provincial Italian towns of Albisola and Alba, became physically removed from the metropolis.

Yet both strands were highly politicized at a time when it was fashionable for avant-gardes to disengage from notions of social revolution. The will to keep expressive social revolution at the core of the avant-garde project had preoccupied Jorn's *alma mater*, the pan-European COBRA group of artists and writers (1948–1951). COBRA, an acronym of Copenhagen, Brussels, and Amsterdam, was a common front of groups from those cities, and their thought was a formative influence upon situationism; for example, Constant Nieuwenhuys (or plain "Constant," as he preferred to be called), another leading light of COBRA, joined Jorn as a founding member of the Situationist International.[9] COBRA's political and artistic unruliness was a gesture against the regulation of politics and art, a refusal of both socialist realism and abstraction, the artistic "house styles" of the cold war (fig. 0.2). In Paris, meanwhile, Guy

**Figure 0.2**

*Constant,* A nous la liberté *(To us, liberty), 1949, oil on canvas, Tate Gallery, London. The painting, which typically for a COBRA work combined figurative and abstractive elements, was later retitled* Après nous la liberté *(After us, liberty) in protest against the stasis of postwar politics. Constant's immersion in situationism later led him to virtually abandon painting in favor of architecture, while retaining the sense of playful energy apparent in his COBRA period.*

Debord led the Lettrist International away from its parent, the Lettrist Group (founded 1946), in a conscious attempt to politicize lettrism's esoteric exploration of language.

A copy of the Lettrist International's gloriously low-budget review of politics and art, *Potlatch*, was passed to Jorn in 1954. Hereupon the friendship between the Lettrist International and the International Movement for an Imaginist Bauhaus, and between Debord and Jorn in particular, was cemented by correspondence, copublications, and exchanges of personnel, although it was largely by default that the issue of design found itself at the center of a program to revolutionize the practices of art and life. None of the main players in the formation of situationism were designers or architects by profession, and precious few showed any real ability in the area as it was traditionally defined. In 1954 the architect and designer Ettore Sottsass, Jr., already a rising star, was drawn into the Imaginist Bauhaus, only to leave three years later in disbelief at the situationist movement's increasing aggression and lack of professionalism.[10] "A movement formed by geniuses like you and your French friends is out of my depth," he wrote sarcastically in his resignation note to Jorn.[11] It was an attitude that mattered not one jot to those who remained loyal to situationism. The benign professionalism of architecture and design had, in their opinion, led to a sterilization of the world that threatened to wipe out any sense of spontaneity or playfulness.

Situationists hankered instead after the "pioneer spirit" of modernism. They were nostalgic for a time when artists, architects, and designers had pursued disparate, open-ended experiments; for a time when the conditions of modern life—above all, the relationship between "man and machine"—had been addressed head-on; for a time when fundamental shifts in thought, like those engendered by Marx, Freud, and Nietzsche, still felt fresh and vital; and for a time when general revolution was

**Figure 0.3**

*"Maximum and normal horizontal work surfaces," illustration from Raoul Vaneigem, "Commentaires contre l'urbanisme,"* Internationale situationniste, *no. 6 (1961). The diagram, used as an example of design's rationalization and reification of the body, was derived from U.S. industrial designer Henry Dreyfuss's ergonomic and anthropometric studies.*

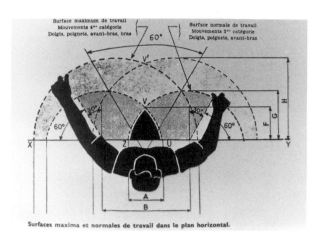

regarded as necessary, even inevitable. The situationists were hazy about the precise dates of this golden age, but they assimilated a cornucopia of sources—from the arts and crafts movement and the Deutscher Werkbund to expressionism, cubism, futurism, constructivism, De Stijl, the Bauhaus, dadaism, and surrealism.

The situationists were acutely aware of the task bequeathed them by such august predecessors: "there has been a notable progression from futurism through dadaism and surrealism to the movements formed after 1945," Debord announced to the founding meeting of the Situationist International. But he warned his audience that "at each of these stages . . . one discovers the same totalistic will for change; and the same rapid crumbling away when the inability to change the world profoundly enough leads to a defensive withdrawal."[12] The pioneer avant-gardes seemed either to have become self-critical to the point of virtual dissolution, like dadaism and surrealism, or to have abandoned programs of outright revolution in order to procure patronage.[13]

This, situationists believed, had been the fate of the modern movement in architecture and design. Sometime in the 1920s, at the Bauhaus, in the pages of Le Corbusier's modernist manifestos, and through the 1928 foundation of the Congrès Internationaux d'Architecture Moderne (International Congress of Modern Architecture), the modern movement had cleaned up its image, systematically sidelining unruly and eccentric

expressionisms in favor of a "functional," "rational" program for universal clean living (fig. 0.3). Functionalism and mass production, once embraced as ways of delivering innovative "good design" to the masses, seemed to have gradually merged with the productivist values of capitalism and state communism, workers remaining appendages to the machine rather than its masters.

*Internationale situationniste* assessed the legacy of functionalism:

**Its positive contributions—the adaptation to practical functions, technical innovation, comfort, the banishment of superimposed ornament—are today banalities. Yet although its field of application is, when all is said and done, narrow, this has not led functionalism to adopt a relative theoretical modesty. In order to justify philosophically the extension of its principles of renovation to the entire organization of social life, functionalism has fused, seemingly without a thought, with the most static conservative doctrines (and, simultaneously, has itself congealed into an inert doctrine).[14]**

*Figure 0.4*

Modern movement rationalism, rooted in the belief that the problems of the real world could be resolved by reason, had started out as a deeply humanist project, championed by the left and dedicated to the fostering of social progress and democracy. But for situationism, this sort of progress had come at an unacceptable price. Rationalism had insisted that collective interest take priority over individual interest. Situationist radicals felt differently: genuine social progress did not subsume the individual, but maximized his or her freedom and potential.

COBRA artists despised the rationalist grid, so beloved by Piet Mondrian and Le Corbusier, as a metaphor for the regulative practices of the state. In 1948 Constant compared it to the "objective, abstracting spirit of the bourgeois world," and Christian Dotremont related it five years later to "the order which rules in Warsaw" (fig. 0.4).[15] The triumph of reason had left no space for imagination or expression: writing in the first edition of COBRA's journal, Michel Colle mourned the disappearance of expressionist and surrealist tendencies in architecture, complaining that, under "the pretext of putting a little order and discipline back into architectural expression," Le Corbusier and his allies had instituted an architecture of "right angles" and "cadaverous rigidity."[16] In Colle's judgment, the rationalization of the environment was having the very opposite effect upon mass consciousness from that once promised by the *Gestalt* and behavioral theories of the modern movement.

Colle noted "the state of total and passive submission" experienced by "the man in the street placed before the architectural phenomenon," and he felt that the Corbusian concept of the functional "machine for living in," rather than liberating the common man, was interring him as a component of functionalist society. "We have been given the machine for living in, where very often nothing is sacrificed to the only truly human parts of life, to poetry and to dream. There is worse: for our intransigent rationalists, a residential building can be nothing other than the superimposition of four, ten, any number of linked machines for living in. . . . The ambiance is overwhelming: at the end of his day, man quits his factory for working in for his factory for eating and sleeping in."[17]

As a dramatic reversal of this contemptible domestic Taylorism, Günther Feuerstein submitted his 1960 proposals for "impractical flats" to SPUR, the German section of the Situationist International.[18] By declining labor-saving devices, devising tortuous routes through his apartment, and fitting it with noisy doors and useless locks,

Feuerstein refused to allow his own home to become another cog in the mechanized world. It would no longer protect him from the environment nor the sensations of his own body: ripping out his air conditioning and throwing open his windows, he could swelter, shiver, and struggle to hear himself think above the roar of the city; later he might bump and hurt himself against one of the myriad sharp corners in his flat, and sit at his wobbly table and on his uncomfortable sofa. Or he might unwind by throwing paint against the walls and drilling holes through them, filling out his flat with traces of his own ideas and history.

And so situationism took over the negotiations between reason and imagination, and between the individual and the social, that André Breton had once tried to pursue with Le Corbusier, when Breton had proffered his opinion to Le Corbusier that modernist functionalism was "the most unhappy dream of the collective unconscious," a "solidification of desire in a most violent and cruel automatism."[19] Although the impact of rationalism on building production between the wars had invariably been controversial and relatively limited, at least outside France, Holland, and Germany, a new generation of modern movement zealots was emerging after the Second World War. Rationalism's transcultural aspirations had been clear ever since Henry-Russell Hitchcock and Philip Johnson titled their classic 1932 survey of modern architecture *The International Style*, and as postwar European reconstruction got underway, the "International Style" was poised to live up to its name, becoming the paradigm of successive schools of architecture and public planning departments throughout Europe and the United States.[20]

Perhaps the most radical of the schools was that planned by the Swiss sculptor Max Bill, an ex-Bauhaus student and publisher of the third volume of Le Corbusier's *Oeuvre complète*.[21] In 1953, Bill approached Asger Jorn, interned in a tuberculosis sanatorium with his ex-COBRA colleague Christian Dotremont, offering work at his "new Bauhaus," the Hochschule für Gestaltung at Ulm, Germany. Bill would rue the day he made the offer, since Jorn, who had worked in Le Corbusier's studio in 1937–1938 (executing mural decoration for the Pavillon des Temps Nouveaux), seized the opportunity to renew the debate with rationalism. The overtly rationalist, even technocratic syllabus planned by Bill sparked an antagonistic debate between the two men during 1954, spilling over from private correspondence into the very public arena of the Tenth Triennale of Industrial Design in Milan.[22]

Jorn's summary of his dispute with Bill—in three lines, extracted from their correspondence in early 1954—illustrated well the situationist struggle to retrieve the pioneer spirit of the modern movement. "Bauhaus is the name of an artistic inspiration," Jorn wrote to Bill. "Bauhaus is not the name of an artistic inspiration," Bill replied, "but the meaning of a movement that represents a well-defined doctrine." "If Bauhaus is not the name of an artistic inspiration, it is the name of a doctrine without inspiration—that is to say, dead," Jorn concluded.[23] Jorn accused Bill of misrepresenting the ideals of the original Bauhaus in order to guarantee the continued status of rationalism and functionalism as modernist paradigms. As Jorn pointed out, expressionist tendencies had been eminently represented at the Bauhaus, and rationalism had only been the passing outcome of an ongoing artistic experiment, artificially terminated when the Nazis closed the school in 1933.[24]

If Bill's Bauhaus couldn't accommodate alternatives to rationalism, then Jorn's would. By 1955 Jorn's International Movement for an Imaginist Bauhaus had set up shop as a new meeting place for fringe and dissident artists, at the studio of artist Giuseppe Pinot-Gallizio in Alba, Italy. Max Bill's resignation from Ulm was announced the following year "with pleasure" by *Potlatch*, which had been monitoring Jorn's mission for two years.[25] Supplemented by various theoretical writings of 1955–1956, the debate with Bill provided a nucleus for Jorn's sprawling situationist treatise *Pour la forme: ébauche d'une méthodologie des arts* (In defense of form: outline of a methodology for the arts), published by the Situationist International in 1958.[26]

Situationism was not quite alone in its thoroughgoing reassessment of modernism. The American urban historian Lewis Mumford, for example, had been a severe critic of urban technological culture since the 1920s, influencing not only the situationists but many professional planners and architects as well. But his solutions, founded upon his admiration of the garden city principles of Ebenezer Howard,

were antithetical to the crackling urban energies embraced by the young guns of situationism. The big city was about to gain one of its greatest advocates in Jane Jacobs, whose passion for metropolitan life and despair with the planners and architects meddling with it were all the more impressive for being less highly strung than situationist writings; her book *The Death and Life of Great American Cities* was published in 1961.[27] For the time being, situationist sensibilities were most akin to those of the young British artists and theorists gathered around the Independent Group, which met from 1952 to 1955 as a forum for avant-garde discussion at London's Institute of Contemporary Arts (ICA), and which affected ICA policy for a decade or more to come.

In many ways it seems a relatively short hop from the positions staked out by situationism to the Independent Group and its associated architectural pressure group Team 10. The Situationist International cheekily used the ICA's Dover Street building as its London address.[28] Ralph Rumney, a founding member of the SI, was an ICA regular—in his "psychogeographical report" on Venice, he related his exaggerated horror at coming across the "Dover Street playboy," former Independent Group convener Lawrence Alloway, on the Rialto Bridge.[29] When it expelled Rumney, the Situationist International lost its direct link with the ICA, though it enjoyed the presence in London of its ally, the Scottish writer Alexander Trocchi, whose Project Sigma campaigned for a British version of the Imaginist Bauhaus. The Situationist International held its conference in

**Figure 0.5**

*Le Corbusier, Villa Stein, Garches, France, 1927. The building, one of Le Corbusier's "machines for living in" and an icon of rationalism, was still the subject of considerable discussion among architects in the late 1940s and early 1950s.*

London in 1960, taking the opportunity to attend a meeting about situationism at the ICA, chaired by former Independent Group member Toni del Renzio.

For both the situationists and the Independent Group, the International Style's pretensions to represent the universal truth of technology were now history. As the plaster rendering cracked on Le Corbusier's 1927 Villa Stein, the likes of Independent Group architects James Stirling and Alison and Peter Smithson and Independent Group historian Reyner Banham were confronted by the plain evidence that a modern movement icon had been built by bricklayers, not machines (fig. 0.5).[30] Rationalism was not quite as rational as was once thought: its so-called "machine aesthetic" was really a fashion, not a necessity. *Potlatch* called it a "neo-cubist crust" or "scab," offering a withering review of the trend among young French rationalists to "daub" their buildings with color.[31] The mere abandonment of the whiteness considered *de rigeur* by interwar rationalism did not redress the architecture's propensity to deteriorate, nor disguise the "spiritual and creative poverty" of "the daubers," "their lack of plain humanity."[32] For both situationists and Independents, it was time to discover some new truth that might replace the dishonesty of rationalism.

And similar routes out of the impasse occurred to both. They agreed that it was time to rediscover the original impulses of modernism. Jorn recognized the worth of modernism's humanist impulse to obtain "a true ambiance, created to the measure of man"[33] through the unification of the

arts under the umbrella of architecture, while Alison and Peter Smithson blamed the demise of modernism not upon its pioneers but upon the lumpen mass of followers. Indeed, Le Corbusier himself seemed to be revising the principles of modern architecture in light of the excesses of rationalism, anticipating the spirit of "informality" that characterized many of the postwar avant-gardes, from COBRA and abstract expressionism to the so-called *art autre* (other art).[34] The informal architectural approach proposed by the Smithsons, dubbed the "new brutalism," could be recognized stylistically by its uncompromising exploration of the structures and textures of modern architecture; but it aspired as well to a much larger humanist agenda, addressing not just architecture but culture at large. Jorn's demand that modern building should express "a source of poetic sensation" now found an analogue in new brutalist manifestoes: "Brutalism," the Smithsons wrote in 1957, "tries to face up to a mass-production society, and drag a rough poetry out of the confused and powerful forces which are at work."[35] The happy suggestion was that the postwar world of mass production and mass society actually harbored all sorts of diversions from pure rationality, both in architecture and in everyday life. Situationist and Independent Group interest in mass culture was exemplified in a neo-dadaist sentimentality about everyday objects, a fascination with advertisements and magazines, a desire to intervene in fashion, a recognition of popular music as a valid culture, and attentiveness to unplanned places, buildings designed without architects, and industrial design.

By the late fifties, indeed, interest in the everyday life, space, and culture of the masses was mushrooming in British and American pop art and in French *nouveau réalisme,* though rarely in as serious and confrontational a way as the situationists would have liked (fig. 1.3). COBRA and the Imaginist Bauhaus had always appreciated the connection between their anarchic critique of rationalism and the politics of the hard left, and Debord and the Lettrist International pushed for the formulation of a full-blown revolutionary pro-

gram addressing the culture of everyday life. In 1956 the Lettrist International sent Gil J. Wolman to Alba, to attend the "First World Congress of Free Artists." Organized by the Imaginist Bauhaus, the grandly named World Congress boasted no more than a dozen delegates, but crucially it found the common ground "relative to urbanism and to the uses to which it can be put" that would unify the Situationist International the following year.[36] In short, the Situationist International aimed to convert avant-garde interest in everyday space and mass culture into a revolution.

There was an urgency in all of this. The Parisian built environment had not encountered a stylistic revolution as authoritative as modernism since the Renaissance, and the Lettrist International, sensing that modernism's functionalist and rationalist tentacles were about to squeeze its Left Bank bohemia to death, insisted that politico-artistic struggle be played out at the ultimate level—that of the city itself. "Political economy, love, and urbanism are the means that we must command for the resolution of a problem that is above all of an ethical order," the Lettrist International announced, as it busied itself with creating a framework for direct intervention in the human environment.[37] Between 1954 and 1956 *Potlatch* introduced its readers to the nexus of ideas that this book explores: *psychogéographie* ("psychogeography"), *détournement* ("diversion"), *dérive* ("drift"), *situations* ("situations"), and *urbanisme unitaire* ("unitary urbanism").[38]

For a fuller picture of the revolutionary politics of the Situationist International, readers should consult other literature on situationism, and, of course, the movement's own texts. But in this book I concentrate on the early situationist program and so try to save it from the obscurity to which it was later banished by the Situationist International—in 1964 Debord was openly embarrassed by "the fantasies left over from the old artistic milieu."[39] Contradictions in the Situationist International's artistic program had occasionally been admitted to until, in the early 1960s, situationist "hard-liners" demanded that such contradictions be resolved. "There is no such thing as 'situationism' or a situationist work of art," Raoul Vaneigem declared in 1962, shortly after joining the movement. "Our position is that of combatants between two worlds—one that we don't acknowledge, the other that does not yet exist."[40] No longer would the Situationist International tolerate prerevolutionary attempts to design the architectural form, or indeed any form, of postrevolutionary society. The intensely critical turn that situationist theory took after the first few editions of *Internationale situationniste* effectively terminated the direct situationist interest in art and urbanism, leaving Constant's amazing vision—of the situationist city as a "New Babylon"—out in the cold.

In any case, it seemed that the Situationist International quickly lost control of its architectural theory, which seeped into various avant-garde attempts to reinvent modernism as "structuralism," "experimental architecture," and "anti-design." Even though some of the "old artistic milieu" rallied in 1962 as the Second Situationist International, its journal *The Situationist Times* showed little interest in the building of the situationist city. The Second Situationist International returned to the countryside, building its base in a Swedish farmhouse which it proclaimed as the "Situationist Bauhaus."[41]

## The organization of this book

This book considers situationist design theory in three main parts. Situationism was predicated upon a critique of the environment as it currently existed, and this critique is outlined in the first part, "The Naked City." The second part, "Formulary for a New Urbanism," examines situationist principles for the city and for city living; and part three, "A New Babylon," describes the designs actually proposed for the situationist city.

I hope that this makes the book fairly easy to follow. But in case it settles readers' ideas about situationism too much, I end this introduction by siding with my imaginary Pro-situ detractors. Early situationism was never quite as containable as this book might make it seem. When the word "situationist" was first published, *Potlatch* insisted that "in their final development, the collective constructions that please us are only possible after the disappearance of bourgeois society, of its distribution of products, and of its moral values."[42] Situationism was founded upon the belief that general revolution would originate in the appropriation and alteration of the material environment and its space. Activities that have not shared this aim have a poor claim to being situationist: that this book could provoke a round of dilettante "situation constructing" in schools of art and architecture is a prospect too dreadful to contemplate.

And if in taking this stance I seem to be treating my subject a little too seriously, I ought to contrast it with the sublime attitude of situationists themselves. Architecture featured in Guy Debord's earliest writings for the Lettrist International and in his last film, *Guy Debord: son art et son temps* (1994).[43] At the beginning of his career, architecture seemed to Debord to be bursting with revolutionary potential, but at the end he represented it as if its possibilities had tragically expired. Even the removal of the excesses of modernism, the film noted, has become a meaningless spectacle, with stage show demolitions of the high-rise estates in which a generation of working-class people had been interred. Debord, inevitably a central figure in this study, apparently took his own life shortly after completing the film, dying with the same charisma that he enjoyed when living.[44]

# REALITIES OF DESIGN AND SPACE LAID BARE

### Nurturing the "real life" of the city

One only appreciated the desperate need to take action over the city, situationists felt, once one had seen through the veil of refinement draped over it by planning and capital. If one peeled away this official representation of modernity and urbanism—this "spectacle," as situationists termed the collapse of reality into the streams of images, products, and activities sanctioned by business and bureaucracy—one discovered the authentic life of the city teeming underneath.[1]

It was this sense of the spectacle as the barrier, rather than the gateway, between the avantgarde and the making of a better world that straightaway put situationism at odds with comparable avant-garde attitudes. Some members of Britain's Independent Group, for instance, argued that mass consumption and the capitalist spectacle were things that intellectuals would simply have to come to terms with if they were to appreciate the revolution of space taking place in the electric city. In his 1959 "City Notes," Independent Group ex-

convener Lawrence Alloway started out in apparent accord with situationism by refuting the idealism of the rationally planned city. "Nowhere are 'permanent' formal principles less likely to survive intact," Alloway reckoned, "than in the crowded, solid city. . . . The past, the present, and the future . . . overlap in a messy configuration. Architects can never get and keep control of all the factors in a city which exist in the dimensions of patched-up, expendable, and developing forms."[2] Yet Alloway reached conclusions diametrically opposed to those of situationism, complaining that the only problem with the spectacle of London's electrically billboarded Piccadilly Circus was its inferiority to equivalent American displays. "Related to the neon spectacle," Alloway enthused, "are other aspects of the popular environment," such as "the LP environment at airports, restaurants, bars, and hotel lounges, of light and long-lived pop music that extends radio and TV sound outside the house and into a larger environment."[3]

For situationists, such phenomena were little more than the untrustworthy glamorization of state and corporate power, unrelated to the requirements of ordinary people and their more fully lived lives. "Many techniques do more or less markedly alter aspects of everyday life: the domestic arts . . . also the telephone, television, the recording of music on long-playing records, mass air travel, etc.," Guy Debord admitted in 1961. "But on the whole this introduction of technology into everyday life—ultimately taking place within the framework of

**Figure 1.1**

*"Tonight, the spectacle at home," "Unconscious advertising," illustration from* Internationale situationniste, *no. 8 (1963). Situationists recognized in television an explosion in the power of the "spectacle" of modernity sufficient to affect the perception of real space.*

modern bureaucratized capitalism—certainly tends rather to reduce people's independence and creativity. The new prefabricated cities clearly exemplify the totalitarian tendency of modern capitalism's organization of life: the isolated inhabitants . . . see their lives reduced to the pure triviality of the repetitive combined with the obligatory absorption of an equally repetitive spectacle."[4] Dumbstruck by the condition of modern Paris, Debord drew on a speech from *Macbeth* to endow his critique of the spectacular city with the proper sense of tragedy: "from any standpoint other than that of police control, Haussmann's Paris is a city built by an idiot, full of sound and fury, signifying nothing."[5] Situationists Attila Kotányi and Raoul Vaneigem described more recent attempts at urbanism and its associated spectacle as "nothingness"—"Urbanism is comparable to the advertising propagated around Coca-Cola—pure spectacular ideology"—while *Internationale situationniste* provided case studies of the way in which the spectacle had even invaded the bleak new social housing programs.[6] The estates had been used as locations for fashion shoots and for the testing of prefabricated plastic "bistro-clubs," "a seductive showcase" designed, the journal claimed, "as an instrument of supplementary control on the way to the total surveillance of production and consumption," even accommodating rising youth delinquency. "The candidly avowed recourse to the aesthetics of the shop window is perfectly illuminated by the theory of the spectacle: in the de-alcoholized bars, the consumers themselves become spectacular."[7] The new estates were experimental spaces for the refinement of the electronic spectacle, "atomized to the extreme around each television receiver, but at the same time stretched to the exact dimension of towns" (fig. 1.1).[8]

Vaneigem refused to distinguish the urbanism of communist and capitalist states: "Urbanism and information are complementary in both capitalist and 'anti-capitalist' societies; they organize silence." In both the East and the West, he claimed, "the ideal urbanism is the projection in space of a social hierarchy without conflict. Roads, lawns, natural flowers, and artificial forests lubricate the workings of subjection and render them amicable." It had to be understood that urbanism regulated the body and mind as well as architecture. "In a novel by Yves Touraine," Vaneigem recalled, "the State even offers retired workers an electronic masturbator; economy and happiness find themselves complete."[9]

Situationists never denied that the city of power and capital was seductive. It had fascinated avant-gardes before them, from the impressionists

Figure 1.2

Page from Asger Jorn with Guy Debord, Fin de Copenhague, 1957, sceenprinted book. The book, purportedly collaged together after a single trip to a Copenhagen newsstand, lampooned the experience of modernity.

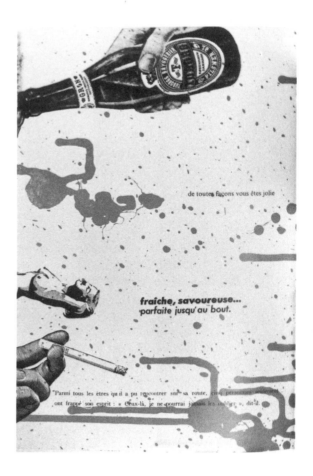

to the futurists. But situationists insisted that the spectacle was merely a manufactured wonderment, a hype that concealed real processes of exploitation. Situationists noted the apparent blunting of class awareness in the West at large (by 1956 there were more white-collar than blue-collar workers) amidst the economic expansion fueled by Marshall aid in Europe and the Monnet Plan in France, growth that massively increased the average worker's purchasing power for consumer goods and leisure.[10] But the result was an increase in a standard of living only narrowly defined, situationists argued. Asger Jorn and Guy Debord satirized the empty heart of the spectacle in their 1957 book *Fin de Copenhague* (End of Copenhagen), collaged from newspapers and magazines collected on a single visit to a Danish newsstand (fig. 1.2), providing a pointed contrast with Richard Hamilton's famous Independent Group collage from the previous year, *Just What Is It That Makes Today's Homes So Different, So Appealing . . . ?* (fig. 1.3).[11] Hamilton, tongue only just in cheek, celebrated the consumer spectacle and its future, whereas Jorn and Debord were optimistic as to its *fin*, its end and supersession. In *Fin de Copenhague* Jorn and Debord gave the spectacle just enough rope to hang itself by, presupposing that a critique of "spectacular" society was already present within the language of that society.

This was the situationist technique of *détournement* in action. *Détournement* can be translated most simply as "diversion," though at

the loss of the nuances encoded in the original French—"rerouting," "hijacking," "embezzlement," "misappropriation," "corruption," all acts implicit in the situationist use of society's "preexisting aesthetic elements."[12] Taking their cue from the wayward nineteenth-century French writer Isodore Ducasse (the "Comte du Lautréamont"), who had insisted "Plagiarism is necessary. Progress implies it," the situationists looked forward to a new "people's aesthetic" built out of the ruins of the spectacle. Jorn and Debord tried to show the way in their collaborative collages. Western capitalism, they realized, was taking a risk by dangling the

**Figure 1.3**

Richard Hamilton, Just What Is It That Makes Today's Homes So Different, So Appealing?, *1956, collage, Kunsthalle, Tübingen. Hamilton's famous image testified, like Debord and Jorn's* Fin de Copenhague, *to the impact of consumerism upon Western Europe.*

spectacle under people's noses. What if spectators transgressed the rules of consumerism by stealing and redistributing its products and images, for themselves, making good its vacuous promises of a better world? As a page of *Fin de Copenhague* read, "Whatever you want, it's coming your way—plus greater leisure for enjoying it all. With electronics, automation, and nuclear energy, we are entering on a new Industrial Revolution which will supply our every need, easily . . . quickly . . . cheaply . . . abundantly," an affirmation that quickly dissolved into a veiled threat that spectacular leisure and technology had already been earmarked by the situationists for "détourned," revolutionary use: "and *voilà*, your life is transformed! WORDS TAKE ON A NEW SENSE."[13]

By 1963 the Situationist International was declaring its intention "to negate 'Pop Art' (which is materially and 'ideologically' characterized by *indifference* & dull complacency)."[14] Yet many overlapping shades of opinion remained between the apparent polar opposites of the "pop" Independent Group and "militant" situationists. The Independent Group, never more than a discussion group, had been even less capable of presenting a homogeneous front than the situationists. Despite the exclamatory tone of its title, the famous 1956 manifesto of Alison and Peter Smithson—"But Today We Collect Ads"—shared little of their Independent Group colleague Richard Hamilton's unconditional enthusiasm for commercial art.[15] Indeed, in all their writings the

Smithsons came across in rather the same way as Guy Debord or Raoul Vaneigem—intellectuals who, if not quite of the old school, retained much of its arrogance, and its belief that the intelligentsia still had a central role to play in the shaping of society. Sink or swim: one either stayed abreast of "popular culture" by collecting its ads, or popular culture would engulf any contribution one had to make as architect or revolutionary.

These more aloof elements of the Independent Group and situationism shared a determination to penetrate the outward, spectacular, commercialized signs of mass culture and explore its interior. There one examined the everyday patterns of life, in particular people's use of buildings and urban space, a version of popular culture as "folk"-based rather than commercially based that was in keeping with the mood of new sociologies.[16] In Britain, "conscience-stricken middle-class intellectuals" had been permanently affected by the findings of Mass Observation, the major survey of working-class behavior carried out in the 1930s and 1940s, and the Smithsons were familiar with the sort of street-level studies that would lead to the publication of Michael Young and Peter Willmott's seminal *Family and Kinship in East London* (1957).[17] On the Continent, meanwhile, sociological thought was being profoundly affected by the work of the French Marxist Henri Lefebvre. The influence of his *Critique de la vie quotidienne* (Critique of everyday life), published 1946, was imported into COBRA by Christian Dotremont, and

**Figure 1.4**

*"Patterns of Association and Identity" (detail), collage of Nigel Henderson photographs of children playing in London's East End, arranged by Alison and Peter Smithson for the* CIAM Grille *(1953), later reproduced in* Uppercase 3 *(1961) and* Urban Structuring *(1967). The Smithsons used the photographs as reminders to architects of the supposed vitality of working-class street life, an attitude that had resonances with situationism.*

then into the Situationist International by Debord, Michèle Bernstein, and Vaneigem.[18] Debord was also fascinated by the dramatic urban social geography of Paul-Henri Chombart de Lauwe, who published his revealing *Paris et l'agglomération parisienne* (Paris and the Parisian agglomeration) in 1952.

Such sociologies led to a heightened awareness of the real social structuring of the city, of the complex way in which cities are divided into distinct quarters, based on class occupation or function, self-contained yet reliant upon other components in the urban machine. Of course, city planners and administrators were well aware that cities are subdivided, and indeed that they had to be if they were to function efficiently. But sociology now implied that traditional planning, which had grown up under a rationalist umbrella, reduced the intricacy of city structuring to fallaciously simplistic levels. In page after page, Chombart de Lauwe's dissection of Paris revealed mind-boggling subtleties in the uses and characteristics of the city, which were, moreover, subject to change over time. Young and Willmott meanwhile illustrated self-managed patterns of social association within a single working-class area of London—Bethnal Green—that had taken generations to develop, and a few years for planners to destroy.

The broad sweeps of the rationalist imagination, which had aspired to tailor the city with Cartesian precision, suddenly looked like butchery. Debord, Jorn, and the Smithsons alike sought ways

of illustrating and addressing the social ecology of the city, professing an empathy with the habitual behavior of the city's lowly. The Smithsons borrowed photographs of children playing in the streets of Bethnal Green, snapped by their Independent Group colleague Nigel Henderson, to demonstrate "patterns of association and identity" (fig. 1.4).[19] The situationists, who seem to have had difficulties getting on with "everyday" citizens, preferred to experiment on themselves, analyzing the factors affecting their mood, behavior, and choice of route as they wandered their "drift" (*dérive*) through the city.

Situationists and Independents felt that indigenous living patterns were best nurtured through the "clustering" of the city.[20] In 1956 and 1957 Debord and Jorn cut up street maps of Paris, in the process identifying some indigenous working-class zones worthy of study and preservation pending the formulation of anything superior (fig. 1.5). The Smithsons, never ones to underrate their own abilities, felt that they had already hit upon something better than the working-class quarter

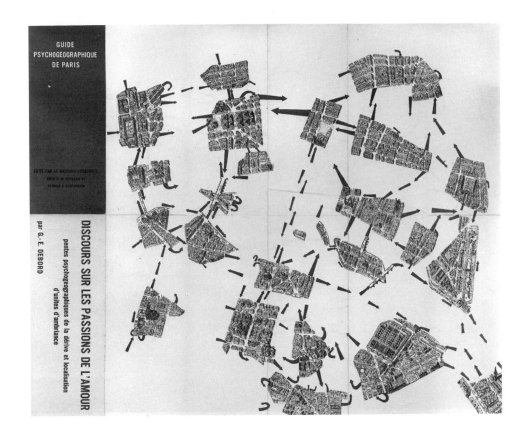

**Figure 1.5**

*Guy Debord with Asger Jorn,* Guide psychogéographique de
Paris: discours sur les passions de l'amour, *1956, screenprinted map. The map was collaged from the* Plan de Paris
à vol d'oiseau *(1956), a magnificent perspectival rendering
of the city (fig. 2.16). The publication of the* Guide *was
soon followed by another Debord and Jorn psychogeographic map of Paris,* The Naked City *(fig. 1.32).*

**Figure 1.6**

*Peter Smithson,* Cluster City, *1952, reprinted in*
Uppercase 3 *(1961). Alison and Peter Smithson regarded
the cluster model as empathetic to the complex indigenous lifestyles of the city. Its pattern was like an echo of
the situationist "drift" through the city, and it anticipated
the plan of New Babylon, the situationist city designed by
Constant (cf. fig. 1.12).*

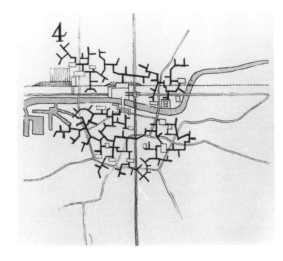

**Figure 1.7**

Le Corbusier, Unité d'Habitation, near Marseilles, 1947–1952. The Unité was the touchstone of modern architecture in the decade after the Second World War, mellowing rationalism and trying to compress the various functions of the city—residence, commerce, and leisure—into a single block.

"as found." In sketches from 1952, Peter Smithson developed Le Corbusier's 1930s projects for the linkage of housing blocks into seamless wholes, and when he and his wife entered the 1952 competition to redevelop working-class housing in the Golden Lane area of the City of London, they presented the "cluster" as a megastructural web (fig. 1.6). Individual dwellings and, by an architectural leap of logic, individual inhabitants, would be jelled together into an organic whole.

In the 1950s the Smithsons, who found work difficult to come by, and the situationists, the most marginal of all the marginal avant-gardes, must have realized that there was little chance of reforming the entrenched interests of those rationalist architects and planners who were restructuring cities throughout the world. Instead they targeted the unsound theoretical foundations of that restructuring, codified in the 1930s and more than due for revision.

## Beyond the rational city

By far the most influential codification of rationalist planning was the 1933 Athens Charter, the lengthy manifesto issued by the official representative body of modernist architecture worldwide: the Congrès Internationaux d'Architecture Moderne, better known simply as CIAM. Drafted by CIAM delegates pondering "The Functional City" during a sea cruise from Marseilles to Athens, the Charter was splendidly isolated from urban reality, managing to be both dogmatic and generalized in its clauses. As Reyner Banham summarized it, the "persuasive generality which gave the Athens Charter its air of universal applicability concealed a very narrow conception of both architecture and town planning and committed CIAM unequivocally to: (a) rigid functional zoning of city plans, with green belts between the areas reserved to the different functions, and (b) a single type of urban housing, expressed in the words of the Charter as 'high, widely-spaced apartment blocks wherever the necessity of housing high densities of population exists.'"[21]

Actually, the founding fathers of CIAM had paid scant attention to the Charter since its drafting, and faint attempts were made to redress its problems—notably at CIAM's 1951 meeting in Hoddesdon, England, which tackled "The Urban Core," an issue woefully neglected by the Charter.[22] The biggest imprint upon the Charter had been made by Le Corbusier, who revised and republished the Charter in 1943, but as his landmark 1947–1952 Unité d'Habitation residential block near Marseilles showed, he was also steadily abandoning functionalism, rationalism, and even urbanism for more organic and self-contained structures (fig. 1.7). Nonetheless, he had bequeathed some very persuasive images to his rationalist followers. As well as the Charter, his 1935 ratification

**Figure 1.8**

Le Corbusier, maquette of the Plan Voisin, 1925. Le Corbusier's epochal though unrealized vision for Paris embodied the Cartesian excess that situationists pledged to obstruct.

of the rationalist city, *La ville radieuse* (The radiant city), had proven an unforgettable book, and his 1925 Plan Voisin project to raze central Paris and replace it with ranks of cruciform towers, connected to the rest of the city by urban motorways, was a vision that still intrigued postwar planners and tormented situationists (fig. 1.8).

Debord's 1959 "Situationist Theses on Traffic" was part manifesto and part satire on the Athens Charter's functionalist dogma. By far the greatest threat to the urban mix demanded by the anti-CIAM lobby was the Charter's demand for strict zoning and ease of traffic circulation: "Zoning that takes account of the key functions—housing, work, recreation—will bring order to the urban territory. Traffic, the fourth function, must have only one aim: to bring the other three usefully into communication."[23] Debord's theses on traffic instead

*"The progress of the sickness": "Core-garage" project by Januz Deryng, illustration to anon., "Urbanisme comme volonté et représentation,"* Internationale situationniste, *no. 9 (1964). Deryng proposed placing massive underground automobile garages at regular intervals beneath Paris. For situationists, the rise of the commuter journey by private motor car exemplified the dissolution of the old city.*

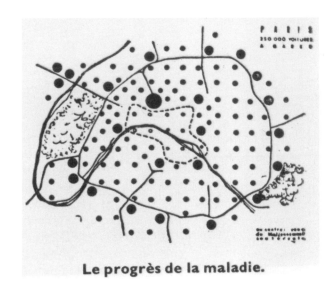

Le progrès de la maladie.

promoted "unitary urbanism" (*urbanisme unitaire*). "Unitary urbanism acknowledges no boundaries; it aims to form a unitary human milieu in which separations such as work/leisure or public/private will finally be dissolved."[24] In fairness, Le Corbusier recognized motorized traffic as a potential social and urban ill, but unitary urbanism was critical of any urbanism that failed to profoundly alter the *function* of vehicles within the city. "The mistake made by all urbanists is to consider the private automobile . . . essentially as a means of transportation," Debord joked, playfully subverting the rationalism of the Athens Charter. "Commuting time, as Le Corbusier rightly pointed out, is a surplus labor that correspondingly reduces the amount of 'free' time"; in which case, Debord deduced, "we must replace travel as an adjunct to work with travel as pleasure."[25] And so, in his *New Babylon Bulletin*, Debord's one-time situationist colleague Constant poured over the findings of Great Britain's milestone 1963 Buchanan Report on *Traffic in Towns*, only to advocate the development of machines for joyriding.[26]

The horrors of postwar planning were epitomized by its servile submission to the pretended logic of the private car. In Debord's opinion, "The breaking up of the dialectic of the human milieu in favor of automobiles . . . masks its irrationality under pseudopractical justifications."[27] To illustrate the point, *Internationale situationniste* reproduced an example of cutting-edge urbanism, a "core-garage" project by Januz Deryng, which admitted to operating on the principle that "the parking lot dictates urban planning" (fig. 1.9). Thanks to this triumph of postwar prosperity management, *Internationale situationniste* noted laconically, "each of the one hundred million Frenchmen that De Gaulle anticipates by the end of the century will find his car at its designated spot."[28] 1950s and 1960s Paris witnessed car parking on public thoroughfares for the first time, the installation of expressways on the left and right banks of the Seine, and the construction of Paris's epochal orbital motorway, the Boulevard Périphérique—at an average cost per kilometer equivalent to 1,000 housing units or 1,800 hospital beds, some of which could have been occupied by victims of the Boulevard's daily average of an accident for every kilometer.[29] In 1968 Pierre Couperie, a historian of Paris, cheerlessly assessed the impact of traffic on the city: "In 1963 there were more than 1,700,000 cars for 330,000 parking spaces. The sidewalks were overrun, the streets permanently choked. . . . The most essential services were sacrificed to the big-money interests of a minority, for in Paris the automobile is a social symbol more than a means of transport. Aside from the din . . . in ten years the death rate from lung cancer has doubled and chronic bronchitis increased by 20 percent."[30]

Postwar developments in public transport, meanwhile, actually exacerbated the disintegration of traditional city life. Couperie described the Parisian experience: "With the failure of public transport, more than half the population travels more than an hour a day. The sudden discharge of thousands of suburbanites by some stations paralyses certain districts."[31] Paris's prestigious RER (Regional Express System), begun in 1961, encouraged the dispersal of traditional (usually working-class or immigrant) Parisian communities into the suburbs as fast as it relieved congestion around the old railway stations. The old marketplace of Les Halles, for example, epicenter of situationist Paris, was demolished and excavated for the central exchange of the RER, much as Amsterdam's Nieuwmarkt was eventually cleared to make way for a new Metro terminus.

In the mid-sixties Amsterdam's Provo group (short for *provocatie*—"provocation"), which counted Constant among its select core membership, formulated the sort of radically simple solution to urban transport that was loathed by authorities intent upon modernization.[32] The White Bicycle Plan proposed that the car be supplanted in Amsterdam by 20,000 bicycles, their white livery indicating that they were at the disposal of any passing Amsterdammer in need of transportation. The Plan overlooked the problem of cycle maintenance, even if its overall failure was due not least, it is said, to police confiscations. But one upshot was a popular critical alertness among Amsterdammers to the impact of rationalist urbanism, and especially its correlation with transport policy. The Metro was developed from the late sixties to the mid-seventies to link central Amsterdam to the giant suburb of Bijlmermeer, the last word in 1960s residential planning, and destined to become the last place in Amsterdam where Amsterdammers wanted to live. The massive opposition to the Metro was due not only to its incredible cost but to its anticipated impact, making way for big business by forcing indigenous Amsterdammers, through a combination of rent hikes and demolitions, out to the suburbs. Resistance, organized around the heirs to the Provo phenomenon, the Neighborhood Committees, would have made a situationist proud. And, as the Nieuwmarkt clearances were completed in a quasi-military police operation, it provoked the authorities into revealing the full capacity for violence underwriting the Dutch state and its seemingly peaceable and tolerant Western neighbors.

The willingness of planners to pander to the insatiable demands of motorized traffic, rather than simply abolish it, only indicated to the situationists that "those who believe that the particulars of the problem are permanent want in fact to believe in the permanence of the present society."[33] So situationist critique was root-and-branch, exposing the cozy hearth-and-home ideology at the heart of CIAM, one which had insisted that "the home, that is to say the shelter of the family, constitutes . . . the nucleus of town planning."[34] Unitary urbanists, by contrast, felt that "it is necessary to transform architecture to accord with the whole development of society, criticizing . . . condemned forms of social relationships (in the first rank of which is the family)" (fig. 1.10).[35]

But it was the measured architectural methodology posited by the Smithsons and their colleagues, not the mischief of Debord and his comrades, that was to send shock waves through CIAM. Disillusioned by the programmatic complacency of CIAM when they attended its ninth meeting in Aix-en-Provence, France, in 1953, the Smithsons, and their Independent Group friends Gill and Bill Howell and John Voelcker, won the right to organize the program for the next CIAM meeting in Dubrovnik, Yugoslavia, in 1956. Joined by other young radicals—Aldo van Eyck and Jacob Bakema from the Netherlands, Georges Candilis from France, Giancarlo De Carlo from Italy, and Shadrach Woods from the United States—the organizing team for the tenth CIAM conference became known as Team 10. Team 10's campaign to abandon rationalist dogma in favor of a pragmatic approach to each project established the group as a formidable force in modern architecture for some

years to come. Its dismantling of a universal rationalist program for architecture proved incompatible with the CIAM mission: delegates to the Dubrovnik conference recognized that CIAM had come to its end, and something of a posthumous CIAM meeting was held in 1959 at Otterlo, Holland.

In fact Team 10's Aldo van Eyck—a friend of Constant, and the member of COBRA who had endowed the group's exhibitions with a radical and lyrical sense of space—had confronted CIAM with a "Statement against Rationalism" as long ago as its Bridgwater meeting in 1947.[36] "The old struggle between imagination and commonsense ended tragically in favour of the latter," the young van Eyck complained. "But the scales are turning: CIAM knows that the tyranny of commonsense has reached its final stage, that the same attitude which, 300 years ago, found expression in Descartes' philosophy . . . is at last losing ground. Yes, the deplorable hierarchy of artificial values upon which contemporary existence has come to rest is beginning to totter."[37] Yet despite the revolutionary threat implicit in the statement, van Eyck had preferred to reshape space in the here-and-now, under the respectable patronage of De 8 (a Dutch CIAM group), rather than await the revolution. Some unlikely shoulder-rubbing resulted, a van Eyck project finding itself posted in CIAM's proceedings next to one by archrationalist Max Bill, and with van Eyck's Amsterdam playgrounds being compared to the roofscape of Le Corbusier's Unité d'Habitation.[38]

**Figure 1.10**

*Drawing of a bourgeois open-plan apartment, uncaptioned illustration from Uwe Lausen, "Répétition et nouveauté dans la situation construite," Internationale situationniste, no. 8 (1963). The picture summarized the preoccupations of French modernization: the processes of "privatization," identified at the time by Henri Lefebvre, Cornelius Castoriadis, and Edgar Morin in people's desire to retreat from the public realm into the domestic sphere; and, para-doxically, an obsession with "communication" that charac-terized the open plan of domestic space just as surely as it did the free flow of automobile traffic. "And yet," Kristin Ross notes in her account of French modernization, Fast Cars, Clean Bodies (p. 6), "the experience of communica-tion itself, be it understood as spontaneous expression, reci-procity, or the contiguity necessary for reciprocity to exist, was precisely what was in the process of disappearing under the onslaught of merchandise and the new forms of media technologies" (cf. fig. 1.1).*

Sigfried Giedion himself, quasi-official historian to the modern movement and secretary to CIAM, singled out van Eyck's playground as an exemplar of what modern architects should be doing to "humanize" the heart of the city. "A formerly useless piece of waste ground has been transformed . . . into an active urban element," Giedion noted admiringly. "One need only provide the opportunity and we—the public, who are also maybe children of a kind—will know how to use it."[39] Giedion would doubtless have been horrified to realize how well his remark anticipated situationism, and CIAM's new promise to provide for "spontaneous manifestations of social life" at the urban core was to remain largely rhetorical.[40] In the opinion of Team 10's Giancarlo De Carlo it represented a half-sentimental, half-cynical legitimation for the accelerated redevelopment of the city.[41] The old guard of CIAM had little inclination to adopt one delegate's invitation to incorporate into modern architecture the vitality of Parisian street life and of Luna-Parks at night.[42] It was difficult to imagine Giedion riding the Dodgems: immersion in popular culture, and enjoyment rather than frustration at the fragmentary chaos of the real city, was best left to the youngsters.

Writing in 1959, Reyner Banham appreciated CIAM's belated recognition of the need for a multipurpose urban core, but, detecting an old Le Corbusier/CIAM nostalgia for a city as compactly organized as "an egg," he worried that planners working on the British new towns had not yet caught up with the complex ramifications of the

postwar explosion in communications, aspiration, and leisure.[43] Banham's alternative manifesto for a "City as Scrambled Egg" liberally borrowed from situationist unitary urbanism, stripping it of its politics and just as quickly placing it within planning discourse. The result was a bizarre fruit, a cross-fertilization of the Independent Group's love of Los Angeles sprawl with the situationists' love of Parisian compactness. Juxtaposing an aerial photograph of a drive-in cinema with a portion of Debord and Jórn's *Guide psychogéographique de Paris* (fig. 1.5), Banham summarized his manifesto:

**The drive-in cinema . . . was the first of the radically new centers of popular aggregation produced by the diffuse, well-mechanised culture of motorised conurbations, and serves the needs of a large and well-defined public—so large and well-defined that together with other facilities such as swimming pools, shopping-centers, schools, etc., it can be used to manipulate and direct movements of population from hour to hour. But the growth of centers of aggregation for activities that do not need large plant or equipment cannot be manipulated by such techniques. The forces that cause jazz-men, wig-makers, sports-car enthusiasts or sculptors to collect in one area rather than another are not understood—but a start could perhaps be made with some such technique as Guy Debord's theory of Psycho-geographical drift.[44]**

Yes, the situationists looked forward to pleasurable speed and mobility through the city at

**Figure 1.11**

*Aldo van Eyck, Amsterdam Children's Home, Amsterdam, 1958–1960, overhead view. The plan of the building was like a variant of Peter Smithson's "Cluster City" (fig. 1.6) in miniature, and its labyrinthine quality made a conscious attempt to generate the sort of playful interaction considered essential to a more humane architecture.*

large, but not to its degeneration into Banham's motoring conurbation. Yes, they wanted, in Banham's phrase, "a whole lot of special interest belts overlapping and colliding, to their mutual benefit," but not so as to attract the troupes of "brainstormers" that Banham considered essential to the life of the urban core, "the cool jazz connection, action painters, documentary camera crews, [and] advertising copy-writers."[45] Planning toward a cultural apartheid of motorized cruisers and brainstormers denied the social meltdown implicit in situationist unitary urbanism.

Situationists and Team 10-ers alike would nonetheless have agreed with Banham's basic proposal to crack open Le Corbusier's urban egg and step up the heat. The core of Banham's Scrambled Egg City would be a labyrinth negotiated by the pedestrian in ways that confounded the logic of rationalist planning. Not that the drift of the pedestrian confounded all logic: as an alternative to the excessive and often sterile spaces of rationalist planning, Aldo van Eyck proposed that architects plan buildings and cities of "labyrinthine clarity," substituting a strict hierarchy of spaces with a more multifarious order. Labyrinthine clarity would thus grant the individual user of the building or city a relative freedom of choice in the use and discovery of its spaces and places.

It was an approach exemplified by van Eyck's Amsterdam Children's Home, designed in 1955 and built between 1958 and 1960, its spaces

clustering and crisscrossing like a carpet, punctuated by surprise forms and surfaces like colors and mirrors, and generating adventures and chance encounters among the child internees (fig. 1.11).[46] In the race to discover a postrationalist architecture, van Eyck and friends working within the architectural profession kept pace with situationists working outside it. Constant collaborated with van Eyck on a 1953 installation for the "Man and House" exhibition at the Stedelijk Museum, Amsterdam, where they attempted to articulate space through a "spatial colorism" comparable to colorfield painting.[47] For their efforts van Eyck and Constant were jointly awarded the Nederlanse Sikkensprijs architectural medal in 1961. Somewhat belatedly, an article by van Eyck on labyrinthine clarity appeared in a 1963 edition of the *Situationist Times*, though the wandering, layered ground plan of Constant's New Babylon had long since confirmed the proximity of the various "labyrinthine" interests.[48] Constant's plan for a situationist city synthesized the Amsterdam

**Figure 1.12**

*Constant*, North New Babylon, *1959, watercolor on collage,
Gemeentemuseum, The Hague. Constant's New Babylon
represented the most ambitious version of the labyrinthine
cluster principle, a single, continuous structure spreading
across the city and countryside.*

Children's Home with Peter Smithson's Cluster City and expanded both to an improbable scale (fig. 1.12).

The explosive, utopian implications of situationism proved ultimately tangential to Team 10's bid to revive modern architecture, and Team 10's replacement of one set of concrete visions with another was distasteful to many situationists. Team 10 was right to pay attention to "patterns of association," a situationist might have argued, but it was wrong to then congeal those patterns into fixed "place-forms." The choices left to the inhabitants of a Team 10 structure, as they scurried along its burrows, had in effect already been made by the designers. New Babylon, by way of contrast, was designed by Constant to accommodate an ever-changing panoply of forms and effects chosen by the New Babylonians themselves.

Clearly there was something of a clash of philosophies here, the situationists asking architects to renounce their master visions at the earliest opportunity, Team 10 asking architects to press on until the very fundamentals of habitat had been discovered. Rejecting the anarchic, expressionist impulses of COBRA, van Eyck sought precise relationships between architectural form and socio-psychological need, and by the 1960s his quest was associated with the structuralist movement.[49] The structuralist ethnologist Claude Lévi-Strauss claimed to find basic structures underlying all cultural processes, and archi-

tects impressed by this believed that they were engaged in the creative search for archetypal solutions. If human "patterns of association" were governed by the basic structure of primordial relationships, then so would their container, the architectural "place-form."

Nothing could be further from the spontaneity idealistically demanded by the situationists. Yet Team 10's work retained a situationist ring to it. A rallying cry like that delivered by van Eyck to Team 10 in 1959—"Instead of the inconvenience of filth and confusion, we have now got the boredom of hygiene . . . mile upon mile of organised nowhere"—could almost have been lifted from the pages of Internationale situationniste.[50] And indeed, as the sixties wore on, Continental members of Team 10, notably van Eyck, Candilis, De Carlo, and Woods, became ever more pessimistic about the role of the architect within a capitalist and bureaucratic society.[51] By 1967 Woods was writing in a vein so radical that it might have been acceptable even to situationists. "Our weapons become more sophisticated; our houses more and more brutish. Is that the balance sheet for the richest civilisation since time began?"[52] In 1968, the year of the political chaos that the situationists claimed to have sparked, Woods assisted students in the removal of his own work from the Milan Triennale.

His colleague De Carlo was meanwhile attempting an analysis of the ideological legitimation of modern architecture that would, for all intents and purposes, equate with situationist lore. He reviewed the consequences of CIAM's Frankfurt Statutes of 1929, where functionalist *Existenzminimum* ("minimum existence") standards had been formulated:

**Today, 40 years after the Congress, we find that those proposals have become houses and neighborhoods and suburbs and then entire cities, palpable manifestations of an abuse perpetrated first on the poor and then even on the not-so-poor: cultural alibis for the most ferocious economic speculation and the most obtuse political inefficiency. And yet those "whys" so nonchalantly forgotten in Frankfurt still have trouble coming openly to the surface. At the same time, we have a right to ask "why" housing should be as cheap as possible and not, for example, rather expensive; "why" instead of making every effort to reduce it to minimum levels of surface, of thickness, of materials, we should not try to make it spacious, protected, isolated, comfortable, well equipped, rich in opportunities for privacy, communication, exchange, personal creativity. No one, in fact, can be satisfied by an answer which appeals to the scarcity of available resources, when we all know how much is spent on wars, on the construction of missiles and anti-ballistic missiles, on moon projects, on research for the defoliation of forest inhabited by partisans and for the paralysation of the demonstrators emerging from the ghettos, on hidden persuasion, on the invention of artificial needs, etc.[53]**

## From "plenty" to "excess"

The meanness of "legitimate" architecture noted by De Carlo in 1968 confounded the lifestyle predictions made by the avant-garde only a decade or so earlier. The Independent Group had looked forward to a consumerist "aesthetic of plenty," and the situationists, always optimistic about "détourning" the power of production and consumption toward the revolution of everyday life, had envisaged a society not merely of "plenty" but of outright "excess."

A new grass roots culture, it was assumed, would be created through appropriation. The Independents let their eyes wander over the goods of postwar popular culture and decided to take whatever they wanted. Richard Hamilton, John McHale, and Eduardo Paolozzi constructed their own aesthetic out of fetishized automotive details and fragments of commercial illustration; Banham and Alloway invited the intelligentsia to take unabashed pleasure in science fiction; the Smithsons found a future for socially conscious architecture in cars and mobile homes and kitchens from the United States. It was an attitude that had affinities with the situationist technique of *détournement*. *Détournement* would provide for a society of pleasure instead of the stoicism and sacrifice of Stalinism or the peer pressure of consumerism. Postwar abundance, in the West at least, suggested that indulgence could be had without risk to the community at large; the profits of capital could be redistributed as greater goods and leisure for all rather than for the few, while commandeered technologies of production took care of work.

Whether these ideas stood up to scrutiny was never really an issue for the avant-garde. It was enough that they dented the traditional esotericism of the intelligentsia, at a time when the American critic Clement Greenberg still held modernism's international center stage with his insistence that popular culture was little short of despicable.[54] And so it was that personalities as different as Reyner Banham and Asger Jorn both felt drawn, for instance, to a reassessment of popular American "Borax" product styling, that antagonist of rationalist industrial design. For Jorn and Banham, industrial design, in effect the lowest tier of the design hierarchy (with architecture in the middle and urban planning at the apex), had to be part and parcel of the reassessment of modernism. Industrial design was, after all, the only tier of creativity fully geared to mass production, supposedly the organizing principle of the modern movement.

For Jorn and Banham, the emergence of such mass-produced frippery as streamlined pencil sharpeners and "organic" home furnishings demonstrated the vulnerability of rationalism to mass demand for less austere styles.[55] In short, what Greenberg dismissed as kitsch Banham and Jorn recognized as a bid to transcend the sterility of everyday life, each fin, chrome strip, and coiling surface of the consumer durable a little flight of

fantasy into the realms of science fiction and the surreal. Rationalism, they felt, hid from consumer demand behind a bogus neoplatonic aesthetic of form following function, forcing designs that served a multiplicity of needs to fit a single aesthetic.[56]

It was not even that Jorn shared Banham's genuine fondness for Borax and organicism—Jorn regarded the latter as a debasement of natural form, and he certainly had no truck with the untrammeled capitalism that had produced the former. But like Banham, he wanted to defend the rights of "ordinary people" to make their own choices of objects, to expect artists and designers to behave as consultants and providers rather than dictatorial tastemakers, and to enjoy a material world of change and spontaneity. This last demand answered a concern for playfulness and festivity that was increasingly fashionable among intellectuals. Henri Lefebvre's notion of the "festive" as a transcendence of everyday life, and Roger Caillois's sociology of play and leisure, came in the wake of Johan Huizinga's classic *Homo Ludens* (first published in 1938) and the interwar literary criticism of Mikhail Bakhtin. Like Bakhtin, situationism emphasized the subversive power of "carnivalization"—the opportunity for unofficial and popular elements to playfully invert social and cultural conventions by elevating the everyday and "uncrowning" the elite. "With the disappearance of the exceptional personal performance," Constant wrote in 1948, "'genius' will become public property and the word 'art' will acquire a completely new mean-

**Figure 1.13**

*Asger Jorn, work from the International Ceramics Meeting, Albisola, 1954, reprinted in the Imaginist Bauhaus journal Eristica, 1956. As something of a protest against the rationalist sensibilties dominant in the design profession, Jorn dispatched the products of his International Ceramics Meeting to the Milan Triennale of Industrial Design. The explosive anthropomorphism of Jorn's figures was in marked contrast to Le Corbusier's disciplined Modulor man (fig. 1.20).*

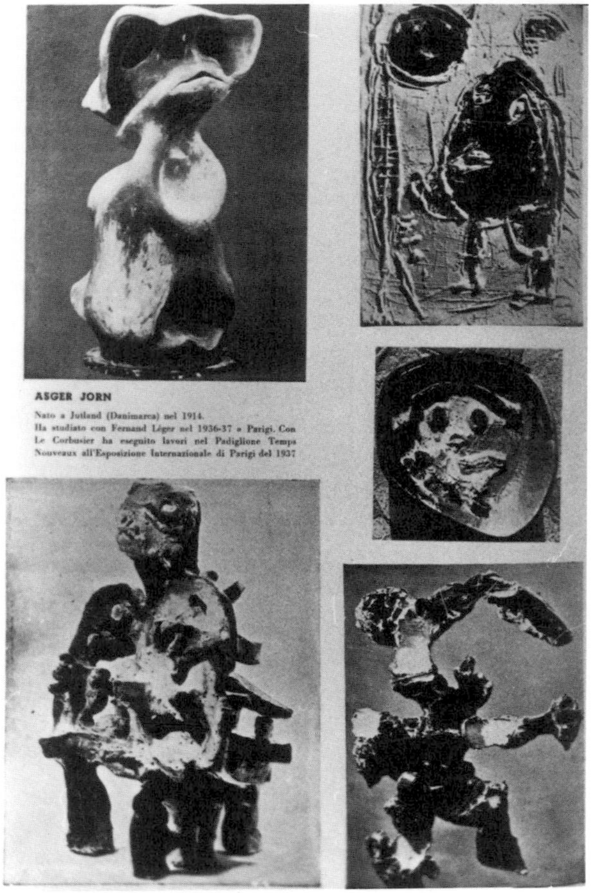

ing."[57] Huizinga's thesis, which was more widely distributed and readily acknowledged than Bakhtin's, had a different emphasis, positing that the wellspring of all culture, or at least all great culture, was the instinct for play. Here indeed was a cultural metatheory jolly enough to rival the sobriety of rationalism, and Jorn illustrated the culture clash in 1954 by bringing some playful Imaginist Bauhaus ceramics with him to a Milan Triennale otherwise dominated by rationalist "good form" (fig. 1.13).[58]

Even so, it seemed to Independent Group and situationist theorists that rationalism had been correct in identifying mass production and technology as motors of cultural transformation, and as assets that the avant-garde would have to seize if it was to shape the modern world according to its own vision. With the Industrial Revolution long in England's past, the Independent Group felt that the modernizing forces of technology and consumerism were ushering in "the revenge of the elementary school boys," exposing the traditional English ruling class as hopelessly outmoded and creating opportunities for those schooled in the movies rather than the classics.[59]

But the feeling of Continental situationists, operating in countries like France, Italy, and even Holland and Germany, where modernization was very much a recent and ongoing experience, was that technology and consumerism were consolidating rather than undermining the ruling class. Technology and production would have to be

fought for, just as Marx had said, in the streets and in culture. In 1957 Debord called upon the groups preparing to unify as the Situationist International to rise to the challenge set out by the basic Marxist proposition of dialectical materialism—that change in society's productive and economic base begins to outpace the cultural resistance of society's superstructure. "Our era," Debord said, "is fundamentally characterized by a lagging of revolutionary political action behind the development of modern possibilities of production which call for a superior organization of the world."[60]

Jorn fleshed out the debate on mass production in the first issue of *Internationale situationniste*. Automation, he wrote, "is now at the heart of the problem of the socialist domination of production and of the preeminence of leisure over labor time." It "contains two opposing perspectives: it deprives the individual of any possibility of adding anything personal to automated production . . . and at the same time it saves human energy by massively liberating it from reproductive and creative activities. The value of automation thus depends on projects that supersede it and open the way for expression of human energies on a higher plane." Before closing, Jorn summarized the heart of situationist ambition: "The sleeping creator must be awakened, and his waking state can be termed 'situationist.'"[61]

That capitalist consumerism had tapped the possibilities of production first was a matter of some regret, though Independents and situationists alike believed that there was still room for avant-garde maneuver. Consumerism was brilliant in creating and meeting transitory gratifications; but for all the rhetoric about consumer power, the direction of consumerism was really decided by capital, and the alienating, one-way battery of goods from capitalist to consumer did little to satisfy the human needs for spontaneity, play, and creativity

that the Huizinga-inspired avant-garde regarded as fundamental. "Modern man is stifled in these television-, frigidaire-type necessities," Jorn lamented, while his colleagues observed how "in our time functionalism . . . is attempting to entirely eliminate play, and the partisans of 'industrial design' complain that their projects are spoiled by people's tendency toward play."[62] They tried to envisage an avant-garde intervention: "We obviously have no interest in encouraging the continuous artistic renovation of refrigerator designs." No; "the only progressive way out is to liberate the tendency toward play elsewhere and on a larger scale."[63]

If the avant-garde could only reconcile the dichotomies of the consumer regime, then it might achieve a postwar utopia. Some Independent Group members looked to new ideas coming out of information theory, like feedback and spectator intervention, as ways of narrowing the gap between the producers and consumers of culture and its artifacts. Situationists believed that consumerism's economy of commodity exchange could be replaced by a more daring mode, of exchange as gift. The Lettrist International's journal *Potlatch* took its name from a Northwest American Indian tradition that had been studied by the French anthropologist Marcel Mauss in his classic essay on "The Gift," and which had delighted Huizinga: the redistribution of goods in fierce competitions of generosity.[64]

Walter Benjamin's dictum—that artistic apparatus "is better the more consumers it is able to turn into producers, that is, readers or spectators

**Figure 1.14**

*Opening of Giuseppe Pinot-Gallizio and Giors Melanotte's* Cavern of Anti-Matter *(1958–1959, oil and resin on canvas, private collection) at the Galerie René Drouin, May 1959. The* Cavern *is occupied by Pinot-Gallizio, his son Melanotte, gallery owner Drouin, and a model wearing a dress made, like the* Cavern, *from the "industrial painting" developed by the artists at the Imaginist Bauhaus.*

into collaborators"—could almost have served as a situationist motto.[65] At the Imaginist Bauhaus in 1958–1959, Giuseppe Pinot-Gallizio and his son Giors Melanotte explored mass production as a means of deflating the manufacturing cost and commodity value of art, so preparing it for general "potlatched" distribution. As it turned out, their "industrial painting" (*pittura industriale*)—painting on a continuous roll, sold by the meter—was a William Morris wallpaper for the abstract expressionist age. Far from being industrial, it looked, and was, distinctly crafts-based, painterly, and expressionist.[66] Nonetheless, Pinot-Gallizio and Melanotte realized that it was possible to produce industrial painting in sufficient quantities to "wallpaper" whole rooms, and they toured industrial painting and its associated "environment," or "Cavern of Anti-matter," through European galleries (fig. 1.14).[67] The reality of industrial painting—impressive, though not astounding—mattered less

than what it stood for. Just as rationalist architects between the world wars had coveted mass production as a metaphor for revolutionizing the production of buildings, situationists now looked to the mass production of art to revolutionize the production of space. Pinot-Gallizio's confidence in the power of situationist art to transform everyday life was boundless, conjuring up as a mere beginning visions of the Italian *autostrade* (freeways) repainted in bright colors.[68]

The supreme environment, however, and the supreme art machine, was invented by Pinot-Gallizio's Imaginist Bauhaus colleague Constant. Pinot-Gallizio, who was a local left-wing councilor, owned a piece of land in Alba where Gypsies made camp, and in 1956 he invited Constant to design a permanent encampment, a system of movable partitions within a common shelter (fig. 1.15). Constant, who was already working on designs for an Imaginist Bauhaus pavilion, took up the idea enthusiastically, and activity on the Gypsy Camp quickly expanded into the megastructure of New Babylon, an infinite, inhabitable container for mass-produced environments, fabulous technologies, and endless artistic exchange.

Constant's thinking had affinities with another "postindustrial" notion, proposed by Banham. From 1955 Banham nursed a theory of "Other Architecture" ("une architecture autre") which, taking its cue from the informal trends in painting collected in Michel Tapié's 1952 book *Un art autre*, was initially devised as an architectural

alternative to rationalist orderliness.[69] Banham now tacked onto Other Architecture the proposition that inhabitants define their own environments by a fluid and playful selection of objects, services, and technologies, rather than submit to a monumental architecture imposed by the architect. Though clearly inspired by consumerism, Other Architecture's demand for high-performance, life-supporting goods and systems was beyond anything that contemporary consumer capitalism could offer, and looked forward to the birth of a new consumer.

In the mid-fifties, only the American radical designer and theorist R. Buckminster Fuller had much to offer Banham's Other Architecture, and it would be some years before anyone got a glimpse of the new consumer. In the event, the latter was

modeled by Banham himself, placed in a pneumatic plastic Environment Bubble in the April 1965 edition of *Art in America* (fig. 1.16).[70] Banham had the designer François Dallegret to keep him company there, but Other Architecture looked rather lonely even so, typifying a postindustrial condition that today survives among millions of Internet surfers sitting alone in their bedrooms. It was a condition implicit in the very definition of postindustrialism provided by Alain Touraine, the sociologist who emerged as the leading French theorist of modernization during the halcyon years of situationism. "Those who are 'home-centered' and who own a radio, a television, a record-player, magazines, are bypassing the social hierarchy of their community, in order to make direct contact with broader social

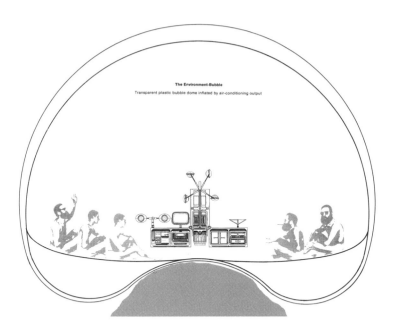

**Figure 1.16**

Reyner Banham and François Dallegret, "The Environment
Bubble," illustration from "A Home Is Not a House," Art in
America, no. 53 (April 1965). Banham's vision of an "Other
Architecture," informally assembled from the detritus of
consumer technologies, provides an intriguing comparison
with situationist architecture.

**Figure 1.17**

Installation view of the Sistema 45 range of office furniture,
designed by Ettore Sottsass for Olivetti, 1969. Sottsass's
departure from the Imaginist Bauhaus more than a decade
earlier marked the dissemination of situationist ideas into a
wider design philosophy, characterized by a new informality.

realities and values," Touraine argued in 1959, breaking ranks with those intellectuals nostalgic for a popular culture of authentic, immediate, community-based working-class experiences.[71] Threatened with a postindustrialism of voluntary alienation, it was no wonder that situationists insisted that the technological revolution be highly sociable and personable.

Given the common fascination with consumption and eclecticism, it is not surprising that the situationists and the Independent Group have since been regarded as sources of a postmodern sensibility. The situationist model of culture falling into either spectacular or anti-spectacular camps, and the Independent Group model of culture as one "long front," both had the effect of leveling the traditional cultural hierarchy of highbrow and lowbrow.[72] Both models' lack of deference to high culture was one in the eye for "university culture" and class distinctions of taste. This "postmodern" sensibility regularly resurfaced in situationist texts—a 1960 manifesto suggested that the breakup of aesthetic orthodoxy and hierarchy would be a necessity of the future situationist world. "Since everyone will be, so to speak, a situationist, we shall see a multidimensional plethora of new trends, of experiments, of 'schools,' all radically different, and this *no longer in succession but simultaneously.*"[73]

But claims on situationism as a postmodern source need to be qualified. Situationism would have abhorred postmodernism's celebration of the meaningless forest of consumer signs and objects. One likely bridge between situationism and post-

modernism was the breakup in aesthetic decorum presided over by the so-called "anti-design" of the 1960s. Italian "anti-designers," like Ettore Sottsass (a member of the Imaginist Bauhaus) and Joe Columbo (a member of the nuclear art movement, associated with the Imaginist Bauhaus), were doubtless influenced by the attention that situationism paid to the larger emotional relationship between humans and objects, design and behavior (fig. 1.17). They attempted to soften industrial design almost in the manner prescribed by Jorn, making increasing use of organic, fantastic shapes and textures, color, popular references, new materials, and flexibility. But the choices created by the designs of Sottsass and Columbo were essentially consumerist rather than political. Standard domestic and business interiors were made to look more relaxed, without attacking the fact of their existence. The "fun" iconography of anti-design did not affect its servicing of industry and consumerism nor, therefore, the type of alienated society of which industrialization and consumerism are constituent parts.[74]

## Carving out the spaces of culture and politics

The determination to address fundamental issues about the politics of space, rather than simply rearrange the furniture, so to speak, separated situationists from anti-designers just as it separated them from most avant-gardes. So when in 1960 the Situationist International finally put in its appearance at the old London home of the Independent Group, the ICA, it was as *agent provocateur* rather than as ally. Jorn's biographer, Guy Atkins, described the foot-stamping, dadaist atmosphere at the meeting convened by former Independent Group member Toni del Renzio:

**Instead of beginning with the usual compliments, [Maurice] Wyckaert [acting as situationist spokesman] scolded the ICA for using the word "Situationism" in its Bulletin. "Situationism," Wyckaert explained, "doesn't exist. There is no doctrine of this name." He went on to tell the audience "If you've now understood that there is no such thing as 'Situationism' you've not wasted your evening. . . ." Wyckaert ended as he had begun, with a gibe at the ICA. "The Situationists, whose judges you perhaps imagine yourselves to be, will one day judge you. We are waiting for you at the turning." There was a moment's silence before people realised that the speaker had finished. The first and only question came from a man who asked "Can you explain exactly what Situationism is all about?" Wyckaert gave the questioner a severe look. Guy Debord stood up and said in French "We're not here to answer cuntish questions." At this he and the other Situationists walked out.[75]**

"We are waiting for you at the turning": while a comparison of situationism with other avant-gardes enables it to be positioned within a wider discourse, it also alerts us to an ideological gulf. The "turning" that the Situationist International loitered on, theoretical coshes in hand, was that of revolution. No postwar avant-garde aspired to the mantle of revolutionary radicalism more fervently than the situationists.

All the same, both situationism and the Independent Group can be interpreted together as prototypical new-left reactions to the assassination of politics, the vulgarizing of culture, and the atrocious coerciveness presided over by the Soviet Union. In the 1950s Western intellectuals, only recently traumatized by Fascism, learned that they had been duped by Soviet Communism as well. Rather than clear the air, Krushchev's 1956 denunciation of Stalin, as the Situationist International prepared to unify, was offset by the Soviet invasion of Hungary, confirmation of a deadening weight that could be felt in the West as well through the agency of the Communist Party. Henri Lefebvre's gradual and painful departure from the PCF (French Communist Party) between 1956 and 1958 was a very public example of the crisis in Western Marxism. With the German Democratic Republic's hasty erection of the Berlin Wall in 1961, the perversion of Communist revolution attained its tangible form: here was a barricade, all right, ostensibly keeping the forces of bourgeois reaction out in order to pen citizens in.

Situationism and the Independent Group were reactions as well to the pseudo-neutrality of high modernism, whose apostle Clement Greenberg had led the exodus from realist practices and Marxist criticism in the arts. The neutrality of Western intellectuals did not seem credible when Western states were actively engaged in a cold war with the East: landing in Korea in 1950, the United States embarked on its crusade against a supposed Communist conspiracy. The Western European states that the postwar avant-gardes grew up in seemed to be turning their power inward, reluctantly foregoing empire to concentrate resources on social and urban reconstruction. In 1949, the year in which the Netherlands was finally driven out of Indonesia, the private viewing of COBRA's Stedelijk Museum exhibition ended in fistfights over the political insinuations of the speeches.[76] Of the Western states, France was perhaps the most traumatized by the loss of empire, humiliated by its defeat at the hands of the Vietnamese at Dien Bien Phu in 1954, only to have the United States adopt the conflict as its own. In the same year France embarked upon the so-called "dirty war" with its Algerian colony, which lasted until 1962 and left a permanent imprint upon the membership and work of the Lettrist and Situationist Internationals.[77] Even Britain, whose 1945–1951 Labour government put a brave face on reduced British status—heroically inventing a welfare state and a Festival of Britain—retained its physical presence in Egypt until 1956, and in Arabia until 1967, as it stumbled into the most violent years of its ongoing civil war in Northern Ireland.

Casting around for a new utopia, the Independent Group looked toward America, the French Sartrian existentialists toward China, science fiction utopians—heads turned upward by the launch of Sputnik in 1957—toward outer space. But perhaps only the situationists squared up to the fact that utopia was in neither Russia, America, China, nor space. It was, by definition, nowhere, and would have to be imagined and pieced together in their own backyards—in COBRA's artists' colony at Bregneröd, Denmark, at the Imaginist Bauhaus in Alba, in the Lettrist International's Parisian Left Bank, and eventually in Sweden, at the Situationist Bauhaus's farm, Drakabygget.

In the 1950s, genuinely exploratory political philosophy was virtually an avant-garde activity by definition, and perhaps all the more vibrant for it, putting cultural politics on new footings. It developed a healthy skepticism about the East-West posturing of cold war politics, shifting attention away from large party and state groupings toward the small group experiences of everyday life and space. There were, nonetheless, differences of attitude and outlook. For the Independent Group, disengagement with the politics of the old left entailed an abandonment of knee-jerk criticism, admitting that it *was* possible to enjoy an American film or magazine without necessarily supporting America's foreign policy in Korea. In its more enlightened moments, the Independent Group was well aware of the precariousness of such an attitude. "If we go on voting Labour like this," John McHale once quipped to Independent Group partner Magda Cordell, "we shall destroy our own livelihood."[78] Situationists would certainly have regarded the ICA circle's ease with the spectacle as risky and probably complicit. The situationists went the other way, frantically trying to reinvest in a class consciousness against the cynicism of cold war attitudes and the big politics of party and state.

For the situationists, a relentlessly critical state of mind had to confront all hegemonic cultural forms, whatever their origin, domestic or foreign, left or right, Eastern or Western. It was not enough for the intellectual simply to admit to enjoying American mass culture, nor to decoratively rearrange it, pop art style, into artistic products for distribution on the conventional art market. This merely elaborated the spectacle. The situationists wanted to believe in the possibility of a cultural sphere *outside* the spectacle of capital, party politics, and imperialism.[79] The situationists were certain, of course, that *they* stood outside the spectacle, and that they could lead the populace out of it as well. The fact that "75%" of workers aspired to leave the estates erected by planners revealed "a first resistance" that would simply "have to be supported and enlightened by a revolutionary organization."[80] True, the average worker seemed more set on moving to the sort of "detached house with a garden" being built by the car manufacturer Renault than on taking up residence in a situationist city, but the Situationist International was to remain confident in its ability to liberate the workers' revolutionary "instinct for construction."[81]

Capital, situationists argued, may have become more sophisticated, reorganizing itself as a consumer spectacle, blurring the distinction between producers and consumers, and ingratiating itself with sections of the working class. Socialism and Communism, meanwhile, may have become less sophisticated, clinging to the clichés of party discipline and centralization. But the idea that class struggle had somehow disappeared, as it had from the discussions of the Independent Group, the situationists considered naive at best. And though the situationist preoccupation with class might have seemed rather old-fashioned, their version of dialectical materialism was nonetheless much racier than that of traditional Marxism. When the situationists identified the slippery spectacle as their enemy, they abandoned the comfortable certainties of monolithic social, economic, political, and material formations. Society's new dialectics were dazzlingly fast, even playful. Proponents of traditional dialectical materialism, *Potlatch* claimed, had become trapped by their own "unconditional exaltation of fixed forms."[82] The capitalist and bureaucratic spectacle, the situationists argued, had no fixed form, so neither could its resistance.

And so, rather aptly for an age of resistance movements in the former empires, situationism developed a guerrilla mentality, launching "raiding parties" on the power of the spectacle. The raids would be dispatched from the literal and metaphorical space carved out by situationism. Situationist space existed literally in the situationist safe havens—the unsanitized parts of Alba, Paris, Amsterdam, London, and Munich where the Imaginist Bauhaus, Lettrist International, and Situationist International felt at home. And it existed metaphorically in culture, amidst the serendipitous disorganization of expressionist art, old books, boozing, Hegel and Marx. Indeed, while Independent Group members believed that culture would be reinvigorated by the forces of commercialism, the situationists "détourned" fragments of *ancien* tradition as weapons against *nouveau* Philistine materialism. "The literary and artistic heritage of humanity should be used for partisan propaganda purposes," wrote Debord, something of a connoisseur in everything from his reading to his food.[83] It was an attitude with its roots in the Marshall Plan era, when the French left chose to drink wine instead of Coke as an act of defiance against "Coca-Colonisation." Perhaps even more than the English avant-garde, most situationists were fiercely cultivated individuals choosing to "rough it," one foot in the militancy of wartime Resistance and postwar austerity, rather than succumb to the comforts of the spectacle. As Debord was lamenting by 1988, "Beyond a legacy of old books and old buildings, still of some significance but destined to continual reduction . . . there remains nothing, in culture or in nature, which has not been transformed, and polluted, according to the means and interests of modern society."[84]

*Détournement* would permit anyone to take part in the raids on official culture, weakening the polarization between "author" and "reader," nullifying the importance of attribution, originality, and intellectual property. "Clashing head-on with all social and legal conventions," Debord claimed, *détournement* "cannot fail to be a powerful cultural weapon in the service of a real class struggle. The cheapness of its products is the heavy artillery that breaks through all the Chinese walls of understanding."[85] The experiments in *détournement* that situationists carried out on literature, political theory, and film (all of Debord's films were built around *détournement*) were intended as just the start. The situationists aimed to eventually "détourn" bits of city.

This inclination to transgress the boundaries found in culture and cities also characterized the work of Henri Lefebvre, which was so seamlessly assimilated by situationism, and vice versa, that for the purposes of this discussion it is hardly possible or useful to distinguish the two.[86] Lefebvre admitted to being inspired by Constant's work of the early fifties, and he eventually confessed to "a sort of unfinished love affair with the situationists."[87] Like many situationists, Lefebvre came from a surrealist background, and the cornerstones of his thought and those of the situationists were remarkably similar. Following Huizinga, both looked to play, spontaneity, and festivity as necessities of daily life, oppositional forces to bureaucratic planning. Above all, they sought to understand that moment when people gain insight into the rationalized and alienated patterns of their everyday lives. Lefebvre's interpretation of the eruptive "moment" as embodying "fleeting but decisive sensations (of delight, surrender, disguise, surprise, horror or outrage) which were somehow revelatory of the totality of possibilities contained in daily existence" could stand just as well for the situationists' notion of the "situation."[88] Both Lefebvre and the situationists looked to the declaration of the Paris Commune as history's sublime "moment" and "situation," when ordinary citizens decided to become self-governing. "The Commune was the biggest festival of the nineteenth century," the second situationist thesis on the Paris Commune declared. "Underlying the events of that spring of 1871 one can see the insurgents' feeling that they had become masters of their own history, not so much on the level of 'governmental' politics as on the level of their everyday life."[89] The 1936 election victory of the French Popular Front, and the liberations of 1945, were comparable moments of euphoria and *fête* actually present in the memories of Lefebvre and of many situationists.

By the early 1960s, however, Lefebvre and the situationists had become antagonistic toward one another. Intellectual competitiveness, as ever, was one provocation, as when Lefebvre failed to acknowledge the essay on the Commune written for him by the situationists. The fundamental disagreement, however, was over revolutionary praxis. When Debord was invited to talk to Lefebvre's Group for

Research on Everyday Life about the "Perspectives for Conscious Alterations in Everyday Life," he sent a tape recording rather than attend in person, implying that the academic space of the Center of Sociological Studies was the last place in Paris where conscious alterations in everyday life might actually occur.[90] The situationists regarded Lefebvre's voluminous academic dissection of revolution as inherently suspect: the point of studying the "moment" or "situation" was to provoke it again in the future, not to adapt it as a seminar topic. Marxist geographer David Harvey writes how Lefebvre "provocatively though not altogether unfavourably depicted them [the situationists] as romantics"; the situationists, in turn, accused Lefebvre "of failing to appreciate the revolutionary potential of their own tactic of creating 'situations' as opposed to what they saw as Lefebvre's more passive stance of experiencing 'moments' when they happened to arise."[91]

The situationists almost certainly drew their inspiration for creating, as well as simply experiencing, "situation," from Jean-Paul Sartre.[92] The very word *situation* derives from Sartrian existentialism, which in the years after the war emerged as the most influential humanist philosophical movement in France and probably in Western Europe. Sartre argued that life is a series of given situations which affect the individual's consciousness and will, and which must in turn be negotiated by that individual. Situationism now presupposed that it was possible for people to synthesize or manage these situations as an act of self-empowerment. "The life of a person is a succession of fortuitous situations," Debord complained, "and even if none of them is exactly the same as another the immense majority of them are so undifferentiated and so dull that they give a perfect impression of similitude. We must try to construct situations, that is to say collective ambiances, ensembles of impressions determining the quality of a moment."[93]

Though Lefebvre's loyalty to empirical rigor kept situationism at arm's length, he no doubt sympathized with its spirit. Like the situationists, Lefebvre disliked specialization. Structuralism was one example that he singled out for criticism. In his opinion structuralism, rather than redressing the failures of formalism and functionalism in the way so recently promised by Team 10, actually joined them as a partial model mechanistically applied by architects.[94] Lefebvre and the situationists agreed that a "totalizing," holistic approach—a merging of specialisms—was needed to adequately diagnose the sicknesses of the city.

The situationists, however, were more willing than either Team 10 or Lefebvre to extend criticism of specialization even to their own professional practice. Jorn idealized "the free artist" as "a professional amateur," and openly questioned the legitimacy of avant-gardism itself, inasmuch as it constituted another specialism.[95] This ostentatious self-criticism allowed the situationists always to play the radical card: no matter how intelligent or useful the contributions of non-situationists might be, they were inherently compromised by their production and distribution within the milieu of the spectacular establishment (such as academia) or bourgeoisie rather than within the "free" situationist alliance. "The greatest revolutionary idea concerning urbanism is not itself urbanistic, technological or aesthetic," Debord concluded in his theses on "The Organisation of Territory." "It is the decision to reconstruct the entire environment in accordance with the needs of the power of the Workers' Councils, of the *anti-statist dictatorship* of the proletariat, of enforceable dialogue."[96] This enabled the Situationist International to relegate Lefebvre to a trendy 1960s wave of political, sociological, semiological, and psychological readings of the urban environment (like those of Jane Jacobs, Kevin Lynch, Françoise Choay, Gillo Dorfles, and so on). All that situationists could do with those readings was "détourn" them, leaving the Situationist International alone in opposing the spectacular edifice in its totality, armed with a group political program and constrained neither by allegiance to academic rigor and objectivity nor to existing systems of planning and construction.

Lefebvre came in for increasingly rough handling from the situationists. In 1961, reviewing a recent Lefebvre article in the *Revue française de sociologie*, *Internationale situationniste* insisted that Lefebvre had not gone far enough in his critique of the teams of architects and sociologists who were working on urban problems. "Lefebvre's article too greatly validates work which certainly has its utility, and its merits, but in a perspective radically different from ours. The title of his article, 'Experimental Utopia: For a New Urbanism,' . . . straightaway contains all the equivocation. Because the method of experimental utopianism . . . obviously has to embrace totality, that's to say putting it into action would not lead to a 'new urbanism,' but to a new usage of life, to a new revolutionary praxis."[97] By this time disagreement over whether it was possible to address urbanism without revolutionizing the totality had opened rifts within the Situationist International as well, the French section rapidly sidelining the sorts of unitary urbanism envisaged by the Dutch and German sections.[98]

Identify the places in which revolutionary situations might be constructed, the Parisian situationists insisted, rejecting architects' attempts to merely "improve" the city through urban design. Look to the spaces of class struggle, not just at its unfolding through time, the French situationists challenged other Marxists.[99] David Harvey believes that it was this challenge that Lefebvre "tacitly countered" in his later work on urbanization and the production of space, reframing his idea of the "moment" as spatio-temporal rather than just temporal.[100] Lefebvre's sequence of major statements on urban space came late—Le droit à la ville (The right to the city) did not appear until 1968, and the Critique d'espace quotidienne (Critique of everyday space) not until 1974—although other intellectuals, in particular those gathered around

the Utopie group, founded 1967, were busy blending Lefebvre's measured discussions of urbanism with the more polemical and intuitive approach of the situationists.[101] Lefebvre came to recognize the need for a praxis in urban studies if, as Marx had demanded, philosophy was to change the world rather than merely interpret it, and his proposed praxis—"synthesizing objective analysis and 'experimental utopia,'" and the deployment of "the 'imaginary' in the production of new concepts of urban life"—was resonant with situationism.[102]

### Urbanism and power

In the France of the 1950s and 1960s, Lefebvre and the situationists were confident that dominant power resided in the state, its capital, and its media; that social interests were more or less class-based; and that the dynamics of society—whether one looked at the production of time or the production of space—could still ultimately be explained through an updated dialectical materialism. "All space is already occupied by the enemy, which has even reshaped its elementary laws, its geometry, to its own purposes," Kotányi and Vaneigem concluded on behalf of the Situationist International.[103] Some years earlier, Potlatch had started to publish Jorn's neo-Marxist analyses of architecture. "Architecture is always the ultimate realization of a

**Figures 1.18, 1.19**

*Oscar Niemeyer and Lúcio Costa, Brasília, 1956–1963: the ministries, congress domes, and twin secretariat towers at Three Powers Square, and the Highway Axis passing through residential districts. Brasília was one of the modern movement's most extraordinary achievements, and as such was despised by the situationists. Like the Ensemble Maine-Montparnasse in Paris (fig. 1.29), it was briefly featured in Guy Debord's film* La société du spectacle *(1973).*

mental and artistic evolution," he argued, because "it is the materialization of an economic stage. . . . Creating an architecture signifies constructing an ambiance and fixing a way of life."[104] He was determined that the struggle between the "Apollonian" forces of ruling-class order and the "Dionysian" forces of underclass energy should become visible in architecture.

It is not difficult to see why architecture and space, and more particularly the relationship between the modernist aesthetic and the restructuring of society, preoccupied Lefebvre and the situationists. Even as mainstream modernism was on the wane in avant-garde architectural circles, it was reaching its apogee in building production worldwide. Two massive projects of the sixties, Le Corbusier's Chandigarh in India and Lúcio Costa and Oscar Niemeyer's Brasília in Brazil, conjured up administrative centers in the desert in ways that confirmed mainstream modernism's transition from the rational to the extraordinary, from the revolutionary to the bureaucratic (figs. 1.18, 1.19). Brasília, *Internationale situationniste* declared, represented "the architecture of functionaries, the instrument and the microcosm of the bureaucratic *Weltanschauung.*"[105] Rationalist reconstruction and redevelopment was undertaken with particular zeal in France, as Lefebvre and the Parisian situationists were only too well aware, haunted by key areas of the program: the bleak *grands ensembles* (housing schemes) built around the peripheries of French cities, the projection of a series of *villes*

*nouvelles* (new towns), and the plans to reshape Paris as a modernized European hub.

Rationalism was already situationism's *bête noire*, but, to make the provocation even more unbearable, French postwar rationalism was of a particularly uncompromising strain. The impact of the new architecture upon the French popular imagination could be gauged, for instance, by the dystopian vision of Jean-Luc Godard's film *Alphaville* (1965).[106] The peculiarly repetitive nature of the new architecture was a side effect of the French mastery of system building, a highly efficient way of building usually achieved by hanging standardized units on reinforced concrete frames, a technique considered to combine modernity with economy. Of course, this construction was being carried out not by the pioneers of rationalism, but by a younger generation seizing the opportunity to finally impose something of the visions of the masters that they had learned in the seminar room. The ambitions to build the city in the sky, renew housing, and reorganize traffic circulation were all still there, but, despite considerable planning powers, projects tended to be piecemeal, the astonishingly utopian, "clean sheet" visions of the twenties and thirties, like Le Corbusier's Plan Voisin for Paris, now something of an anachronism.

In truth the situationists were among the most megalomaniac heirs of *urbanisme*, aspirants to the remaking of the city, while Le Corbusier's postwar work was marked by a steady transition into intensely humane and organic work. But it was easy for them to set up Le Corbusier as the whipping boy, laying every ill of rationalism at the feet of the aging master himself by interpreting him solely on the basis of his interwar work.[107] After all, even the scaled-down ambition of postwar reconstruction could produce some audacious schemes, and it was undoubtedly the cursed legacy of Le Corbusier and his CIAM colleagues that had inspired it all. In desperation *Potlatch* issued a "Boycott Order" against the 1956 "Radiant City Festival" event held in Marseilles, a celebration of Le Corbusier's vision organized under the state patronage of the Ministry of Reconstruction and Urbanism that aimed to impose, the International Lettrists claimed, an official unity upon an avant-garde that ought to be vital and independent.[108]

What counted as legitimate and benevolent social planning for Le Corbusier, CIAM, and the generation of planners that was their offspring, represented the bourgeois reorganization of space to the situationists. In 1923, claiming that "big business is today a healthy and moral organism," Le Corbusier had justified urbanism as a choice between "architecture or revolution," concluding that social frustration was a result of the workers' inability to transfer the rationality of the workplace to home life and leisure.[109] His version of radical change was carried through not by the populace but by the visionary architect-dictator, capable of planning people's lives by first organizing the spaces and places in which they were acted out: factories, offices, apartment blocks, sports halls, and cars.

"Urbanism renders alienation tactile," Debord and Jorn claimed.[110] *Potlatch* compared Le Corbusier's architecture to the programs, stretching from Plato's *Republic* to the early nineteenth-century mystic Pierre-Simon Ballanche's plan for a "City of Atonement," to design not just the fabric of the city but the social, spiritual, and economic minutiae of its everyday life.[111] *Potlatch* dismissed Le Corbusier as a "cop" and nicknamed him Le Corbusier-Sing-Sing after the notorious prison. He was, indeed, "le Protestant modulaire" (the modular Protestant), as if the fashionable Corbusian modular system for proportioning buildings was somehow inherently theocratic, an architectural straitjacket tailored for Le Corbusier's ideal man (fig. 1.20).[112] Anticipating claims made by Henri Lefebvre, Michel de Certeau, and Michel Foucault that control and surveillance are a principle of organization in the modern world, the Lettrist International declared that modernist architecture "has never been an art" and that "it has on the contrary always been inspired by the directives of the police." The lettrists became ever more hysterical: "today the prison has become the model habitation, and the Christian ethic triumphs without response, when one realizes that Le Corbusier aspires to *suppress the street*. And he's proud of it. There indeed is the program: life definitely partitioned in closed blocks, in surveilled societies; the end of chances for insurrection; automatic resignation."[113]

Debord and Jorn's illustration of the principle was less sophisticated than the Benthamite panop-

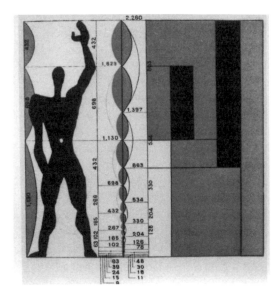

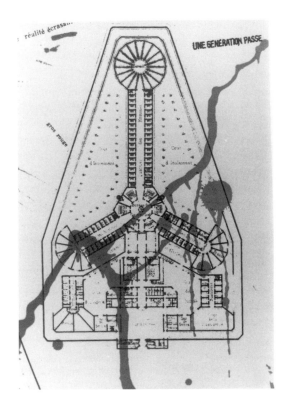

ticon prison later chosen by Foucault, but it made the point well enough, the plans of a nineteenth-century prison workhouse floating through the tortured space of their *Mémoires* (fig. 1.21).[114] Obsessive control, bequeathed by a succession of urban authorities, seemed to govern the most innocent spaces of everyday life, even in the Lettrist International's neighborhood pleasure park: "One can discover at a single glance the Cartesian organization of the so-called 'labyrinth' of the Jardin des Plantes and the inscription that announces it: GAMES ARE FORBIDDEN IN THE LABYRINTH. One could not seek a clearer summary of the spirit

of a whole civilization."[115] Evidence of the complicity of architecture and authority came easily to hand. *Internationale situationniste* published a clipping from the newspaper *Le Monde* discussing Interpol's "plans to create . . . a 'bureau of criminal prevention' . . . to provide architects, engineers, builders and other specialists with the wide range of techniques developed and endorsed by the police in order to prevent criminal offenses."[116]

The situationists' ability to "détourn" evidence like this made urban planning feel suddenly unsettling. Urban redevelopment and housing in postwar France, partly prompted by migration from the countryside as the nation continued to shift its economy from an agrarian to an industrial and commercial base, were perhaps the most visible reminders of the presence and power of welfare capitalism at a time when the French state was anxious to secure consensus.[117] Against the background of the loss of Indochina and the outbreak of the Algerian war, France under the Fourth Republic was governed by a string of unstable coalitions, with police troops prowling the streets of Paris in 1955–1956 in an attempt to "keep the peace." The competition between the left and right wings of mainstream French politics was stabilized for less than a decade by De Gaulle's Fifth Republic, constituted in 1959.

Barely deterred by the unpopularity of the *grands ensembles*, De Gaulle's government stepped up plans for redevelopment both in Paris and in the provinces. "One can only admire the ingenuity of our ministers and our urbanist architects," A.-F. Conord commented in *Potlatch* in 1954. "So as to avoid a complete rupture of consensus, they have put in place some model slums, the plans of which serve the four corners of France. . . . It is the 'barrack' style."[118] Later that year *Potlatch* claimed that the French authorities were using an earthquake in the Algerian city of Orléansville as a pretext for the creation of "a premeditated ghetto" that would relocate the indigenous population to the outskirts of the city in "vaguely neo-Corbusian barrack-block housing," much as Algerian immigrants would find themselves ghettoized on the fringes of Paris in the early 1960s.[119] *Internationale situationniste* continued to provide such case studies, citing the notorious *grand ensemble* of Sarcelles, built for blue-collar habitation, and the *ville nouvelle* of Mourenx, to substantiate its claim that planners were using housing to literally stratify workers according to their social and economic status (figs. 1.22, 1.23).[120] Mourenx's sudden appearance in his rural homeland of southwest France shocked Lefebvre as well into a deeper examination of the production of space.[121] The town's population was bound by exclusive employment to the gas fields and petrochemical complex of Lacq, *Internationale situationniste* explained, and labor and social relations enforced at Lacq were being carefully reproduced in housing at Mourenx: single people were housed in towers, married people in horizontal blocks, families in semi-detached dwellings, employees with high salaries enjoyed a villa to themselves, while managers lived in completely different cities. The journal compared the new style of housing to the cold war fashion for nuclear shelters (fig. 1.24): a survival without life, isolating the "disenfranchised" from their bureaucratic masters in Paris.[122]

**Figure 1.22 (top)**

*"Captive nature: At Sarcelles, the landscape 'reservation' magnanimously reconstituted by urban planners,"* illustration from anon., *"Urbanisme comme volonté et représentation,"* Internationale situationniste, *no. 9 (1964).*

**Figure 1.23 (bottom)**

*"The town of Mourenx,"* illustration from anon., *"Critique de l'urbanisme,"* Internationale situationniste, *no. 6 (1961). Despite the initial popularity of* grands ensembles and villes nouvelles *like Sarcelles and Mourenx, situationists correctly predicted their long-term social and architectural failure.*

No one could deny that urban reorganization has been a stock response among modern states faced with social instability, a process usually involving slum clearance and the improvement of communications. Thesis 172 of Debord's *Society of the Spectacle* quoted Lewis Mumford's *The City in History*: "With the present means of long-distance mass-communication, sprawling isolation has proved an . . . effective method of keeping a society under control."[123] Situationists believed that the priority of reconstruction was the viability of government rather than the improvement of living conditions. Constant, for example, dismissed the Corbusian *ville verte* (green city) as a "quasi-social space" where "roads, logically formed for circulation, are only marginally used as places of encounter."[124] The situationists, following generations of revolutionaries and avant-gardists before them, identified the street as the space of "real life" in the city.[125] What was needed, Constant argued, was not the opening of excessive urban space but its infilling: "if an intimate relation between environment and behavior is to be produced, the built-up area is indispensable" (figs. 1.25, 1.26, 1.27).[126]

The production of excess space only encouraged the capitalist "circulation of things and of human beings trapped in a world of things," too dear a price for fringe benefits like spectacular vistas.[127] This, the situationists claimed, had been the result of Paris's key urbanist projects—Haussmann's, from 1853, and a century later its

natural successor, postwar redevelopment—and so in a sense situationists simply brought the skepticism of the radical intelligentsia up to date. In the time of surrealism, Walter Benjamin had produced a lengthy critique of Haussmannization, and Louis Aragon's anger at ongoing Haussmannesque redevelopments was clearly articulated in his 1926 book *Le paysan de Paris* (Paris peasant).[128]

The passing of time enabled the situationists to see where urbanism had been heading. By 1963 the group had identified the impact upon cities of what we might today refer to as "late capitalism." The development of monopoly capitalism demanded ever greater urban cultural homogeneity—even leveling off extremes of deprivation and ostentation:

**Modern capitalism—concentrated and highly developed capitalism—inscribes onto the scenery of life the fusion**

## Figures 1.25, 1.26, 1.27

Constant, illustrations from "Une autre ville pour une autre vie," Internationale situationniste, no. 3 (1959):

top: *A quarter of a traditional town.* "Quasi-social space: the street. The streets, logically formed for circulation, are only marginally used as places of encounter."

middle: *A Corbusian* ville verte. "Isolated unités d'habitation. Social-minimum space: encounters only occur by chance and individually, in corridors and in the park. Circulation dominates everything."

bottom: *The principle of a covered city.* "'Spatial plan'. Suspended collective habitation; stretched out over all the town and separated from circulation, which passes over and under." This was the solution that Constant pursued in his New Babylon.

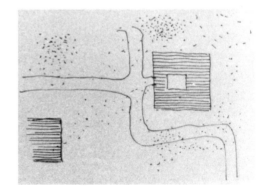

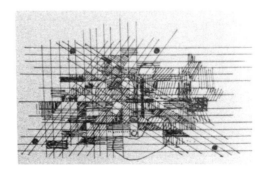

of what used to be opposed as the positive and negative poles of alienation: a sort of *equalizer of alienation.* . . . The new cities are laboratories of this stifling society: from Vällingby in Sweden to Bessor in Israel where all forms of leisure are to be united in one single center, without forgetting the housing project in Avilès that signals the neo-capitalist development now reaching Spain. Simultaneously, the disappearance of the "urban jungle" that corresponded to free market capitalism—in all its lack of comfort, its luxuries, and its adventures—continues apace. The center of Paris is radically restructured by the organization of automobile traffic: the quays transformed into highways, Place Dauphine into an underground parking garage.[129]

### Defending urban mix

If the city was becoming enslaved to late capitalism, then sooner or later its cultural mix, its "margins," its ethnic and working-class ghettos, would disappear. Between 1954 and 1974 the number of workers living within the Ville de Paris declined by 44 percent, displaced by rebuilding and rent-hiked gentrification to the suburbs beyond the Boulevard Périphérique, while the number of inhabitants belonging to the *cadres supérieurs* (management classes) increased by 51 percent.[130] In the later 1950s, Parisian situationists, who in the early part of the decade could still take the remarkable socio-architectural unevenness of their city for granted, made a last tour of the old neighborhoods, recording them for posterity, fastidiously avoiding the fluid traffic of the boulevards in favor of the still pools and backwaters of the city.

The situationist "drifter" was the new *flâneur* (the Parisian "stroller," dandy spectator of the urban scene who had emerged in the early nineteenth century and was later celebrated in the writings of Charles Baudelaire). Like the *flâneur*, the drifter skirted the old quarters of the city in order to experience the flip side of modernization. And situationist writing carried over some of the *flâneur*'s cavalier attitudes; page upon page passionately denounced alienation and extolled revolution, but the reader was only directed toward a deeper understanding of the ghetto-dwellers' real lives with a nonchalant wave of the hand. Situationists mythologized the poor as fellow travelers on the urban margins, treating the ghetto as an urban asset rather than an urban ill. "We hold that the so-called modern town-planning which you recommend," the lettrists told *The Times* newspaper in London, "is fatuously idealistic and reactionary. The sole end of architecture is to serve the passions of men." The projected demolition of London's Chinatown, they went on, "must obviously make England more boring than it has in recent years already become."[131]

The group provided some splendidly facetious descriptions of Paris's various ethnic *quartiers*. Jacques Fillon joked about establishing an "alter-

native travel agency," providing tours of cultural "others" that could be reached on foot from the Lettrist International's headquarters near the Place de la Contrescarpe. Of the Chinese quarter, our guide simply noted that "the inhabitants are very poor. They prepare complicated dishes, of little nutrition and strongly spiced." He located the working-class stronghold of Aubervilliers, on the northeast edge of the city, thus: "Having taken the route toward the north, a two-hour walk, one arrives at a place called Aubervilliers, a plain cut with unusable canals. The climate there is cold, and snow falls frequently. . . . The inhabitants, very poor, speak fluent Spanish. They await the revolution. They play the guitar and they sing."[132]

And while situationists' alertness to the class and racial conflict that produced ghettos was fitting in an era of increasing residential segregation—de facto in, say, Chicago, and explicit in South Africa—their own encounters with the ghetto could be immature or deliberately provocative, delighting in the *frisson* of long and loud drinking sessions in Yiddish, Polish, and Algerian bars.[133] Only occasionally was this half-real, half-imagined situationist city infringed by socioeconomic practicality; *Potlatch* was once moved to complain that the Abbépierre's emergency Red Cross winter shelter had spoiled the view at a favorite lettrist haunt, the Square des Missions Etrangères.[134] Effortlessly merging the legacies of avant-garde revolutionary with those of *flâneur* and *précieux* (the dandy's seventeenth-century

**Figure 1.28**

*Derelict frontages of the former Rue Sauvage, 13th Arrondissement. The Lettrist International "campaigned" for the preservation of the Rue Sauvage as an increasingly rare example of Paris without spectacle. It has since disappeared from street maps, to be absorbed into apartment blocks and the sidings of the Gare d'Austerlitz.*

ancestor), the International Lettrists played up their role—"Do you honestly believe a gentleman can amuse himself in Soho?," they asked the editor of *The Times*.[135] Like new gentlemen of leisure, promoting their "revolutionary" motto of *Ne travaillez jamais* (Never work), they reserved a sort of *ancien* disdain for the petit-bourgeois areas of Paris.[136]

"We are not attached to the charm of ruins," the Lettrist International once emphasized in its "campaign" to save the scruffy Rue Sauvage at the back of the Gare d'Austerlitz in the 13th Arrondissement. "But the civil barracks which are erected in their place have a gratuitous ugliness that calls for the dynamiters."[137] For the Lettrist International, the Rue Sauvage was not so much a candidate for straightforward conservation as a reference point for assessing the impact of perfunctory urban redevelopment. Today, only traces

**Figure 1.29**

*Lopez, Beaudoin, and de Marien, Ensemble Maine-Montparnasse, Paris, 1966–1973. Debord's footage of the Ensemble, for his 1973 film* La société du spectacle, *testified to the reshaping of an area that had served as the headquarters to the bohemian avant-garde in the first half of the twentieth century. Once it was completed, most Parisians considered the spectacular height of the Tour Montparnasse to be an unacceptable intrusion into the Parisian skyline.*

of Rue Sauvage can be detected in frontages and cobblestones, and by the 1970s the 13th Arrondissement as a whole was being transformed from its traditional mix of factories and working-class housing into a modernist swath of new housing and offices, centered on the Place d'Italie (fig. 1.28).

Its fate was sealed in the very years of situationism's formation, from the early 1950s to the early 1960s, when the most serious plans for the future of Paris were being drawn up. The scale of postwar redevelopment planned for Paris in those years, once the urgent need to rebuild towns destroyed in the *départements* (provinces) had been met, was unprecedented since Haussmann. It has been estimated that at least a third of the old Ville de Paris disappeared. The plans of which situationists would have first been aware were those of the Conseil Municipal de Paris, intent upon the removal of the officially designated *îlots insalubres* (insalubrious blocks) as a way of renewing Parisian habitation and of improving traffic circulation. In addition, the return to power of De Gaulle in 1958 accelerated policies that envisaged Paris redeveloped as a rapidly expanding tertiary center servicing Europe as a whole. The slick and slightly vacuous image of the new Paris was pondered in Debord's film *La société du spectacle* as the camera swept Raymond Lopez's Ensemble Maine-Montparnasse, a business complex for 21,000 people, with a tower boasting fifty-six floors but no other architectural distinction, a development

approved unanimously by the Conseil Municipal (fig. 1.29).

A massive plan, Haussmannian in ambition, neo-Corbusian in style, led by the Gaullist councilor André Thirion in the early 1950s, proposed the redevelopment of "peripheral" *quartiers* and the removal of the indigenous working-class population from a large triangular district bounded by Gare Saint-Lazare, Gare du Nord, and Place de la République to "nearby suburbs," making way for commerce and for the creation of a new urban

**Figures 1.30, 1.31**

*Before-and-after models of the redevelopment of the Îlot Dupin, Rue Saint-Placide, 6th Arrondissement, c. 1958. Part of the so-called "Reconquest of Paris" and complete by 1961, this replacement of architectural jumble by a modern municipal slab block typified the sort of redevelopment that the situationists disliked.*

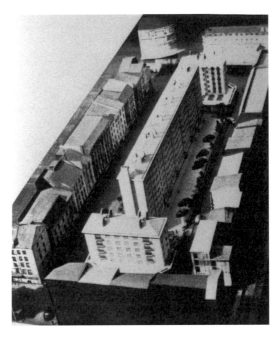

motorway network with roads fifty to sixty meters wide. The plan was defeated only narrowly in 1951, and schemes continued to flow through the Conseil Municipal and the superior Préfecteurs throughout the fifties. Between 1953 and 1958 the Conseil was guided by the Corbusian principle of "reconquering the sun" through the *ville verte*, the instrument so bitterly criticized by the situationists, and in 1954 Lopez, backed by the councilor Bernard Lafay, launched a new round of modernization proposals tackling the first ten

arrondissements of Paris, the historic core of the city.[138] The Conseil's vacillation ultimately pleased no one. The numerous, if relatively minor, incursions that were realized disrupted the urban grain. For example, the Îlot Dupin in the 6th Arrondissement, a couple of blocks away from the lettrist haunt of Square des Missions Etrangères, cleared the preferred situationist urban scene of tight, jumbled buildings and spaces in favor of a slab block with off-street parking (figs. 1.30, 1.31). Meanwhile the massive schemes for housing around the Parisian

**Figure 1.32**

*Guy Debord with Asger Jorn,* The Naked City: illustration de l'hypothése [sic] des plaques tournantes en psychogeographique [sic], *1957, screenprint. This, the second and simpler of Debord and Jorn's psychogeographic maps (compare fig. 1.5), was by far the most famous image to come out of situationism, and perhaps deservedly so. Its arresting,* *matter-of-fact design simultaneously mourned the loss of old Paris, prepared for the city of the future, explored the city's structures and uses, criticized traditional mapping, and investigated the relationship between language, narrative, and cognition.*

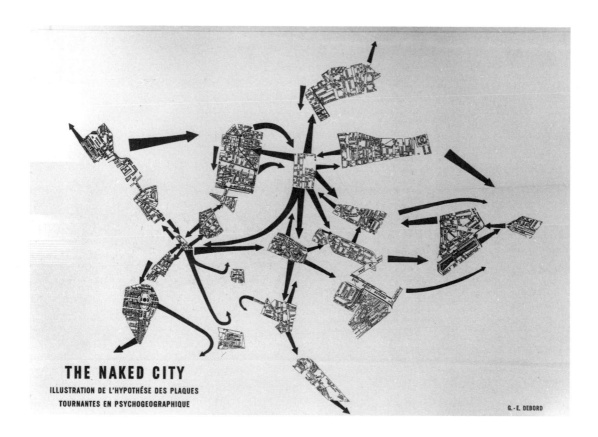

periphery—in 1954 alone the Conseil approved the construction of about four thousand flats—failed to stem the city's housing problem, a frightening compound of escalating rents, immigration, overcrowding, and inadequate sanitation. "New housing was on the average too small, often badly constructed ($1/4$ of these 'new slums' should be destroyed), and always too expensive," the historian Pierre Couperie noted in 1968. "Because of this, in 1966 from 15,000 to 30,000 new dwellings were vacant, unsold despite the persistent crisis. . . . At the same time, the irresponsible choice of automobiles over adequate housing aggravated these evils and created new ones."[139]

**Figure 1.33**

Cassan and Albert, University of Paris Faculty of Sciences (later the Universités Paris VI–Paris VII), Paris, begun 1962. The construction of the Faculty flattened the site of the old Halle aux Vins (wine market) featured in Debord and Jorn's psychogeographic maps.

detective work by borrowing the title of *The Naked City* from the famous 1948 drama-documentary film of detectives at work in New York City. Watching the film *The Naked City*, M. Christine Boyer has noted, one has the impression of an urban space reconstructed, of a city that was otherwise on the brink of disappearance, "no longer experienced directly by pedestrians" as it became "abandoned for the suburbs, fragmented by urban renewal, and tormented by the automobile."[141] Debord and Jorn's *Naked City* conveyed much the same effect.

Each case study of the subsequent redevelopment of the Parisian "Naked City," it seems, illustrates the verity of situationist claims that *urbanisme* represented a drive to rationalize, homogenize, and commercialize the socioeconomic diversity of Paris. The right-hand edges of the *Guide psychogéographique* and *The Naked City* showed the Gare de Lyon, now surrounded by the office developments that were encouraged near main railway stations by the strategic plan for Paris in the early 1960s.[142] Across the Seine, in the 5th Arrondissement, the maps included the old Halle aux Vins (the wine market, built in 1664 and rebuilt 1808–1819). Only five years after the maps were made, the serried wine stores, separated by tree-lined avenues that bore names as romantic as Rue de Champagne, Rue de la Côte d'Or, and Préau des Eaux de Vie (Champagne street, Gold coast street, Courtyard/playground of the waters of life), would be evicted for the University of Paris's Faculty of Sciences on the Rue Jussieu (fig. 1.33).

To some extent Debord and Jorn's situationist maps, the *Guide psychogéographique de Paris* of 1956 and *The Naked City* of 1957, served as guides to areas of central Paris threatened by redevelopment, retaining those parts that were still worth visiting and disposing of all those bits that they felt had been spoiled by capitalism and bureaucracy (fig. 1.32).[140] The deductions were made by "drifting" around the city, looking for evidence about the condition of contemporary Paris; Debord and Jorn emphasized the rigor of their

The attentive pedestrian can still find pieces of the walls of the Halle aux Vins on the fringes of the new Université, where the cash to finish the demolition of the old and construction of the new dried up. Here is old Paris ravaged by Cartesian excess. Exactly as the situationists seemed to be warning us, the social is implicated in the aesthetic: Jussieu's nightmarish corridors, vertiginous stairwells, and campus deserts, fashioned from *béton brut* to meet the demand for popular higher education, barely conceal an indifference for their users.

In 1959 it was officially decided to preserve the "urban and social tissue" of the core, but in a way that was barely less distasteful to situationists. They were not the only critics sickened by the policies of André Malraux, De Gaulle's new Minister of Culture, whose passion for sanitizing and gentrifying the old as a complement to the new presented an official image of the city just as surely as wholesale reconstruction.[143] And then there was the issue of what was "officially" historic. Since opinion over the role of historic buildings transcended party division and was only part of a wider debate that concerned traffic and social management, the authorities' hesitation over the extent of renovation and conservation cannot be taken as evidence of a properly conservationist strand in the 1950s, and situationism constituted a lone and ignored voice in the debate. By the 1960s mainstream French conservationist opposition was a little more coherent—consternation over the possible

excesses of modernism was felt in the debate about the height and location of Parisian tower blocks, for instance—but as late as 1965 the influential councilor and journalist Alex Moscovitch would exploit the obsessions with hygiene that dominated French modernization, carrying the day with a lecture impatiently titled with the rhetorical question "Are the slums of Paris sacred?"

**To confuse the old with the ancient, to shed crocodile tears over those dilapidated tumbledowns, stinking and without character, on the pretext that they are two hundred years old, and that during those two centuries they have sheltered generations of scrofula sufferers[144] and consumptive children, is that to create a work of culture, of spiritual elevation, and of good taste? Must it confer the right to treat as "destroyers" and "vandals" all those who are not snobs of restored slums, all those who prefer modern comfort, hours of sunshine, anywhere that authentic masterpieces of architecture are unlikely to be put in peril?[145]**

The Marais, a fabulous and historic slum composed of rotting aristocratic *hôtels particuliers* (residential mansions), and briefly home to situationists Guy Debord and Michèle Bernstein, appeared as chunks floating in the northeast corners of the situationist maps.[146] Unlike, say, the Halle aux Vins, the Marais was generally recognized as worthy of conservation, its fate being debated within the Conseil Municipal from as early as 1946. The president of the Conseil Municipal

**Figure 1.34**

"Internal currents and external communications of Les Halles," figure from Abdelhafid Khatib, "Essai de description psychogéographique des Halles," Internationale situationniste, no. 2 (1958). Khatib's report was one of the few psychogeographic accounts to be published in Internationale situationniste.

in 1946–1947, a self-proclaimed admirer of Haussmann, had suggested that historic buildings could be simply moved out of the way, rebuilt, perhaps, around the Marais as a sort of open-air museum, precisely the sort of solution dreaded by the situationists, who complained of the tendency "to restore a few old urban spots as sights of touristic spectacle, a simple extension of the principle of the classical museum by means of which an entire neighborhood can become a *monument*."[147] No such official patronage extended to the Marais's neighbors, the decrepit Beaubourg (literally translated it means "beautiful village," an irony that doubtless delighted situationists) and the marketplace of Les Halles, placed at the very centers of the situationist maps. At the time, the spectacle of modernization had bypassed this part of Paris. It was a recognizably working-class area, where pedestrians rather than motorized traffic had priority on the streets, and where commercial exchange still took place over transitory market stalls, or in small shops, rather than in the chic boutiques or monolithic department stores a little further north and west. Here in the center of late-fifties Paris, Debord and Jorn correctly identified a gap in the Parisian spectacle.

Its vulnerability merited its celebration. Since the 1930s the Parisian authorities had been determined to modernize the area. The Plateau Beaubourg section of Îlot no. 1, once designated as the worst slum in Paris, was razed to the ground in the 1930s, much as Haussmann had flattened the medieval quarter on the Île de la Cité, on the pretext that it was an unsanitary harbor of prostitution and tuberculosis. The Plateau was left as wasteland and used as a truck park during market hours for Halles, which was scheduled to move out to the suburbs as part of the regional plan.[148]

Planners toyed with the space throughout the late fifties and sixties. Les Halles, they envisaged, would be demolished and excavated for the central Paris interchange of the new RER Métro, with transformation of the area sure to follow through a combination of state and private capital providing for parking, shopping, and offices. By 1966 a lobby of conservationists and left-wingers, opposed to the loss of low-rent housing and space for artisan trades as well as of historic buildings, was combining to throw the Halles plans into disarray, yet in a sense the battle was already lost. Nothing could save the unselfconscious atmosphere at Halles that the situationists had loved, scrupulously surveyed by Abdelhafid Khatib for

**Figure 1.35**

"*Numerous views of dawn at Les Halles,*" *still from* Sur le passage de quelques personnes à travers une assez courte unité de temps, *dir. Guy Debord, 1959, reprinted in Guy Debord,* Contre le cinéma *(1964). Despite their efforts to* make psychogeography into a reasoned method, Khatib's and Debord's representations of Halles were really love letters to Paris. The market halls were demolished in 1971.

*Internationale situationniste* and panned by Debord's camera in his 1959 movie *Sur le passage de quelques personnes à travers une assez courte unité de temps* ("On the passage of a few people through a rather brief moment in time") (figs. 1.34, 1.35).[149] The market itself, which had met on the site since the late twelfth century, departed in 1968, its place taken for a while by the displays and happenings accompanying the revolutionary May events, providing populist competition for the officially sanctioned Festival du Marais. The market halls were demolished in 1971, ingloriously cleared for "le grand trou," the big hole that was eventually filled in with the RER and a sunken shopping and entertainment center, the somewhat dismal outcome of a planning process that attracted the attention of the biggest names in urban thinking—Henri Lefebvre, Roland Barthes, Philip

Johnson, Tomás Maldonado, Bruno Zevi, Jean Nouvel, and Jean Baudrillard, among many others (fig. 1.36).[150] No amount of expertise in city surgery could put the heart back into Paris.

It was surely no coincidence that 1968 also found President Georges Pompidou personally throwing Beaubourg's fate open to an international architectural competition for a "happening" library, gallery, and cultural center. Remarkably, neither of the winning architects, Renzo Piano and Richard Rogers, was French. Yet the project as a whole was dedicated to the French conception of *la gloire*, that special combination of personal and national vainglory.[151] In fairness to Piano and Rogers, their brilliant building was surely preferable, socially and aesthetically, to most of the megastructures that had competed for the site (fig. 1.37). Rogers even pleaded with the French president himself to preserve Baltard's old glass and green iron Halles market building, a structural exemplar to which Rogers's work paid homage, and no one should doubt the sincerity of Rogers's own radicalism at the time—his 1969 manifesto was the very embodiment of sixties technological utopianism, claiming that "technology offers the possibility of a society without want, where, for the first time, work and learning need only be done for pleasure, and the age-old capitalist morality of earning one's keep, the backbone of the existing power structure, would be eliminated."[152] But the plain fact was that the Centre National d'Art et de Culture Georges Pompidou, a showcase for industrial design, canonically great modern painting, and information, sheathed in a brash functionalism, represented one of the purest and most refined forms of spectacle, an attraction more popular than the Eiffel Tower. Profoundly divorced from the sort of radical local initiative implied by situationist urbanism, Beaubourg seemed to be one more piece of territory lost in the battle for urban space.

Richard Rogers and Renzo Piano, Centre National d'Art et de Culture Georges Pompidou, Paris, 1977. There was a tremendous irony in the way the Pompidou Centre filled the Beaubourg void at the center of the psychogeographic maps: a building and piazza embodying the urban spectacle that situationists had fought, yet at the same time a structure that paid homage to many of the principles of "flexibility" and "participation" that they had promoted.

When writing about the struggle against the spectacle, the situationists were fond of military metaphors, and at Beaubourg one can see why. Were it not for the authoritarian supervision of the Centre's construction by Robert Bordaz, a state councilor whose previous work included the evacuation after Dien Bien Phu, Beaubourg would still be a hole in the ground.[153] Or it might harbor the sort of radicalized population that had put its head above the wall in May 1968, just prior to Pompidou's announcement of the Beaubourg competition. If, as the situationists claimed, the May events were evidence of a spontaneous popular will, then the Centre Pompidou looked like a blatant attempt to manage that will. Even Rogers's biography noted that "the police presence was still overwhelming in Paris in 1971—none of the Piano & Rogers team had ever seen so many armed police on the streets."[154]

In 1977 Jean Baudrillard, who as a member of the Utopie group a decade earlier had been profoundly affected by Lefebvre and the Situationist International, published a text on *L'effet Beaubourg* (The Beaubourg effect) to coincide with the opening of the Centre. Dismissing the Centre as "a monument of cultural dissuasion," Baudrillard cheerily offered the apocalyptic vision of the Beaubourg's steel frame buckling under the weight of the masses.[155] Within the Beaubourg machine, he felt, humanism would finally collapse into populism. Since the Second World War the situationists and others had been demanding the space and technology for spontaneous popular culture. In the wake of an attempted revolution, the state had, in effect, called the avant-garde's bluff.[156] In 1989 the Beaubourg hosted the retrospective exhibition on the Situationist International.

**From the rational to the sublime**

"Architecture is the simplest means of articulating time and space, of modulating reality, of engendering dreams," stated Ivan Chtcheglov, a brilliant and disturbed nineteen-year-old International Lettrist, in one of the manifestoes of situationism, the "Formulaire pour un urbanisme nouveau" (Formulary for a new urbanism), a beautiful document written in 1953.[1] Situationists promised that their architecture would one day revolutionize everyday life and release the ordinary citizen into a world of experiment, anarchy, and play.

In the meantime situationist architecture remained largely in the mind, awaiting activation through revolutionary modes of production, and situationists were left to draw their inspiration from the raw material of the existing city. "That which changes our way of seeing the street," Debord said at the inaugural meeting of the Situationist International, "is more important than that which changes our way of seeing a painting"; and psycho-geographic drift altered the situationists' percep-

tions of the street at the same time as it completed its taxonomy of the modern city.[2] Psychogeography was playful, cheap, and populist, an artistic activity carried out in the everyday space of the street rather than in the conventional art spaces of the gallery or theater. "The importance attributed to the street in French cultural discourse conveys a sense of the general desire for a culture that is more open, fun-loving, and free-wheeling, as opposed to the allegedly stifling, pompous and enclosed world of high culture," Brian Rigby claims in his history of French popular culture; "the street is the privileged site which unites the quotidian and the festive."[3] Since the nineteenth century the city had been recognized as the absolute locus of modernity, sociability, and revolutionary change; now the city streets of Amsterdam, London, and above all Paris would double as situationist galleries, their meanings unstable and hotly contested.

Postwar modern architecture had been spellbound by the slab block erected between 1947 and 1952 by Le Corbusier in Marseilles. He called it the Unité d'Habitation. But situationists demanded a quality beyond that of mere habitat; they sought out the *unité d'ambiance*—an area of particularly intense urban atmosphere.[4] The chunks of Paris represented on Guy Debord and Asger Jorn's situationist maps, the *Guide psychogéographique de Paris* and *The Naked City*, were deemed to be such unities of ambiance, and in effect the situationists' insistence on the special qualities of these *loci* ("singular places") within the turmoil of the city revived the French school of urban geography founded by Marcel Poète in the 1920s.[5]

Many unities were attractive for their social composition, supporting concentrated artisan, artist, or student populations, but social composition alone was not enough. Nor was any particular architectural style. "The slightest demystified investigation," insisted Debord, "reveals that the qualitatively or quantitatively different influences of diverse urban decors cannot be determined solely on the basis of the era or architectural style, much less on the basis of housing conditions."[6] The unities of ambiance were constituted by many things, especially the "soft," mutable elements of the city scene: the play of presence and absence, of light and sound, of human activity, even of time, and the association of ideas. The "hard" elements, like the shape, size, and placement of masonry, gently articulated the softnesses in between.

This sounds rather abstract, and it was barely fleshed out by the written analyses offered by the situationists. In 1958 the Situationist International dispatched Abdelhafid Khatib to fully report on what made Les Halles such an exemplary unity of ambiance.[7] Yet the reader of his report slowly realized that in some couple of thousand of words, bolstered by a sprinkling of Chombart de Lauwe-style maps, complex descriptions of street patterns, and a careful survey of the area's socioeconomic diversity, Khatib had not found the source of ambiance after all. The report was no more and no less than what it said

it was, a "description" of Halles rather than its explication.

Michèle Bernstein's short description of the Square des Missions Etrangères in the 7th Arrondissement, which appeared in *Potlatch* in 1955, was as good an introduction as any to the ineffable qualities of a small unity of ambiance, and the Square survives sufficiently intact for today's visitor to sample something of its subtle charm. Typically for psychogeography, Bernstein paid scant attention to function or style. She sketched in the nineteenth-century mansion flats bordering one side of the square as being "of fine appearance," while the impressive, sheer cliff wall of the terrace, sliced through to make way for the Square, was summarily described as being "black" and "ten meters high" (figs. 2.1, 2.2).[8] And though near to the bohemian havens of the Left Bank, the area in which the Square des Missions Etrangères was to be found was bourgeois, endowing the place with no obvious socioeconomic complexion other than its unfashionableness. Yet there was something here to haunt the visitor. Missions Etrangères was a terminal point in the city, presided over by "a bust of Chateaubriand in the form of the god Terminus."[9] Spatially the place was intriguing, forking so that, as Bernstein noted, one branch was overshadowed by the cliff wall, while the other branch seemed to penetrate it (fig. 2.3); and to intensify the sense of confusion, Bernstein advised us that Mission Etrangères had to be "besieged at night."[10] The situationist city

**Figure 2.1**

Square des Missions Etrangères, 7th Arrondissement, look-ing north. Michèle Bernstein's analysis of the Square gave us one of the few and brief insights into situationist aesthet-ics. Nineteenth-century mansion flats border one side of the Square.

**Figure 2.2**

Square des Missions Etrangères, looking southeast. The high wall of the terrace, sliced through to make way for the Square, provides a backdrop to the bust of Chateaubriand. On the left is the back of the park shelter (see fig. 2.9).

**Figure 2.3**

Square des Missions Etrangères, looking south. On the right is the terrace wall, breached by the small park's branch to the left, creating an unusual space now occupied by games courts.

Figure 2.4

Claude-Nicolas Ledoux, Rotunda tollhouse, Barrière de La Villette, Place de Stalingrad, Paris, 1786, with the overhead Jaurès-Stalingrad Métro line (and passing train) in the immediate background. Guy Debord and Gil J. Wolman, who discovered the place on a drift through Paris in March 1956, were haunted by its complex effects of space and architecture.

Figure 2.5

Bassin de La Villette/Canal de l'Ourcq, viewed from the Ledoux Rotunda. Guy Debord invited us to compare the view with Claude Lorrain's imaginary views of seaports.

was a constant play of contrasts, between confined and open spaces, darkness and illumination, circulation and isolation.

Guy Debord and Gil J. Wolman, meanwhile, were delighting in their "discovery" of the Ledoux Rotunda. Claude-Nicolas Ledoux's 1786 tollhouse at the Barrière de La Villette, Place de Stalingrad, is an outstanding neoclassical essay in pure architectural form which opens out onto the deep spaces of the Canal Saint-Martin, Boulevard de la Chapelle, Rue d'Aubervilliers, and the Canal de l'Ourcq (figs. 2.4, 2.5).[11] Debord compared the composition of the view to Claude Lorrain's harbor scenes, in which the artist depicted imaginary classical ports and landscapes, their foregrounds packed with the details of port life, their backgrounds recessed into deep seascapes, and the whole suffused by the mysterious golden light of early morning or late evening (figs. 2.6, 2.7). And indeed, once brought to mind, Debord's favorite paintings, the two seaports by Claude Lorrain hanging in the Louvre (*Seaport with Setting Sun*, 1637, and *Seaport with Ulysses Returning Chryseis to Her Father*, 1644), could virtually superimpose their contents onto one's own view down the Bassin de La Villette.[12] Debord, encountering the disused tollhouse as "a virtual ruin left in an incredible state of abandonment, whose charm is singularly enhanced by the curve of the elevated subway line that passes at close distance," loved the massing of architectural variety at Place de Stalingrad, comparing the scene to "the clearly psychogeographic appeal of the illustrations found in books for very young children" where "one finds collected in a single image a harbor, a mountain, an isthmus, a forest, a river, a dike, a cape, a bridge, a ship, and an archipelago" (fig. 2.8).[13]

## Figure 2.6

*Claude Gellée (called Lorrain),* Seaport with Setting Sun, *1637, oil on canvas, Musée du Louvre, Paris.*

## Figure 2.7

*Claude Gellée (called Lorrain),* Seaport with Ulysses Returning Chryseis to Her Father, *1644, oil on canvas, Musée du Louvre, Paris. "I scarcely know of anything but those two harbors at dusk painted by Claude Lorrain—which are at the Louvre and which juxtapose two extremely dissimilar urban ambiances—that can rival in beauty the Paris Métro maps," Debord wrote in his "Introduction à une critique de la géographie urbaine" (1955). Debord's comparison was less visual than conceptual, encouraging his readers to explore the city both real and imaginary. The two paintings also featured in Debord's 1973 film* La société du spectacle.

Significantly, then, the unities embraced eclecticism and a sense of the picturesque, and this oddly corresponded to the influential appeal for picturesque townscaping then issuing from Britain's *Architectural Review*. The *Architectural Review* and *Potlatch* basically concurred that the ideal town would be one where humane, pedestrian social spaces, endowed with mixed architectural compositions and curios, would take priority over any abstract, CIAM-ish principle for purely "rational" planning. On the other hand, the journals were polarized not only by ideology, but by their radically differing interpretations of beauty and of the value of the picturesque. For the *Architectural Review*, the picturesque was a byword for the lyrical and the pleasant, whereas situationism was attracted by the more troubled side of the picturesque—meditative,

exotic, expressive. The *Architectural Review*'s nononsense judgment of beauty and ugliness would have found few followers among the situationists.[14] As Jorn put it, "an era without ugliness would be an era without progress."[15] "All of us agree," the Lettrist International once announced, "to repel aesthetic objection, to silence the admirers of the portal of Chartres. Beauty, when it is not a promise of happiness, must be destroyed"; and where the picturesque was too contrived it was simply dismissed as "annoying."[16] Situationism sought something more demanding in its aesthetics, Bernstein taking a delight in "a kiosk of great

**Figure 2.8 (top)**

*Didactic map for children, representing a wide variety of geographic features. Illustration for Ivan Chtcheglov's "Formulaire pour un urbanisme nouveau,"* Internationale situationniste, *no. 1 (1957). Debord compared the massing of effects in such maps to the experience of exemplary urban spaces like the Ledoux rotunda.*

**Figure 2.9 (bottom)**

*Shelter at the Square des Missions Etrangères, looking west. Bernstein's admiration of the structure typified the situationist acceptance of ugliness.*

**Figure 2.10**

*Giovanni Piranesi,* Carceri, *plate VII, second state, 1760, etching. Piranesi was a vital source for the situationists' psychogeographic sublime, and his vision would later be invoked in Constant's renderings of New Babylon (see fig. 3.26).*

**Figure 2.11**

*"Le Facteur" Ferdinand Cheval,* Palais Idéal, *Hauterives, France, 1879–1905, with a portrait of the architect. Cheval's self-built marvel was a situationist icon.*

dignity which looks for all the world like a station platform and has a medieval appearance" sited slap in the middle of the Square des Missions Etrangères (fig. 2.9).[17]

It was, for Bernstein, a sort of latter-day folly. For the original picturesque planners of the eighteenth century, the allusions of the folly "were meant to move the viewer to salutary states of awe, melancholy, joy or terror"—in other words, to

an experience of "the sublime."[18] *Potlatch* consistently recommended sources for the sublime, suggesting visits to the two best surviving examples of picturesque gardening around Paris, the Désert de Retz and the Parc Monceau, and inviting readers to compare two recognized masters of the sublime, Claude Lorrain and the printmaker Giovanni Battista Piranesi (fig. 2.10).[19] "Piranesi," the journal announced, "is psychogeography in the staircase. Claude Lorraine is psychogeography in his presentation of a palatial *quartier* and the sea."[20] By a neat turn, the poetic and awesome architecture depicted by Piranesi in the *Vedute* (Views) of ancient and modern Rome, and his terrifying and dramatically lit *Carceri d'invenzione* (Imaginary prisons), had fascinated Claude-Nicolas

*Figure 2.12*

*Guy Debord with Asger Jorn, page from* Mémoires, *1959, screenprinted book.* Mémoires' *collage of text, maps, and illustration evoked the sense of reverie appropriate to psychogeography.*

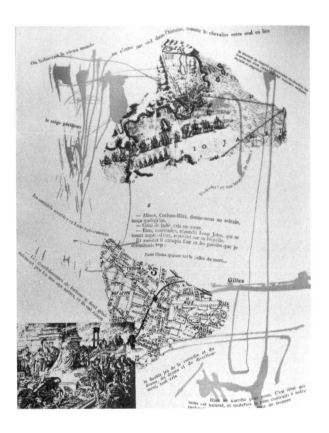

Ledoux, Charles Baudelaire, and another situationist hero—the English romantic writer Thomas De Quincey, who had "drifted" through London in his 1821 *Confessions of an English Opium-Eater*. *Potlatch*'s list of sublime sources carried on, raising Le Facteur Ferdinand Cheval—the French postman who built a personal exotic palace in his spare time—to the supreme honor of "psychogeography in architecture" (fig. 2.11). Edgar Allan

Poe, pioneer of the macabre and of the detective story, and *flâneur*, was deemed psychogeographic "in landscape."[21]

Eighteenth-century theorists had advocated the picturesque and sublime as stimulants to reverie. Then the intention had been to overcome the excessively ordered universe envisioned by the Enlightenment, so it seemed to follow that the sublime could induce new flights of fancy in a mid-twentieth-century city reshaped by the Enlightenment's progeny, modernism. Psychogeography directed us to obscure places, to elusive ambient effects and partial artistic and literary precedents for the sublime. If we felt frustrated at the effort required to put them all together, we had missed the point. Psychogeography was a reverie, a state of mind conjured up in Debord and Jorn's *Mémoires*, which left readers with the task of negotiating Jorn's inky dribbles through Debord's collage of text, maps, and illustration (fig. 2.12). It represented a drift from the ideal and the rational to the extraordinary and revolutionary.

### Making sense of psychogeography

The eighteenth-century picturesque and sublime had paid homage to nature, depicting it as a force poised to subsume or overwhelm humanity, at odds with the pastoral vision of people at ease in an

*Figure 2.13*

*Le Corbusier, drawing of the Cité Contemporaine pour 3 Millions d'Habitants, 1922. In this classic image of modernism, Le Corbusier presented the ideal city as uncannily clean, unpeopled, and ordered, as if time itself could be arrested. Situationists found the image chilling; Constant's zestful renderings of the situationist city conveyed a very different sensation of the urban future (compare fig. 3.3).*

ideal landscape. By analogy, the situationist city was at odds with the Corbusian vision of people at ease in an ideal urban landscape, a place where the struggle with nature, with the body, with space, and with class had inexplicably come to an end. Le Corbusier's Ville Contemporaine (Contemporary city) was forever contemporary only by freezing time and ending history (fig. 2.13). In psychogeography all the struggles were acute again, making a nonsense of the Corbusian fantasy of the city as something abstract, rational, or ideal. Debord reported that "the primarily urban character of the drift, in its element in the great industrially transformed cities—those centers of possibilities and meanings—could be expressed in Marx's phrase: 'Men can see nothing around them that is not their own image; everything speaks to them of themselves. Their very landscape is alive.'"[22]

As its name implied, psychogeography attempted to combine subjective and objective modes of study. On the one hand it recognized that the self cannot be divorced from the urban environment; on the other hand, it had to pertain to more than just the psyche of the individual if it was to be useful in the collective rethinking of the city. The reader senses Debord's desperation to negotiate this paradox in his "Théorie de la dérive" (Theory of the *dérive*), a key document first published in the Belgian surrealist journal *Les lèvres nues* in 1956 and republished in *Internationale situationniste* in 1958. The drift, Debord explained, entailed the sort of "playful-constructive behavior" that had always distinguished situationist activities from mere pastimes. The drift should not be confused, then, with "classical notions of the journey and the stroll"; drifters weren't like tadpoles in a tank, "stripped . . . of intelligence, sociability and sexuality," but were people alert to "the attractions of the terrain and the encounters they find there," capable as a group of agreeing upon distinct, spontaneous preferences for routes through the city.[23]

One of Debord's priorities in hedging the role of spontaneity and chance in the drift was to create distinctions with its better-known surrealist precedents. "An insufficient awareness of the limitations of chance, and of its inevitably reactionary use, condemned to dismal failure the celebrated aimless ambulation attempted in 1923 by four surrealists, beginning from a town chosen by lot," he noted.[24] Debord had some tolerance for surrealist methods (he was amused by a friend who "had just wandered through the Harz region of Germany while blindly following the directions of a map of London"), but while situationists made it their business to disrupt the bourgeois worldview, they had no wish to problematize all instrumental knowledge and action. Surrealist automatism was, they felt, creatively and politically exhausted, "a genre of ostentatious . . . 'weirdness.'"[25]

Debord was resigned to the fact that "in its infancy" drift would be partly dependent upon chance and would have to accommodate a degree of "letting go."[26] The psychoanalyst Jacques Lacan had claimed that surrealist play oscillated between intention and automatism, and much the same could have been said about psychogeographic drift.[27] Debord and Wolman themselves decided that the drift was a combination of

chance and planning that reached various stages of equilibrium.[28] In his concern that "letting go" might collapse back into surrealist automatism, Debord overlooked the fact that drifters could not completely "let go" even if they wanted to. Psychogeography was formed and validated by a situationist group discourse and culture that couldn't be just blanked out at will. In fact Debord presented the situationist maps of Paris and the "theory of the *dérive*" precisely in order to ratify group activity, codifying all sorts of overblown psychogeographic techniques.[29]

The result—an organized spontaneity—was something of an oddity, and it certainly didn't collate much real data. "A bar, for example, which is called At the End of the World at the limit of one of the strongest unities of ambiance in Paris, is not there by chance," *Potlatch* pleaded. "Events only belong to chance if one does not know the general laws of their category."[30] With its detective-style iconography, Ralph Rumney's situationist photographic record of Venice's streets, made as he stalked American Beat author Alan Ansen, looked suitably systematic (fig. 2.14). But it failed to yield anything remotely like "data," its author struggling to explain the significance of his encounters with children and with old acquaintances, account for the romance of Venice, and identify "sinister," "depressing," and "beautiful" zones. Rumney clearly lacked seriousness, leaving us uncertain whether his project was a failure or a wholesome pursuit of situationist play. At one point he attrib-

**Figure 2.14**

*Ralph Rumney,* Psychogeographic Map of Venice *(detail), 1957, photographic collage. The document was a rare, if flawed, visual record of a psychogeographic drift.*

uted Ansen's eccentric behavior in the photographs to the fact that he was "aware of the photographer and is showing off," and there was a note of capitulation to the impalpability of "psychogeographic" data as Rumney admitted that his report might have benefited from being conducted by "one more competent than the author."[31] Announcing his expulsion shortly after, the Situationist International regretfully noted that Venice had "closed in on the young man."[32]

In fairness, psychogeographers recognized that theirs was a necessarily inexact science, dealing with imprecise data. *Potlatch*, discussing recent tendencies in poetry, noted the failure of fixed literary form and then implied a link to the failure of fixed political and urban forms.[33] To seek fixed form was folly, the journal noted, since it denied the serendipitous processes that create literature, politics, and cities alike. And in any case, even if permanently fixed form could be discovered and isolated, it would be an impediment to the dynamics of creativity. So in their *Mémoires*, Debord and Jorn cheerfully resigned themselves to urban relativity, noting that "these ambiguities do not owe anything to psychology—cities are born from interferences of situations—the influences follow each other surpassing each other while meshing."[34] "The sectors of a city are, at a certain level, decipherable," Debord admitted in his 1961 film *Critique de la séparation* (Critique of separation), as the viewer was shown aerial views of Paris. "But the personal meaning they have for us is incommunicable, like all that clandestinity of private life regarding which we possess nothing but pitiful documents."[35]

The situationists wanted to keep a grip on reality nonetheless. The commentary of Debord's film *Sur le passage de quelques personnes à travers une assez courte unité de temps* dreamily recollected the experience of the drift: "It was a trompe-l'oeil reality by means of which one had to discover the potential richness of reality," as if the special, unreal conditions of the drift might occlude a more profound insight into the city; a page of *Mémoires* complained about "false stonework—trompe l'oeil—never enough—never satisfying."[36] The Debordist element reacted quickly against those situationists for whom the mysteries of the drift were going beyond cool reasoning and heading down the same magic road as postwar Bretonist surrealism. In 1956 *Potlatch* attacked a "faction, comprising sometimes the most advanced in the search for a new behavior," which found itself "drawn to the taste of the unknown, mystery at all cost" and "to diverse occultist conclusions which border on theosophy." The article's tone became menacing: "The analysis and the representation of this last tendency eventually brought us to

put an end to the relative political freedom which we had up till now mutually accorded ourselves."[37]

As in the stoic tradition of the male artist presented with the female nude, a degree of resistance to the charms of psychogeography was applauded. From the outset psychogeography was regarded as a sort of therapy, a fetishization of those parts of the city that could still rescue drifters from the clutches of functionalism, exciting the senses and the body. "We will play upon topophobia and create a topophilia," the Situationist International profligately promised,[38] and the overwhelmingly male-dominated group's penchant for girlie illustrations gave its architectural commentary an especially odd cast. A page of Debord and Jorn's *Mémoires* drew upon the old metaphor of the landscape as a female body (fig. 2.15). The chunks of female bodies, disarmingly chopped up, were "moving accidents"—"accidents" like the rolls and dips of the landscape, perhaps, or "moving" in the emotional sense, or in the way that they were encountered on the move, on the drift. The experience of delving bodily into the urban landscape was like being "half-buried between the mounds of Easter Island."[39] Another of Debord's metaphors, in distinctly poor taste, suggested that the drifter could rape the night streets of London's East End— "Jack the Ripper is probably psychogeographic in love."[40] The linkage of sexual prowess to the city and to revolution was completed by a famous piece of situationist-inspired May '68 graffiti: "I came in the cobblestones."[41]

**Figure 2.15**

Guy Debord and Asger Jorn, page from Mémoires, 1959, screenprinted book. "Détourned" soft porn pictures of women were a frequent motif in situationist work, usually drawing attention to capitalism's ghastly capacity to make a spectacle even of the human body. The "détourned" images nonetheless conferred their capacity to titillate onto situationism, adding to its peculiarly risqué and seductive quality. In this page from Mémoires, the female body is compared to the cityscape, effectively appropriating the body for situationist psychogeography.

So psychogeography offered a sense of violent emotive possession over the streets. Exotic and exciting treasures were to be found in the city by those drifters able to conquer her, able to overcome the exhaustion and euphoria of the drift. "In 1953–1954," Chtcheglov boasted, "we drifted for three or four months; that's the extreme limit, the critical point. It's a miracle it didn't kill us."[42] In this will to possess the city there was something more than mere fetishization. Like the imperialist powers that they officially opposed, it was as if situationists felt that the exploration of alien quarters (of the city rather than the globe) would advance civilization. More poignantly for the handful of female or non-European psychogeographers, the drift could momentarily defy the white patriarchy of urban space-time, the likes of Michèle Bernstein and Abdelhafid Khatib "reclaiming the night": Khatib was twice arrested for breaking the police curfew imposed on Algerian residents.[43] Reports on psychogeography were presented as if they were produced by a military rather than an artistic avant-garde.[44] As well as having a nautical derivation, Debord borrowed the idea of drift from military tacticians, who defined it as "a calculated action determined by the absence of a proper locus."[45] For Clausewitz it had been an "art of the weak," for von Bülow a maneuver "within the enemy's field of vision."[46] The power of psychogeography, it seemed, lay precisely in its intoxicating combination of subjective and objective—fetishistic and militaristic—approaches to urban exploration. Psychogeography

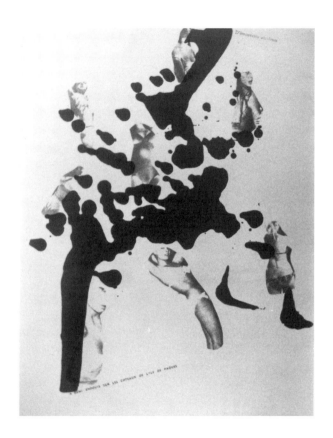

was merely a preparation, a reconnaissance for the day when the city would be seized for real. The drift, Debord explained, "takes on a double meaning: active observation of present-day urban agglomerations and development of hypotheses on the structure of a situationist city."[47]

### A passion for maps

Now that the drift offered a new way of surveying urban space, a new means of representing space on paper would have to be found. The 1956 *Guide psychogéographique de Paris* (fig. 1.5) and 1957 *Naked City* (fig. 1.32) served as alternative maps of Paris, Debord and Jorn representing the surreal disorientation of their drifts around Paris by scattering the pieces of map and the arrows showing their routes.[48] Maps had traditionally been made by those wishing to impose order upon the city: "without extraordinary assistance, how do you think that a private person could have emerged from this labyrinth?," Louis XIV's engineer had demanded to know as he introduced the new "scientific" survey of Paris in 1652.[49] In their maps, by stark contrast, Debord and Jorn attempted to put the spectator at ease with a city of apparent disorder, exposing the strange logic that lay beneath its surface.

The maps that situationists stared into became aids to reverie, suggestive of possible living environments. *Potlatch*'s editors imagined "the inviting aspect of certain localities in Ireland and elsewhere, which are shown on general geography maps in color or on partial Ordnance Survey maps with scales and cross hatchings; the determination of a passionate *organism* destined to function in this environment."[50] Situationist maps accordingly declared an intimacy with the city alien to the average street map. The narration to the opening sequence of the 1948 film *The Naked City*, an aer-

ial view of lower Manhattan tracking northward, must have summed up the mood, the penetrating realism, and the sense of humanity that Debord and Jorn sought in maps: "As you can see, we're flying over an island, a city, a particular city, and this is the story of a number of its people, and the story, also, of the city itself. It was not photographed in a studio. Quite the contrary . . . the actors played out their roles on the streets, in the apartment houses. . . . This is the city as it is, hot summer pavements, the children at play, the buildings in their naked stone, the people without makeup."[51] Rather than float above the city as some sort of omnipotent, instantaneous, disembodied, all-possessing eye, situationist cartography admitted that its overview of the city was reconstructed in the imagination, piecing together an experience of space that was actually terrestrial, fragmented, subjective, temporal, and cultural.[52]

"One measures the distances that effectively separate two regions of a city," Debord noted, "distances that may have little relation with the physical distance between them."[53] But although Debord and Jorn made the physically coherent depiction of the city disappear their scalpel, they were not disillusioned with mapping itself. They were just unhappy with the structures and imperatives mapped out in the maps they chose to sacrifice: the depiction of a seamless Parisian spectacle by Blondel la Rougery's magnificent *Plan de Paris à vol d'oiseau* (Bird's-eye plan of Paris)—source of the *Guide psychogéographique*—and the banal indexing of the *Guide Taride de Paris,* sliced up to create *The Naked City*

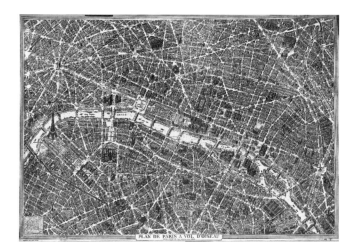

**Figure 2.16**

*Blondel la Rougery,* Plan de Paris à vol d'oiseau, *1956, drawn by G. Peltier. This huge and extraordinary map, the source of Debord and Jorn's* Guide psychogéographique de Paris, *came complete with its own booklet. The back cover insisted that "no work of comparable importance has been accomplished, for a capital, since the famous Turgot plan published in 1739," doubtless a fair claim, though its unconditional celebration of "The Spectacles" of Paris, which it carefully listed, was just inviting trouble from the situationists. It was a brave man, even so, who finally set to work on the map with a scalpel.*

**Figure 2.17**

*Page from the* Guide Taride de Paris, *1951, showing the 1st Arrondissement. The Taride street atlas became the source for Debord and Jorn's* The Naked City.

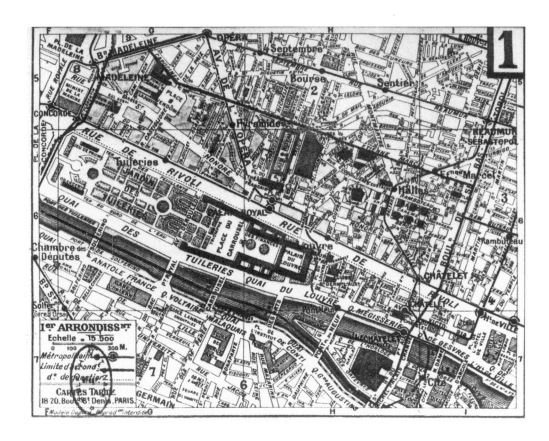

*"The residential units of the sector," from Paul-Henri Chombart de Lauwe,* Paris et l'agglomération parisienne, *vol. 1 (1952). Part of a case study of the Wattignies district in the 12th Arrondissement, the map was made by Louis Couvreur, a researcher working with Chombart de Lauwe. Its striking appearance, and its attempt to isolate the components of the city at large, were emulated in Debord and Jorn's* The Naked City.

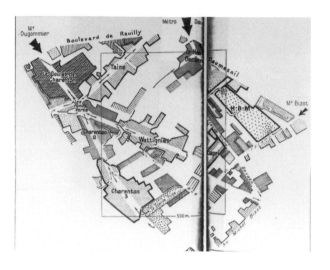

(figs. 2.16, 2.17).[54] The disturbed grid lines of the *Guide Taride*, still visible in the fragments composing *The Naked City*, emphasized the incompatibility of Cartesian logic with the real experience of the city.

"With the aid of old maps, aerial photographs and experimental drifts, one can draw up hitherto lacking maps of influences, maps whose inevitable imprecision at this early stage is no worse than that of the first navigational charts," Debord insisted, trying to sound confident that his intuitive passion for Paris could be usefully reconciled with more conventional geographies, sociologies, and cartographies.[55] It was a brave claim. Debord drew overambitious parallels with the work of Paul-Henri Chombart de Lauwe and Chicago geographer Ernest Burgess: "ecological science—despite the apparently narrow social space with which it limits itself—provides psychogeography with abundant data."[56] *The Naked City* even adapted the rather abstract appearance of Chombart de Lauwe's map of the Wattignies district of the 12th Arrondissement (fig. 2.18).[57] But Chombart de Lauwe's map only *looked* fractured, and while its arrows had some relation to situationist arrows, both in appearance and in function—showing flows in and out of the *unité residentielle* (residential unit)—they said little about the relationship between the Wattignies unity and the city's other "unities," an all-important relationship in psychogeography.[58] Nor, for all its fascinating detail, did Chombart de Lauwe's geography tell situationists what the city *felt* like: Khatib championed situationist methods over "other means, such

as the reading of aerial views and plans, the study of statistics, of graphs or the results of sociological enquiries," since these "are theoretical and do not possess that active and direct side" inherent in situationist approaches. "The situationists seem capable . . . not only of redeveloping the urban milieu, but of changing it almost at will," he noted, rejecting the notion of a scientific objectivity that would consider the city and its observer as discrete and disinterested.[59]

So *Internationale situationniste* tried another juxtaposition, between an aerial photograph of Amsterdam ("an experimental zone for the drift") and a 1656 *précieux* "map of the land of Feeling," alerting readers to the possibility of mapping states of consciousness and feeling during the drift (figs. 2.19, 2.20).[60] The *précieux* had mapped their ideal of tenderness as a debate between love and friendship; the situationists mapped the drift as a "discourse on the passions of love," the subtitle of the

**Figures 2.19, 2.20**

"Map of the land of Feeling, 1656" and "An experimental zone for the dérive: The center of Amsterdam, which will be systematically explored by situationist teams in April-May 1960," illustrations for anon., "Urbanisme unitaire à la fin des années 50," Internationale situationniste, no. 3 (1959). The juxtaposition emphasized the intimacy between environment and human emotion that was central to psychogeography.

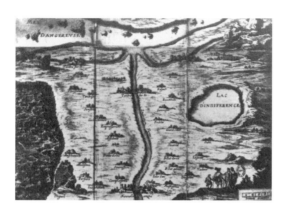

**Figure 2.21**

Métro map of Paris, c. 1955.

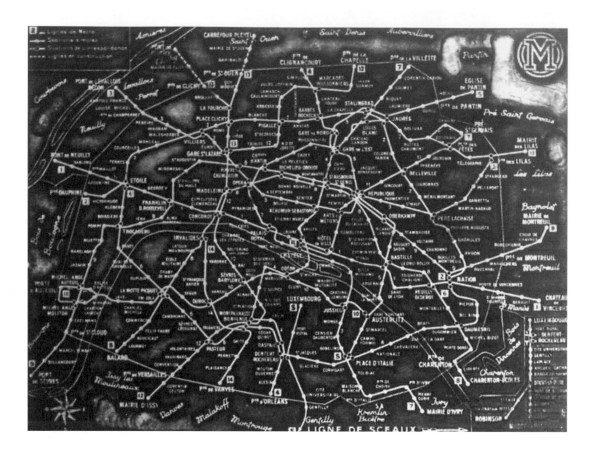

*Guide psychogéographique*, reminiscent of the way André Breton had compounded his excursions through Paris and through a love affair into his surreal novel *Nadja*.[61] No map, it seemed, could be read dispassionately. When Debord drew our attention to the wonders of the Métro map of Paris, and when he collaged into *Mémoires* an old map of London's railway network, he might have been construed as offering us some insight into the capital and social growth of cities (figs. 2.21, 2.22).[62] But he more likely enjoyed the way the drifting nets of track

reminded him of psycho-emotional meanderings generally—a little like those that guided Jackson Pollock's drips—and resembled the courses of the drift, which paid so little regard to the internal boundaries of the city. Debord took care to use a map drawn before 1931, the year when London Transport rationalized it.

The drift could cover an area as small as the Gare Saint-Lazare (a "static drift"), but the *Guide psychogéographique* and *The Naked City* mapped the drifts at their grandest.[63] The scale of Thomas

**Figure 2.22**

Guy Debord and Asger Jorn, page from Mémoires (detail), 1959, screenprinted book, reproducing an early twentieth-century map of the London railway network. Debord compared the Paris Métro map to the seaport paintings of Claude Lorrain (figs. 2.6, 2.7) because of "the particularly moving presentation, in both cases, of a sum of possibilities" ("Introduction to a Critique of Urban Geography," 1955)—in other words, their stimulus to the urban imagination. Even though Debord insisted that the beauty of such maps was in their content rather than their appearance, they reminded the viewer of the new trends in art informel and abstract expressionism, like Jackson Pollock's seminal Autumn Rhythm (1950), which were trying to break away from modernism's hard-edge geometry; and, in turn, they evoked the labyrinthine plans for cluster cities drawn by the Smithsons and Constant (figs. 1.6, 1.12). The webs traced by both Paris Métro and London railway maps were of course akin to the routes taken by the situationist drift through Paris and London.

De Quincey's "drifts" across London fascinated the situationists: "seeking ambitiously for a north-west passage, instead of circumnavigating all the capes and head-lands I had doubled on my outward voyage, I came suddenly upon such knotty problems of alleys," De Quincey wrote in 1821, that "I could almost have believed . . . that I was the first discoverer of these *terrae incognitae*, and doubted, whether they had yet been laid down in the modern charts of London."[64] The "northwest passage," like the "drift," was a nautical metaphor—the city imagined as a psychogeographic sea, pushing and pulling the sensitive soul along its eddies and currents. Nautically, there never was a northwest passage to the eastern Pacific (since the Americas are a continuous land mass), but psychogeographers believed that enough channels existed in the capitalist land mass to permit the drift a clean sweep across the city.

In short, the situationist maps described an urban navigational system that operated independently of Paris's dominant patterns of circulation. *The Naked City* helpfully explained itself on the reverse: "The arrows represent the slopes that naturally link the different unities of ambiance; that's to say the spontaneous tendencies for orientation of a subject who traverses that milieu without regard for practical considerations."[65] A sense of the wealth of information included in these maps dawns only slowly. Admittedly, they cover a rather compact portion of the center of Paris, but the infinite care with which they were cut implies that every street inte-

gral to each unity, and every street bordering it, was walked and considered. Here truly were examples of the general postwar mania for systems analysis, for modeling everything from traffic to the economy.[66] The earlier of the two situationist maps, the *Guide psychogéographique*, had, frankly, taken the situationist interest in charting each unity's "exits and defenses" and "fixed points and vortices" to obsessive lengths.[67] Its arrows restlessly danced between, in, and around specific streets, rendering the information almost impossible to absorb. The clean sweeps and sense of composition in *The Naked City*, the later of the two maps, were a result not only of a stylistic refinement, but also of an increasing confidence in psychogeographic judgment and of the need to clarify the shape of the situationist urban system.

It evoked beautifully the way in which some unities of ambiance acted as stations on the drift, junctions in the psychogeographic flow of Paris. The situationists coined a term for these junctions: *plaques tournantes*. The term punned on so many meanings that it is not possible to translate it straightforwardly. A *plaque tournante* can be the center of something; it can be a railway turntable; or it can be a place of exchange (in the same way that Marseilles is sometimes described as a *plaque tournante* for trafficking, or that Paris as a whole has been celebrated as a *plaque tournante* of culture). As a center for markets, drinking, prostitution, and drugs, Les Halles was clearly a *plaque tournante* in all these senses. Zola had described it as "the belly of Paris," an idea incorporated in Khatib's designation of it as "the transition zone of Paris," a place not only of commercial exchange but also of "social deterioration, acculturation, [and a] mixing of populations which is the favorable environment for cultural exchanges."[68] The Plateau Beaubourg next door was shown on *The Naked City* as if it were almost literally a turntable for the drifter, arrows fanning out in seven directions.

Panthéon and Val de Grâce, in contrast, floated almost freely, arrowheads positively recoiling from them. Panthéon is surrounded by an array of university and ecclesiastical buildings then out of favor with situationists, while access to Val de Grâce does indeed require the pedestrian to make an awkward two-step from the so-called "Continent Contrescarpe," virtually impossible without a proper street map, and therefore impractical for the purposes of the drift. From any direction, in fact, it is tricky to access, its perimeter protected by a daunting complex of buildings and railings. Its supposedly psychogeographic qualities only yield themselves to the pedestrian inside the buildings and grounds. If some unities were turntables, others were termini.

The plethora of arrows implied a massive number of permutations for drift, and Jorn and Debord's wish to squeeze so much psychogeographic information onto the map may account for their decision to explode the fragments, freeing room on the paper. If situationists spent as much time drifting as they claimed, then it is possible that all these permutations were tested. And the precision of the maps was achieved only by some tough-mindedness about which streets were truly capable of transforming urban consciousness. "Today the different unities of ambiance . . . are not precisely marked off," Debord complained. "The most general change that the drift leads to proposing is the constant diminution of these border regions, up to the point of their complete suppression."[69]

So some unities of ambiance were lost between the making of the two maps, and many others around Paris did not appear at all. The Ledoux Rotunda (the "Centre Ledoux"), for instance, was nowhere to be seen. One reason was surely the physical problem of psychogeographically mapping Paris right up to its boundaries, a vast project.[70] Arrows at the edges of the maps pointed into space, as if awaiting linkage with further unities. Wolman and Debord, although excited by their discovery of the Centre Ledoux, had been unable to find a satisfactory passage to link it to the rest of the system. Situationists also revised their selections in the light of changes in the fabric of Paris, for psychogeography was nothing if it was not responsive to such changes. In 1956 *Potlatch* regretfully announced that it was no longer worth making the journey to visit their beloved Square des Missions Etrangères or Rue Sauvage: the former because of the erection of temporary buildings in the square, the latter because it was being erased from the cityscape.[71] In effect the maps represented psychogeographic work in progress.

Because of its "annexation" by "the zone of Right Bank-style cabarets," the strip from Rue de la Montagne-Sainte-Geneviève, through Rue Descartes, to the Place de la Contrescarpe itself, headquarters of the Lettrist International, was removed in the second map as a diseased artery that was slowly killing a unity of ambiance.[72] Only its southern part survived, now linked directly to the Left Bank stronghold around Saint-Julien-le-Pauvre.

Debord and Jorn pasted down the chunks of map at some odd angles, as much as forty-five degrees from the mean. Reorienting the chunks in this way helped to represent the drifters' passages across the city as smooth flows.[73] In topological reality, the districts down the left side of the maps (from Banque de France through the Palais du Louvre and across the Seine to the Place de l'Institut, Carrefour de Buci, Saint-Sulpice, and Jardin du Luxembourg) lie along a straight north-south axis. But left like that, the reader of the map would have gained little sense of the supposed vortex of psychogeographical flow around the *plaque tournante* of the little Carrefour de Buci. Debord and Jorn instead kinked the chunks around Buci, showing it as a *carrefour* (crossroads) in a larger sense, a pivot for psychogeographic as well as traffic flows. And Debord and Jorn ruthlessly split areas in order to smooth them into natural passages. According to *The Naked City*, the main body of the Jardin des Plantes showed a stronger tendency toward the River Seine than toward its own annex just across the

road, which was allowed to swing down to the bottom of the map.

The red arrows of the drift were left suspended upon the white space of the paper. One might expect that navigating these blanks, emptied of landmarks, would be problematic. But an assumption of psychogeography was that drifters alert to the feel of the city would find the psychogeographical "slopes" (*pentes*) meeting them as naturally as their last choice of book materialized to them in the library, or as emotions and relationships emerged to them during their day-to-day lives. Like Jorn's inky dribbles through *Mémoires*, the strengths and durations of the psychogeographic slopes were suggested by the weight, shape and patterning of the arrows on the maps. The arrows connecting Beaubourg and Halles, for instance, indicated an indissoluble bond between them. Debord advised drifters to allow themselves to be guided by those features of the street neglected by most pedestrians, like "the sudden change of ambiance in a street within the space of a few meters" and "the path of least resistance which is automatically followed in aimless strolls (and which has no relation to the contour of the ground)."[74] The determinants of drift, apparently, were alternations in emotional and ambient "intensity"; "the appealing or repelling character of certain places"; and the drifter's tendency to "drain" along relatively unresistant paths, the "fissures in the urban network."[75] The Lettrist International even "envisaged a pinball machine arranged in such a way that the play of the lights and the more or less predictable trajectories of the balls" would represent the "thermal sensations and desires of people passing by the gates of the Cluny Museum around an hour after sunset in November," as though drifters were like ball bearings, propelled through the city's channels by the energized "pins" of the unities of ambiance.

"We have since, of course, come to realize that a situationist-analytical work cannot scientifically advance by way of such projects," Debord pronounced, still anxious that psychogeography should develop into a serious discipline.[76] But in his *Mémoires*—the document that contained, in effect, his final reflections on psychogeography—Debord allowed a sense of the drift's romantic, automatist undercurrent to go on record. "A new current carries us slightly toward the left," one page of "détourned" phrases read. "We are just coming across an extremely powerful energy field that information centers have been unable to identify—the earth with its sounds—One needs time to get used to these night walks—They tell us that the continents are solid—A singular place! It's here that the tangled paths pass—The location of this castle is charming—But it's in the interior of the labyrinth, at once bland and beautiful, so sumptuous, dilapidated, disorganized, untidily stacked, luxurious and absurd, with rooms and hearts and gardens."[77]

This, evidently, was not an account of pedestrian circulation that an academic town planner would have recognized. True, academic planners might have sympathized with psychogeography's strenuous separation of the pedestrian and the motorcar—*The Naked City* showed the Rue Pierre et Marie Curie as a loose end with an arrow doubling back, warning drifters of the dire consequences of being swept away by the tides of traffic along the Rue Saint-Jacques. But while town planning separated different forms of traffic for the sake of comfort and efficiency, psychogeography separated them as a way of refusing the mechanistic functioning of the city. Those drifting through the city backwaters would enjoy a sense of encounter with the city, while those being swept along by the crowds in the *grands boulevards* were bound by an artificial imperative of speed, making savings on capitalized time, rushing toward sites of alienated production or consumption.[78]

### Drifting as a revolution of everyday life

It was not that the drift ruled out places of activity in the city. In fact, psychogeographic analysis carefully noted variations in degrees of urban bustle as it attracted and repelled the drifters through the city.[79] But not any sort of spectacular "sound and fury" was acceptable. Tourism, for example, with its crass appetite for ultravisible urban spectacle and nervousness in the dark spaces of the ambient city, was as "repugnant as sports or buying on credit."[80] Most commerce was distasteful, Wolman and

Debord complaining that "the upper section of the 11th Arrondissement" was "an area whose poor commercial standardization is a good example of repulsive petit-bourgeois landscape."[81] The rush to work was disgusting—"never work," the situationists instructed, unwittingly associating themselves with those who, in Reyner Banham's withering remark of the time, "still gush on about the 'vitality' (i.e., crowds of unemployed) of south European city centres," and more wittingly with the radical geographer Elisée Reclus, author of the Paris Commune slogan "Work to Make Ourselves Useless."[82] Situationists regarded the best urban activity as human, unmechanized, and nonalienating, and their texts, films, and maps indicated some possibilities, variously idealizing the marketplaces, like Les Halles or the Rue Mouffetard, the traditional cafés, notably those around Saint-Germain-des-Prés, and the places of student congregation, such as those around the Panthéon.[83]

Psychogeography thus produced a social geography of the city, especially important at a time when social geography was still struggling to emerge from the shadow of academic geography. Against academic geography's "scientific" taxonomy of the physical factors that supposedly determine the character of a space, social geography theorized space as the product of society.[84] It was an approach pioneered in the late nineteenth century by the former Communard Reclus, who recognized in geography "nothing but history in space."[85] Situationists were naturally inclined toward the goals of social geography, which opposed academic geography's reduction of the city to "the undifferentiated state of the visible-readable realm" (to use Lefebvre's disdainful phrase) and to the homogenization of the conflicts that produce capitalist space.[86] Fragmented yet tied together by their arrows, situationist maps explored the very same "three orders of facts"—"class struggle, the quest for equilibrium, and the sovereign decision of the individual"—that Reclus claimed were revealed by the pursuit of social geography.[87]

But it was almost by default, creditable to the eccentricity, complicity, and tenacity of psychogeographical technique, that situationism yielded any worthwhile social geography, excavating a network of anti-spectacular spaces and discourses only by being part of it—café talk and shady goings-on in wastelands, parks, and alleyways. Nor would situationism have had it any other way. The publication in 1960 of *The Image of the City*, written by Kevin Lynch, a professor of urban studies and planning at MIT, marked a rising interest in "cognitive mapping," in the ways in which citizens perceive and interact with their city by first "imaging" it in their minds. 1950s situationist psychogeography, as it set out to study "the specific effects of the geographical environment . . . on the emotions and behavior of individuals," might have anticipated this new interest in the cognitive city.[88] But it was too busy campaigning for politicized and proactive citizenship to be greatly distracted by proper social geography and psychology, deemed of greater interest to the social planners that situationists reviled. And while Debord would have readily admitted that the city reproduced socio-psychological relations, he would have insisted that it was about a lot more besides, rejecting as he did anything sniffing of determinist vulgarity. The city as the terrain of passion was endlessly nuanced, and while a unity of ambiance was partly the product of certain social and capital relations, it was also subject to freak arrangements, to the inscription of ideas, to disuse and misuse, so that it was something idiosyncratic as well—rather as academic geography would have it.

Situationists uncovered the social body of "the naked city" by becoming streetwise. Drifters were effectively vagrants, on the lookout for refuge, and if the claims for three-month drifts were true, the unities of ambiance would have offered places to doss down, like discreet public gardens. The passages of the drift were lined with cheap shops and cafés; the ghettos offered not only an "ambient other" but also nonbourgeois, nontourist costs of living. Sent by the Lettrist International's notorious "alternative travel agency" on a mystery tour through neighboring *quartiers*, one was reminded of that extraordinary sensation of being abroad even when at home. Even in its own *quartier* the Lettrist International was close to nomadism: its headquarters were near the Place de la Contrescarpe, in the 1950s something of a no-man's land where tramps from the banks of the Seine and from the Montagne Sainte-Geneviève could meet without fighting. The situationists were a part of the bohemian youth hanging out in areas like the Panthéon and Saint-Germain-des-Prés, haunts of the transitory student and intellectual population. As Kristin Ross has explained, the bohemian will to link poetic with literal vagabondage, to create a sense of being constantly *dépaysé* (out of place), can be traced back to poet and Communard Arthur Rimbaud, who recognized in laziness a refusal of compartmentalized time, an intensity of physical sensation, and a glorious sense of weightlessness.[89] Coupled with his adolescent impulsiveness, it made Rimbaud a venerable predecessor to the situationists and the insurgents of '68.

Wandering around the city, drifting without destination, neither going to work nor properly consuming, was a waste of time in the temporal economy, in a society where "time is money." If situationist testimony is to be believed, the drift could consume monumental chunks of time; Chtcheglov put the limit at three or four months, and recommended a week as more satisfactory.[90] Debord recommended a day, and even these smaller periods of time, with "an hour or two at the beginning or end of the day" set aside "for taking care of banal tasks," would barely be compatible with a conventional sense of time management: "The times of beginning and ending have no necessary relation to the solar day."[91] Chtcheglov rashly looked forward to a society "where the principal activity is CONTINUOUS DRIFT," where the main

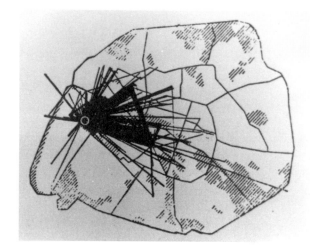

occupation was unproductive of anything except encounters with other people and with places, and of ideas about enhancing those encounters—those "situations."[92] At its best, drift was an unconventionally sociable activity as well, its preferred small-group organization resistant to organized mass circulation and sympathetic to the input of each group member.[93]

Drift therefore became a transgression of the alienated world. "A loose lifestyle and even certain amusements considered dubious that have always been enjoyed amongst our entourage—slipping by night into houses undergoing demolition, hitchhiking nonstop and without destination through Paris during a transportation strike in the name of adding to the confusion, wandering in catacombs forbidden to the public, etc.—are expressions of a more general sensibility which is nothing other than that of the drift," Debord wrote.[94] He suggested games of "possible rendezvous" that would provoke situations, encounters in unfamiliar places in the city, games in which "the element of [spatial] exploration is minimal in comparison with that of behavioral disorientation."[95] Drift had to alert people to their imprisonment by routine. Debord cited Chombart de Lauwe's chart of the movements of a Parisian student as evidence of "the narrowness of the real Paris in which the individual lives" (fig. 2.23).[96] This chart, Debord reckoned, was "modern poetry, capable of provoking keen emotional reactions—in this case, that it is possible to live like that," a pathetic inversion of Baudelaire's euphoria

at the "heroism of modern life."[97] Cutting freely across urban space, drifters would gain a revolutionary perception of the city, a "rational disordering of the senses" of the sort demanded by Rimbaud, encountering both the city's embarrassing contrasts of material wealth and its clandestine glories of popular culture and history.

Situationists had become alert to the possibilities of drifting into the "hidden city" by reading De Quincey. Admittedly, the drama of his "drifts" may have had something to do with the fact that De Quincey was tripping on opium, and the name of this drug, as well as those of marijuana and cannabis, hung in the air on the pages of Debord and Jorn's Mémoires. Like their Beat contemporaries, and their heroin-advocate friend Alexander Trocchi, the situationists regarded "creative" substance abuse as another subcultural and consciousness-altering freedom. Drunkenness was routine, and their London haunt of Limehouse was a drugs ghetto, home to Chinese opium dens. The discovery of the city sublime was a serious business, De Quincey himself complaining that he "paid a heavy price in distant years, when . . . the perplexities of my steps in London came back and haunted my sleep."[98]

### Language, time, and the city

Too much of the city had already been "written" in the language of spectacle, so psychogeographers unashamedly reread situationist meanings into the streets, an old technique of *flânerie*. Charles Dickens, former resident of Limehouse, had restlessly paced the streets of London and Paris, scouring the city for insights into the human condition, and Baudelaire insisted that Paris was "rich in poetic and marvellous subjects" for those sensitive observers drawn to the city's margins.[99] Walter Benjamin heard the call, asking "Who amongst us has not dreamt . . . of the miracle of a poetic prose . . . supple and staccato enough to adapt to the lyrical stirrings of the soul, the undulations of dreams, and the sudden leaps of consciousness? This obsessive ideal is above all a child of the experiences of giant cities, of the intersecting of their myriad relations."[100] Benjamin's attraction toward Baudelaire was partly an outcome of his association with Parisian surrealism; two decades later, situationist writing on the city swung between essentially realistic, political analyses and wildly poetic inscriptions, a technique learned from Louis Aragon's 1926 surrealist book *Le paysan de Paris*.[101] Ivan Chtcheglov's "Formulary" was particularly nostalgic for such texts: "We are bored in the city, there is no longer any Temple of the Sun. Between the legs of the women walking by, the dadaists imagined a monkey wrench and the surrealists a crystal cup. That's lost."[102]

The will to recover the surrealist imagination originated in the Lettrist International's parent group, the lettrists. In a bizarre pictographic book of 1950, *Saint ghetto des prêts*, the leading lettrist Gabriel Pomerand represented the bohemian Left Bank neighborhood of Saint-Germain-des-Prés as, to quote Greil Marcus, "a labyrinth, where every chance encounter with a word, a picture, a building, or a person seethes with legend and possibility, opening into a secret utopia accessible to anyone capable of recognising it" (fig. 2.24).[103] Breaking away from the lettrists, the Lettrist International felt that the obsession with language for its own sake had been taken too far. Pomerand, the Lettrist International felt, had got the equation the wrong way around. He was using his experience of the city as a way of revolutionizing our consciousness of language. Situationists would use their experience of language as a way of revolutionizing

**Figure 2.24**

*Gabriel Pomerand, page from* Saint ghetto des prêts, *1950.*
*Pomerand's lettrist pictographs took the reader on a tour of*
*Saint-Germain-des-Prés, Paris. Lettrism's fascination with*
*language was inherited by situationism.*

our consciousness of the city. "Poetry," the Lettrist International announced, "is in the form of cities."[104]

Still, Pomerand was right to focus upon the role of urban subculture in forming language and consciousness. The extraordinary subcultural life of the Left Bank, centered around the cafés, pointed both to new languages and new modes of living within the city.[105] The punning title of Pomerand's book, which could be interpreted as "our ghetto of lendings" when read out loud, played upon the notion that Saint-Germain-des-Prés had developed its own economy of goods and language. Saint-Germain-des-Prés was the sort of "provisional micro-society" that situationists looked to as a fore-runner of the situationist city, and by celebrating the way that Left Bankers carved out their own space, language, and economy, situationism revived something of the spirit of the 1920s social semi-otics that had been suppressed under Stalinism.[106]

Ferdinand de Saussure, founder of the semi-otic analysis of language, had concentrated atten-tion upon the role of the individual utterance within the larger linguistic system. Social semioti-cians, however, emphasized that language is formed socially, and through time.[107] For them, the individual utterance in itself was less interest-ing than its role within an ongoing dialogue, reply-ing to preceding utterances and anticipating subsequent replies in a "dialogical" chain.[108] Language is thus a carrier for society's values, beliefs, and desires, conscious and unconscious— in other words, it is a vehicle for ideology. The

Marxist had then to regard language as another arena of class struggle.

When *Potlatch* warned its readers that Corbusian rationalism and its attendant "Christian morality" was poised to "triumph without response," they were rallying the avant-garde to fulfill its "dia-logical duty."[109] It seemed that the city and its interpretation had to be contested if it was not to become congealed by the dominant language of capitalism, rationalism, modernization, the "Puritan work ethic," and spectacle. The Lettrist International decided to use chalk inscriptions to "add to the intrinsic meaning" of selected Parisian street names. "These inscriptions will have to extend their impact from a psychogeographic insinuation to subversion in its most simple form," a tactic reminiscent of the "heteroglossia"—the diversity of social voices—beloved by the exponent of subversive "carnivalization," the Russian literary critic Mikhail Bakhtin.[110] Bakhtin had found heteroglossia in the novel; the situationists would write it into the city. Graffiti became regarded as a sign of the "primitive" energy of the everyday life of the "masses."[111] "The chalkings on pavements and walls," Constant insisted in 1948, "clearly show that human beings were born to manifest themselves; now the struggle is in full swing against the power that would force them into the straitjacket of clerk or commoner and deprive them of this first vital need."[112] It was a sentiment echoed by Vaneigem in *Internationale situationniste* some thirteen years later—"What sign should one recognize as our own? Certain graffiti, words of refusal or forbidden gestures inscribed with haste"—and in the compilations of graffiti published to celebrate May 1968.[113]

The subcultural meanings of the proposed reinscriptions deliberately eluded the logic of the dominant discourse of the city. At the Rue Sauvage, for example, *Potlatch* proposed to write a question—"If we don't die here will we carry on further?"—a macabre reference to the lettrist haunt of the Morgue tucked just across the river. "The revolution at night" would be the simple epitaph for the radical sympathies of the residents along the Rue d'Aubervilliers.[114] Thereafter, Lettrist International changes to the signification of Parisian streets only became more obscure and complex, Gil J. Wolman replacing the official street designations made by the Conseil Municipal with complete lines of poetry.[115]

Language was the glue bonding individual, group, and environment together. The intensely personal effect of the reinscriptions emphasized that total revolution starts with subjective feelings shared among associates. As Debord's 1961 film *Critique de la séparation* had explained, "Until the environment is collectively dominated, there will be no individuals—only specters haunting the things anarchically presented to them by others. In chance situations we meet separated people moving randomly. Their divergent emotions neutralize each other and maintain their solid environment of boredom."[116] And so it was no use being half-hearted about the reinscription of the city; the casual passerby was unlikely to find great significance in the Square des Missions Etrangères. One would first have to read Michèle Bernstein's description of the place, be inspired by the desire to reread the square, and become one of her "friends from abroad" (a pun on the name of the square—"foreign missions"). Bernstein avoided ascribing definite meaning or effect to the place, thus forcing us to become complicit with her in the making of meaning.[117]

Which was a neat turn, because attempting to ratify the meanings of the unities of ambiance would have made situationism seem even more ineffable and eccentric than it already was. If we wish to know more, we must descend to the streets ourselves. Khatib issued a questionnaire that invited his readers to forward their own experiences of the city streets and their own demarcations of the unities of ambiance.[118] On those pages of *Mémoires* that refer to the drift, Jorn's inky dribbles and scratches hint at the indeterminacy and effort entailed in rereading the city, as the pages meander through a detritus of novels, philosophies, histories, maps, illustrations, and lettrist writings. Recalling his walks around London with Debord, Alexander Trocchi confirmed the situationist propensity to mythologize the city. "He'd bring me to a spot he'd found, and the place would begin to live. Some old, forgotten part of London. Then he'd reach back for a story, for a piece of history, as if he'd been born there. He'd quote from Marx, or Treasure Island, or de Quincey."[119] *Mémoires*'s sudden bursts of picture and text suggested the rewards of the drift: the flowerings of consciousness, the sudden "comings together" of space and architecture, knowledge and social interaction. Chtcheglov left us with a cautious analogy: "The drift (with its flow of acts, its gestures, its strolls, its encounters) was to the totality exactly what psychoanalysis (in its best sense) is to language. Let yourself go with the flow of words, says the analyst. He listens, until the moment when he rejects or modifies . . . a word, an expression or a definition. The drift is certainly a technique, almost a therapeutic one."[120]

Very likely the drift was an opportunity not just for observation and travel but also for thought and debate between the like-minded, with long periods of silence except for the sounds of the city and the rhythms of the group's footsteps. "The revealing presentations of the big city have come," Walter Benjamin believed, from "those who have traversed the city absently, as it were, lost in thought or worry."[121] Occasionally the "rightness" of the place, people, and understanding would be like that moment when the reader of a complex text suddenly grasps the content of what is being read, only to descend again into the maelstrom of words; it might be as sudden as that moment when the painter stands back from the canvas and realizes that the painting "works," only to succumb to the temptation to alter it. In this way drifting amplified the sense of the dialectics of time pondered by the French philosopher Gaston Bachelard in 1950.[122] Bachelard felt that time is experienced not as a linear continuum but rhythmically, in durations (*durées*) of more or less intensity and activity as mind, body, people, and society interact. It was a rhythm beautifully evoked by the comings-together of image, text, and ink in *Mémoires*.

Drifts, as Debord and Jorn so graphically demonstrated, were radical rereadings of the city—what Michel de Certeau was to call "a pedestrian speech act."[123] They linked the city's "chunks" in new ways, creating a subcultural knowledge versed as much in radicalism and literature as in the distillations of guidebooks and geography. City planners from antiquity to modernism have tried to make the city into a mnemonic (memory aid), mapping into it chains of monuments or sites that would act as a sort of text, reminding the pedestrian of official history and knowledge.[124] As Debord complained, "today cities themselves are presented as lamentable spectacles, a supplement to the museums for tourists driven around in glassed-in buses."[125] The narrative of the drift, however, remained open, contingent, and shifting. The monuments in situationist Paris were not overt, often difficult to identify from situationist maps. Statues compromised by the histories they signified could be reprieved only by their reinscription.

The neat mnemonic of the city would one day be disrupted by the *détournement* of places and objects into the public realm. "Unlimited access to all the prisons. The possibility of making them into tourist stopovers" would foreground deviances that society has attempted to suppress; there would be "no discrimination between the visitors and the condemned." Meanwhile the "abolition of museums, and redistribution of artistic masterpieces to the bars (the oeuvre of Philippe de Champaigne in the Arab cafés of the Rue Xavier-Privas; the *Sacre*, of David, to the Tonneau de la Montagne-Geneviève)" would completely undermine cultural imperialism and elitism.[126] The situationists were equally aware of the ability of the planner to rewrite the meaning of the city through procedures of erasure as well as construction. Like Bataille, and later Foucault, they deplored modernism's *tabula*

*rasa* approach to the city, one that would effectively leave the city without a memory. Urbanism could suppress incidents and places that contradict narratives of authority, just as Haussmann had turned the teeming Île de la Cité into an administrative desert, and just as reactionary fervor had eradicated any traces of the Commune.

But like revolutionaries before them, situationists had no compunction about using the same tactics as the authorities that they rebelled against. They were inspired by the most important act carried out by the Paris Commune's Federation of Artists, which, chaired by the painter Gustave Courbet, had demolished the Vendôme Column, monument to Napoleonic imperialism (fig. 2.25). "Monuments whose ugliness is irretrievable in any part (the Petit and Grand Palais genre) will have to make way for other constructions," the Lettrist International resolved.[127] Its call for the destruction of the portal of Chartres Cathedral invoked French socialism's tradition of uncompromising contempt for organized religion. Situationists considered the church to be an outmoded type not just aesthetically but socially and ideologically: "the cathedral was once the unitary accomplishment of a society that one has to call primitive, given that it was much further embedded than we are in the miserable prehistory of humanity."[128] "While waiting for the closure of churches," the Lettrist International complained about the continued religious connotations of many Parisian street names, and tried in the meantime to avoid the use of the word *saint*

**Figure 2.25**

Destruction of the Vendôme Column, Paris, May 1871, illustration from Internationale situationniste, no. 7 (1962). The Column was demolished, as a monument to Napoleonic imperialism, under the auspices of the Paris Commune's Federation of Artists, chaired by the painter Gustave Courbet. Situationists applauded this brilliantly radical artistic gesture.

in its day-to-day denomination of places: "The names of roads are only passengers," after all, which encourage the "cretinization" of the public imagination.[129]

Yet such was the immanent violence of the Lettrist International's own planned erasure of the signs of urban memory—extending to the names of municipal councilors and Resistance workers (favorite sources of street names in PCF-controlled districts, to accompanying the Party's staple diet of festivals and newspapers), and to the "total destruction of corpses and all headstones" (purportedly representative of a "hideous survival of past alienation")—that some within the lettrist organization itself were unsettled.[130] Debating the role of church buildings, Debord flatly declared himself "in favor of the total destruction of religious buildings, of every faith. (No trace would remain, and the spaces would be used for other purposes.)"[131] Others, however, wished to preserve the traces of a religious heritage, Gil J. Wolman proposing "that churches be preserved but emptied of all religious significance," Michèle Bernstein offering the compromise of churches being only "partially destroyed."[132]

Situationism nonetheless remained fascinated by buildings and places seemingly bypassed by religion, capitalism, and modernization. They served as visible reminders of the relentless processes of history, of class struggle, of the contingency and impermanence of repressive regimes, destined to the same fate as any other socioeco-

nomic arrangement. "The 'new towns' . . . clearly inscribe on the landscape their rupture with the historical time on which they are built," Debord noted; "their motto could be: 'On this spot nothing will ever happen, and *nothing ever has.*' . . . History, which threatens this twilight world, is also the force which could subject space to lived time."[133]

All the unities of ambiance, since restored or renovated, were moldering in the 1950s. Some, like the Marais, Halles, and the Île Saint-Louis (isolated by the Seine and without a Métro station, or, at the time, even a post office) were obstructive to the rational rezoning of Paris; others, like the Jardin des Plantes (replete with the decaying Institut Géologique, closed in 1962 because of disinterest and the degeneration of the exhibits) were specters of past spectacular leisure. Many were memorials to nonfunctioning government. The ruined Ledoux Rotunda had been built to police and profit from the Canal de l'Ourcq, marking the limit of an ideal plan for Paris. Debord and Jorn's psychogeographic maps mischievously included other state buildings of sublime dimensions whose signification had decisively shifted. The Panthéon, resting place of France's great men, was being crushed by its own dome; the Napoleonic Hôpital Val-de-Grâce was crumbling away as fast as France's military reputation in Indochina and Algeria; the Louvre was a royal-court-turned-museum, housing Debord's beloved Claudes; the Marais was a royal-court-turned-slum. To complete the effect, Debord and Jorn systematically purged healthy state bodies

**Figure 2.26**

Giorgio de Chirico, Mystery and Melancholy of a Street, 1913, oil on canvas, private collection. "It is easy to imagine the fantastic future possibilities of such architecture and its influence on the masses," Ivan Chtcheglov wrote in the "Formulary for a New Urbanism" (1953). "Today we can have nothing but contempt for a century that relegates such blueprints to its so-called museums."

**Figure 2.27**

Place des Vosges, 3rd Arrondissement, 1605–1612. Lying at the heart of Henri IV's palatial district, the Place was enjoyed by situationists for its de Chirico–like views, and prior to its steady regentrification the Marais as a whole was appreciated by situationists for its provision of cheap, "authentic" city living.

from their maps, from the Palais de Justice to the Halles Post Office.

"An *empty space* creates a *full-filled time,*" Chtcheglov claimed, promoting the "blueprints" of Giorgio de Chirico as "one of the most remarkable architectural precursors. He was grappling with the problems of absences and presences in time and space" (fig. 2.26).[134] The space of the seventeenth-century Place des Vosges, which boasted de Chirico–like arcaded views, was embraced by situationists as something of a retreat from the crush of major Parisian arteries nearby (fig. 2.27), and the gap of the Plateau Beaubourg, at the heart of Debord and Jorn's maps, marked the passing of one *quartier* while optimistically looking forward to the building of a better one. At Halles, in the absence of spectacle, Khatib noted "a considerable ˌ differentiation between daytime and nighttime ambiances" (see fig. 1.35); in their defense of the Rue Sauvage, the Lettrist International had deplored "the disappearance of an artery little known, and therefore more *alive* than the Champs-Elysées and its lights."[135] Breaking streetlights in 1789 had been the first act of revolution against the surveillance of authorities, and relentless artificial light has historically functioned as an instrument for the extension of the productive and consumptive day. In the spaces of unities of ambiance, on the other hand, drifters could witness the city's codas, "the very border line of two extremely dissimilar urban ambiances" of the sort that Debord found being enacted in his favorite pair of Claude Lorrain seaport paintings (figs. 2.6, 2.7).[136]

"It will be understood that in speaking here of beauty I don't have in mind plastic beauty," Debord went on, pondering his Claudes, "but simply the particularly moving presentation . . . of a *sum of possibilities.*"[137] The absence of spectacle in the unity of ambiance permitted the visitor to imagine it as a revolutionary social space. Even as Khatib gazed upon Les Halles, he projected into it a future situationist social space, in which he would erect "perpetually changing labyrinths with the help of objects more adequate than the fruit and vegetable carts that are the material of the only barricades of today."[138]

## THE CITY REDESIGNED

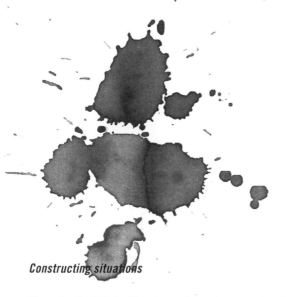

***Constructing situations***

The situationists' ultimate goal was to reconstruct the entire city, though even their immediate ambition to "construct situations" was daunting enough, and in 1957 they committed themselves to it as the Situationist International's "entire program." Constructed situations would be "ephemeral, without a future, passageways," syntheses of those sublime moments when a combination of environment and people produces a transcendent and revolutionary consciousness.[1] This sense of situation had been detected by Henri Lefebvre in his study of the Paris Commune and by situationists in their practice of the drift.[2] The situationists assumed that some sort of "formulary" existed that would permit situations to be produced on demand.

The *situation construite*, the "constructed situation," is best thought of as a sort of *Gesamtkunstwerk* (total work of art).[3] Each constructed situation would provide a decor and ambiance of such power that it would stimulate new sorts of

behavior, a glimpse into an improved future social life based upon human encounter and play.[4] In a paper delivered by Guy Debord to artists preparing to unify as the Situationist International, the mission to construct situations was proposed as an honorable and revolutionary alternative to the creation of traditional artworks.[5] It was, indeed, considered to be a historical necessity, an escape from the alienating physical and social constrictions of traditional art practice—the separation of audience and artist, of production and consumption, within the "art space" of the gallery or theater.

The ambition was admirable and preposterous, carrying no clear notion of how situations would work or what they should look like. The constructed situation would clearly be some sort of performance, one that would treat all space as performance space and all people as performers. In this respect, situationism postured as the ultimate development of twentieth-century experimental theater, the energies of which had been dedicated to the integration of players and audience, of performance space and spectator space, of theatrical experience and "real" experience. "The most pertinent revolutionary experiments in culture have sought to break the spectator's psychological identification with the hero so as to draw him into activity by provoking his capacities to revolutionize his own life," Debord declared.[6]

Futurist and dadaist evenings were famous for their attempts to provoke the audience into active rather than passive participation—"Throw an idea instead of potatoes, idiots!," futurist Carlo Carrà once struck back at his agitated audience.[7] The situationists were well aware of the efforts to take theater beyond entertainment and into revolution. "Pirandello and Brecht have already expressed the destruction of the theatrical spectacle," the first edition of *Internationale situationniste* pointed out, and by its degradation of "the overrated cadaver of Antonin Artaud" the Lettrist International showed its awareness of Artaud's notion of a "Theater of Cruelty," which employed irrationality, spontaneity, and the evocation of primitive rite to defeat theater as mere representation.[8] The constructed situation would plunge its participants into an examination of individual and collective consciousness: redeeming Shakespeare's famous dictum that "All the world's a stage, And all the men and women merely players," the Lettrist International envisaged the construction of situations as a twenty-four-hour tragedy played out for real.[9]

The situationists would measure their success by the degree to which their avant-garde role was minimized. "The situation is made to be lived by its constructors," Debord explained.[10] Conveniently, however, the exact point at which the situationist avant-garde would rescind their role as "auteurs" of the situation, or at which the situation would stop being an autonomous artistic event and become a revolution, escaped scrutiny. The situationists instead diverted criti-

cism onto the multimedia performance art that was emerging elsewhere, refusing it any situationist significance—in 1963 *Internationale situationniste* acknowledged "the 'happenings' produced by the New York artistic avant-garde" only as "a hash produced by throwing together all the old artistic leftovers."[11] The happening, it was argued, was not part of a revolutionary process. A revolutionary transformation of consciousness among its participants was neither its prerequisite nor its result. Not only did it leave the spectacle unchallenged, it was itself a "spectacular" avant-garde activity.

The constructed situation, on the other hand, was conceived solely as part of a cumulative revolutionary chain. In this it was a direct outcome of COBRA, Imaginist Bauhaus, and Lettrist International theory: an investigation of art as a medium for lived experience and social organization. "The new beauty will be of situation," the lettrists had declared, "that's to say provisional and lived."[12] But the situationist process envisaged can barely be claimed to have occurred. There isn't even any evidence that a situation was ever constructed as prescribed. The program that situationists set themselves was so ambitious and uncompromising that it condemned itself to failure. At least happenings took place.

As for the look and feel of the constructed situation, the initial model of the household party was charmingly prosaic.[13] The formula was straightforward, playful, and universal, making the principle of the constructed situation comprehensible to anyone who had ever enjoyed a good night out. "The greatest difficulty . . . is to convey through these apparently delirious proposals a sufficient degree of *serious seduction*," Debord complained.[14] The simplicity of the formula was suggested again by the name of the café that Bernstein and Debord ran for a few weeks in 1958 on the Rue Descartes—La Méthode.[15] The ambiance of parties is born from soft lights, records, and booze, but situationists hesitated over what architectural forms, whether created from scratch or "détourned," might be best in building a constructed situation for real. At least two perceptions of the situationist project were apparent.

One perception was held, for instance, by Constant (who announced himself at the First World Conference of Free Artists as an "ex-artist," by way of a declaration of his commitment to the construction of situations).[16] Constant's situationist city of New Babylon, looking like a cross between constructivism and abstract expressionism, was elastic enough to accommodate the spontaneous popular will of *homo ludens*, and so laden with adaptive technologies that it would have to be built from scratch (see, for instance, fig. 3.3). Another perception of situationism, most typical of the ideas imported from the Lettrist International, expected that an ambient architecture would be created through *détournement*, recycling the old city and existing artistic sources.

Even at the Situationist International's founding conference in 1957, Debord seemed nervous about the sort of city envisaged by his colleagues from the Imaginist Bauhaus. "The comrades who call for a new, free architecture," Debord warned,

**must understand that this new architecture will primarily be based not on free, poetic lines and forms—in the sense that today's "lyrical abstract" painting uses those words—but rather on the atmospheric effects of rooms, hallways, streets, atmospheres linked to the gestures they contain. Architecture must advance by taking emotionally moving situations, rather than emotionally moving forms, as the material it works with. And the experiments conducted with this material will lead to unknown forms.[17]**

Over time, creative differences were raised to the plane of political conflict. Debord and his allies would argue that the priority of the Situationist International was to ensure the social and psychological *conditions* for the construction of situations. Morally, they felt that the actual construction of situations would have to be done by others, and that it was barely possible to predict, let alone dictate, what forms the constructed situation might assume. "The tract 'Construct for yourselves a small situation without a future,'" *Potlatch* had announced, "was actually posted on the walls of Paris, principally in psychogeographically favorable places," as if passersby would decide for themselves how best to respond.[18]

## A "détourned" city

The acceptance of anarchy did not deter situationists like Debord from imagining a "détourned" city, nor coveting the various architectural exemplars that were already to hand. His *Mémoires*, for example, described a "project for a realist urbanism—replace the stairways in Piranesi with lifts—transform the tombs and buildings—align sewers with the planting of trees—recast dustbins in ivory—stack up the shanty towns and build all these cities in the form of a museum."[19] Situationists paid particular attention to so-called primitive architecture, returning to almost Hegelian interests in the origins of building. "The builders have been forgotten, but the inquietudes of the pyramids are resistant to the banalizations of travel agents," *Potlatch* meditated, and *Mémoires* followed up with praise for architecture from "the Aztecs, to the delirious temples of India, to Easter Island, to the great Indian totems of North America—without doubt the greatest architects of all time."[20] Another page was filled with illustrations of such "exotic" exemplars, many of which had inspired the makers of picturesque gardens two centuries before: the Chinese pavilion, the Tartar tent, the tomb, the thatched-roof cottage, the hermitage, the dairy, the philosopher's hut, a variety of defensive architectural forms, stacked and wonderfully ad hoc; and, to bring the ensemble into the twentieth century, the Flatiron Building from New York (fig. 3.1). If we wish to build monu-

ments, the situationists posited, then take the model provided by the follies of the Désert de Retz or Parc Monceau, which attempted, as Monceau's creator Louis Carrogis put it, to "unite in a single garden all times and all places."[21]

Situationists were well aware that their disregard for any conventional sense of "high" and "low," for architectural decorum or uniformity, and their advocacy of a free mixing of architectural sources, had extraordinary aesthetic implications. Debord and Wolman predicted that "the architectural complex . . . will make plastic and emotional use of all sorts of 'détourned' objects: calculatedly arranged cranes or metal scaffolding replacing a defunct sculptural tradition. This is shocking only to the most fanatic admirers of French-style gardens," thus taking situationist aesthetics into a realm beyond even the excesses of the picturesque.[22] Situationists claimed the analogical structure of images that occurs in advertisements and in the poetry of Lautréamont as their inspiration. "When two objects are brought together, no matter how far apart their original contexts may be, a relationship is always formed. . . . The mutual interference of two worlds of feeling, or the bringing together of two independent expressions, supersedes the original elements and produces a synthetic organization of greater efficiency."[23] So when *détournement* is considered in the context of more recent architectural history, a remarkable precedent for the eclecticism of postmodernism emerges. Chtcheglov had understood particularly

*Figure 3.1*

*Guy Debord with Asger Jorn, page from* Mémoires, *1959, screenprinted book, celebrating exemplars of picturesque and "primitive" architectures.*

could fairly boast that *détournement*'s cool reordering of the artistic "text" was an advance upon the grotesque distortions of the "text" perpetrated by surrealism. As if to demonstrate the difference, the Lettrist International's "project of rational embellishments for the city of Paris" began as a revision of an old surrealist paper, André Breton's 1933 "Experimental Researches (On the Irrational Embellishment of a City)." Breton had effectively proposed more spectacle: "Notre-Dame? Replace the towers with an enormous glass cruet, one of the bottles filled with blood, the other with semen."[25] The Lettrist International, on the other hand, wanted to alter the context and use of the existing infrastructure of the city. "Open the Métro at night after the trains stop running. Keep the corridors and tunnels poorly lit by means of weak, intermittently functioning lights. With a careful rearrangement of fire escapes, and the creation of walkways where needed, open the roofs of Paris for strolling. Leave the public gardens open at night. Keep them dark. (In some cases, a weak illumination may be justified by psychogeographic considerations)," the group suggested.[26]

These proposals both confirmed and refuted the old avant-garde excitement about the city of the future. Walkways in the sky would indeed be made available, but the Métro would meanwhile be converted into a catacomb; museums would be abolished and the past eradicated, but they would be replaced not by a new order but by anarchy. The situationists wanted to reassert choice, chance,

well that situationism would have to supersede its modernist precursors not only ideologically but aesthetically as well. "Abstraction has invaded all the arts, contemporary architecture in particular," he noted. "Pure plasticity, inanimate, storyless, soothes the eye. Elsewhere other fragmentary beauties can be found—while the promised land of syntheses continually recedes into the distance. Everyone wavers between the emotionally still-alive past and the already dead future."[24]

True, the surrealists had already tried to counter modernist abstraction. But the situationists and humanist power: "Put switches on the street lamps, so lighting will be under public control."[27] It was this anarchic element that set situationist architectural theory apart. *Détournement* would provide a stockpile of aesthetic elements from which anyone wishing to contribute to the revolutionary city could freely borrow. Once the drift had identified choice features of the existing environment, they could be diverted for situationist use as the "mediocre beginning" of "the complete construction of architecture and urbanism that will someday be within the power of everyone." Anyone could set in train the "displacement of elements of decoration from the locations where we are used to seeing them," taking advantage of the capacity of avant-garde techniques to make everyday things strange. "If *détournement* were extended to urbanistic realizations," Debord wondered, "not many people would remain unaffected by an exact reconstruction in one city of an entire neighborhood of another. Life can never be too disorienting: *détournements* on this level would really make it beautiful."[28]

### A technological baroque

The situationist city was not so much a place of nostalgia, then, as one of romance, dynamism, participation, and passion. The Lettrist International pointed to the amateur architecture of the dadaist Kurt Schwitters and of the Facteur Cheval as evidence that passionate architecture had a place in the twentieth century and beyond. Like the surrealists, the lettrists were thoroughly impressed by Cheval's Palais Idéal (fig. 2.11). That the Palais had been produced by a postman as a continual, playful, expressive outpouring only added to the attractions of the building's fantastic appearance. Moreover, it mixed its sources and references with utter indifference to precedent. It was, in *Potlatch*'s opinion, "the first manifestation of an architecture of disorientation" in the way in which it "'détournes' the forms of diverse exotic monuments, and of a stone vegetation."[29] Cheval's masterpiece was photographed and archived by the lettrists, and Debord had himself pictured standing beneath the Palais's inscription "Where the dream becomes reality," much as Breton had appeared in front of the Palais for his book *Les vases communicants.*[30]

Jorn, who acquired the Lettrist International's pictures of the Palais, took Cheval's lessons to heart when he modified his own house in Albisola, Italy, between the late 1950s and the early 1970s. That Jorn produced the garden in collaboration with his gardener, Umberto Gambetta, made it, in Debord's opinion, the microcosm of a situationist "collective game." Above all, Debord enjoyed its massing of effects—"The painted and sculpted sections, the never-regular stairs between the different levels of ground, the trees, the added elements, a cistern, vines, the most varied sorts of always welcome debris, all thrown together in perfect disorder, compose one of the most complicated and, ultimately, one of the best unified landscapes that one can traverse in the space of a fraction of a hectare. Everything finds its place there without difficulty."[31] Debord was writing in 1974, two years after the official disbanding of the Situationist International, when a melancholic sense of "what could have been" was creeping into his work. "For anyone who has not forgotten the conflicted and passionate relations" of the Situationist International, wrote Debord, or for anyone who "has necessarily remained quite distant from both Situationists and architecture, this [garden] must appear to be a sort of inverse Pompeii: the relief of a city that was not built."[32]

The sense of the baroque running through their aesthetic preferences, from the Palais Idéal to Jorn's garden, was recognized by the situationists themselves, who empathized with the "exemplary" work of "Mad" King Ludwig II of Bavaria, whose most famous work, the fantasy castle of Neuschwanstein in the German Alps, inspired the centerpiece of Disneyland. Ludwig's architecture, Debord felt, had "a baroque character, that one always finds so marked in essays upon an integral art." "In this respect," Debord went on, "it is significant to note the relations between Ludwig of Bavaria and Wagner, who would himself research an aesthetic synthesis"—in other words, the Gesamtkunstwerk, the total work of art.[33]

Maybe, then, Ludwig's fantastic Gesamtkunstwerk at his Grotto of Venus at Linderhof (1876–1877) was an appropriate prototype for the decor of the constructed situation (fig. 3.2). Furnished with stalactites of cast iron coated with cement, it contained a lake fed by a waterfall and a stage hung with a drop scene representing the first act of Wagner's dramatic opera Tannhäuser. Electric light could be controlled to change the colors of the set at will, including the effect of a rainbow. On the lake, which could be ruffled by artificial waves, Ludwig kept two swans and a cockle boat. In his survey of Ludwig's architecture, Michael Petzet has noted that "this 'total' theatre afforded the solitary visitor the complete illusion of stage and auditorium in one, the ultimate improvement on the nineteenth-century peep-show stage; it did not separate the onlooker from the stage by the dark abyss of the empty auditorium," a compression suited to the aspirations of the constructed situation. Petzet describes how, "gliding in his boat over the lake in the middle of the stage, or sitting on the various raised seats at the side, the King experienced an 'action' that consisted only in the change of lighting effects and the change of scenery viewed from different points. . . . Through a peep-hole framed by the grotto wall, the King could even see the real scenery and a nearby castle outside."[34] The editors of Potlatch understood completely the totality of fantastic experience that had been sought by the mad king. "The subterranean river which was his

**Figure 3.2**

Ludwig II of Bavaria, the Grotto of Venus at the Linderhof Palace, Bavaria, Germany, 1876–1877, with cockle boat. This fantastic excursion into the architectural imagination, inspired by the music of Wagner, was the sort of Gesamtkunstwerk that made the "construction of situations" seem like a realistic possibility.

theater or the plaster statues in the gardens signal this *absolutist* enterprise, and its drama," *Potlatch* enthused.[35]

Chtcheglov considered that the new city of situations "would be the baroque stage of urbanism considered as a means of *knowledge* and a means of *action*."[36] It is in Constant's lithographs that we come closest to sensing the baroque atmosphere of the constructed situation, drawing upon the representation of sublime meditative spaces that stretched back to de Chirico, John Martin, Piranesi, and Claude Lorrain (fig. 3.3; compare figs. 2.6, 2.7, 2.10, 2.26, 3.27).[37] Constant's depictions of situationist space were loose, energetic, and suggestive of more than the sum of their parts by their incomprehensible algebraic notation, apparently representative of sound or motion. Some sketches were dissected by speed lines, fusing the baroque to futurism. Constant's world was in perpetual and dynamic motion, its spaces and solids as insecure as those in a cubist painting—or, more specifically, in surrealist developments of cubism, especially the surrealist decor painted by Roberto Matta, like Asger Jorn a 1930s graduate of Le Corbusier's office and sometime participant at the Imaginist Bauhaus (fig. 3.4).

It followed from the Matta influence that the surrealist inheritance would be a significant one. A decorative scheme suggested by the International Lettrist Jacques Fillon in 1955 was deeply reminiscent of the metaphysicism of de Chirico, of the great surrealist shows of the

1930s, of Salvador Dalí's *Happenings* of 1939, and of Frederick Kiesler's architectural models and installations. Three-quarters of a reception room should be elegantly furnished, Fillon thought, while the final quarter would be occupied by a barricade and chicane, protected by loaded guns; suitable lighting and background music would complete the work.[38] Yet Fillon, in common with most situationists, felt that surrealism was a victim of its own success, devalued by overexposure. It was time for situationism to take the next step. Chtcheglov predicted that the new situationist architecture would not just be a matter of *détournement*, but ultimately of a new synthesis with technology and modernity. Referring to the presence in fairy tales and in surrealism of "castles, endless walls, little forgotten bars, mammoth caverns, casino mirrors," he explained that "these dated images retain a small catalyzing power, but it is almost impossible to use them in a *symbolic urbanism* without rejuvenating them by giving them a new meaning. Our imaginations, haunted by the old archetypes, have remained far behind the sophistication of the machines."[39]

Chtcheglov groped instead toward a solution that was almost structuralist in its ambition to distill the essence of architectural language. "We know that a modern building could be constructed which would have no resemblance to a medieval castle but which could preserve and enhance the Castle poetic power (by the conservation of a strict minimum of lines, the transposition of certain others,

**Figure 3.3**

*Constant,* Group Sector, *1962, phototype and ink on paper, Gemeentemuseum, The Hague. Constant's drawings suggested the baroque atmosphere of the constructed situation, thrown into perpetual change by the frenetic energy of its makers.*

**Figure 3.4**

*Roberto Matta,* Eleven Forms of Doubt, *1957, oil on canvas. Matta, who worked at the Imaginist Bauhaus, depicted unstable spatial "situations" similar to those of New Babylon; Constant could also find contemporary explorations of the sublime in paintings by Maria Elena Vieira da Silva and stories by Jorge Luis Borges.*

the positioning of openings, the topographical location, etc.)."[40] Even Debord had been interested in forging this sort of proto-structuralist, technological architecture, and in 1951 worked with Fillon on experiments in neon light and electronic sound.[41] Comparable experiments under the regime of the Situationist International included Walter Olmo's music (reminiscent of Luigi Russolo's noisy contribution to futurism), and Maurice Wyckaert's "'orchestral' projects for assembly-line painting with division of labor based on colour."[42] And of course there was the promised land of Giuseppe Pinot-Gallizio's industrial painting (see fig. 1.14), already spun out in galleries in Turin, Milan, and Paris in 1958–1959 as the *Cavern of Anti-Matter*, its ambiance intensified with mirrors, perfume, music, and female fashion models.

Industrial painting was a proposed medium for the construction of labyrinths, a key motif in the situationist imagination. Legend has it that the Lettrist International was enthralled to discover an entrance into the catacombs on the embankment of the Seine, and the drift had sought a labyrinthine quality in the city itself. Labyrinths seemed to be the ideal environment in which to induce the social interaction necessary for situations, and in which to conjure up the pleasurable fear of the sublime. So in 1959 the Situationist International drew up plans to build a labyrinth in Amsterdam's Stedelijk Museum, through which visitors would drift.[43] Supplemented by the *Cavern of Anti-Matter* and

Wyckaert's "détourned fences," the labyrinth suggested a sort of psychogeographic assault course. The situationists seemed to have in mind the uncanny and paranoiac atmosphere of the surrealist film and the thriller, prescribing, for instance, variable ceiling heights (falling from five meters to a distinctly claustrophobic one meter twenty-two centimeters), variable artificial atmospheric effects (rain, fog, wind, sound and speech, light), and "a system of unilateral doors (visible or possible to handle from one side only)," opening onto rooms which would psychogeographically attract or repel.[44]

But perhaps the most intriguing feature of the Stedelijk plans was the provision of a conceptual bridge between the experience of the gallery and that of the city as a whole. "Its furnishings," the group wrote of the installation, "do not only relate to interior decoration, nor to a reduced reproduction of urban ambiances, but tend to constitute a mixed milieu, never seen, by the mixture of interior characteristics (planned apartment) and exterior (urban)."[45] This play upon the relationship between the Stedelijk's space and the city space of which it was a part became something of an obsession. The psychogeographic course was designed so that it could in theory be extended from its gallery scale of two hundred meters to an urban scale of three kilometers. It was felt that the small labyrinth within the Stedelijk would have to be supplemented by the labyrinth intrinsic to the city as a whole; that the "micro-drift organized in this concentrated labyrinth would have to correspond to the operation of the drift that traversed Amsterdam."[46] The situationists' refusal to recognize the architectural boundary posed by the Stedelijk building was not merely artistic but ideological. Situationist space would not be separated from city space by segregated curatorial space. "The very act of utilizing a museum entails a particular difficulty," the Situationist International admitted, "and the western facade of the Amsterdam labyrinth was a wall specially constructed so as to open a gap in the guise of an entrance: this hole in the wall was required . . . as a guarantee of nonsubmission to the perspective of museums."[47]

There were problems. Even though the three-day drift planned for the city beyond the walls of the Stedelijk was to be particularly sophisticated, employing walkie-talkies to link drifters with "the radio truck of the cartographic team," the situationists were merely refining their practice of drift when their minds might have been more profitably focused on the creation of an installation for the Stedelijk.[48] It is in this light that the reasons for the cancellation of the exhibition require scrutiny. The situationists blamed the Stedelijk's director, Willem Sandberg, for wanting to see the plans for the labyrinth in advance, a straightforward enough request which they deemed typical of "specialists in the research of socioeconomic planning" and which they claimed would have destroyed the "spontaneity" of the installation.[49] Naturally the

museum had to be sure that the plans met standard fire and safety regulations. The situationists found highfalutin reasons for their failure to meet this requirement. They would withdraw from "recuperative" curatorial space, their journal said, so that any future labyrinth would be constructed on waste ground "in direct function with urban realities."[50] Yet situationists regularly exhibited in conventional gallery space, both before and after the Stedelijk episode, which simply fell into a pattern of acrimonious and abortive attempts by the Lettrist and Situationist Internationals to gain recognition on their own terms.[51] Having been severely criticized in 1949 for hosting the enormously controversial COBRA exhibition, Sandberg was hardly an illiberal curator, and he was taking a fresh risk in offering space to a group as fringe as the Situationist International.[52]

At best, then, the cancellation of the installation owed something to insufficient material resources, and at worst to a failure of nerve or even creative imagination on the part of the situationists themselves. The Stedelijk plan as published by *Internationale situationniste* in 1960 was far from comprehensive or complete. Politico-artistic changes already taking place within the Situationist International doubtless played their part as well, the schism over the role of artistic creativity becoming blatant soon after. And if the Situationist International couldn't even decide how to construct a situation, it seemed unlikely that they would agree upon how to transform the city itself.

## Unitary urbanism

The situationist city was to be planned on the principle of "unitary urbanism." The situationists foresaw a city constituted of grand situations, between which the inhabitants would drift, endlessly.

Drifters so far had had to treat the city as a found object. The paths of the drift were subject to obliteration by urban change, like trails in the sand covered by the wind. The drift, *Internationale situationniste* noted,

**furnishes only knowledge that is very precisely dated. In a few years, the construction or demolition of houses, the relocation of micro-societies and of fashions, will suffice to change a city's network of superficial attractions, a very encouraging phenomenon for the moment when we will come to establish an active link between the drift and Situationist urban construction. Until then, the urban milieu will certainly change on its own, anarchically, ultimately rendering obsolete the drifts whose conclusions could not be translated into conscious transformations of this milieu.[53]**

In the city of unitary urbanism, however, urban dynamics would no longer be driven by capital and bureaucracy, but by participation. Unitary urbanism was, then, the final stage projected by the situationist architectural project. In Chtcheglov's famous and idiosyncratic terminology, evoking the romance of life on the ranch, unitary urbanism would be "the hacienda."[54] It was considered so exciting by members of the Imaginist Bauhaus and Lettrist International that they joined forces at the Turin Cultural Union in 1956 to demand that people "demonstrate" in its favor, as if "the future of your children depends on it."[55]

The new city would be "unitary" in several respects. It would primarily be unitary as a social project, ending the capitalist contest for space and prioritization of circulation in order to organize the city for the enrichment of everyday life. In this respect alone unitary urbanism was not actually breaking radically new ground—as recently as 1950 East Germany (the German Democratic Republic) had launched its "Sixteen Principles for the Restructuring of Cities," replacing CIAM's urban principle of "circulation" with one of "culture," insisting on the distinctiveness of urban life, and rejecting the atomization of the city center in favor of "the 'compact city' as a unitary structure efficiently integrating all urban functions and respecting the city's historical dimensions."[56] Of course, no self-respecting situationist was going to own up to being swayed by the directives of East Germany—although it happened that the West German wing of the Situationist International, SPUR, also started demanding a "compact city."[57] It made sense, after all, for situationists to negotiate the propaganda war and "détourn" its best architectural products. As one commentary has explained, "despite the overtly propagandistic and rigidifying effects of East German urban policy in these years, the effort to rethink the city in

**Figure 3.5**

*Alison and Peter Smithson,* Project for Berlin Hauptstadt, *1958, ink, drawn by Peter Sigmond and published in* Uppercase 3 *(1960), showing the growth of pedestrian causeways above the old street grid. This development of Peter Smithson's Cluster City concept had considerable resonance with Constant's New Babylon, since it allowed the city to make a fresh start without wiping the slate clean. The layering of urban history could be made manifest rather than suppressed.*

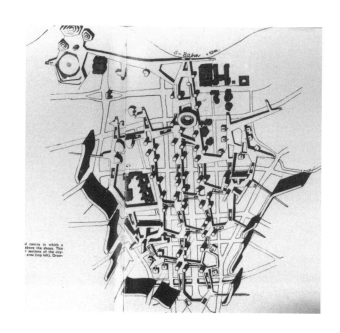

symbolic and historical terms and to overcome the division between architecture and urbanism did produce a serious alternative to Western planning—at least for a few years," SPUR mischievously adopting aspects of East Germany's "Sixteen Principles" only after Nikita Khrushchev had reversed them back in favor of functionalism in 1954.[58] And situationists appropriated aspects of West Germany's architectural propaganda as well. In 1958 the West German government's "Hauptstadt Berlin" (Capital Berlin) competition provocatively invited proposals for the restructuring of central Berlin—including the East German sector of the city. Alison and Peter Smithson's entry to the competition seems to have had a profound influence upon Constant (fig. 3.5; compare figs. 1.12, 3.24).

A more ideologically appropriate antecedent for unitary urbanism existed in the work of Charles Fourier, the nineteenth-century French utopian socialist who had campaigned for the building of a "phalanstery," a "unitary architecture" (*architecture unitaire*) embodying a passionate social harmony (fig. 3.6). Like Fourier's unitary architecture, situationist unitary urbanism was a vision of the unification of space and architecture with the social body, and with the individual body as well.[59] "The imbrications of the *passions*," Walter Benjamin once remarked on the organizing principle of the phalanstery, "were primitive analogies based on the machine, formed in the material of psychology. This machinery, formed of men, produced the land

of Cockaigne, the primal wish-symbol, that Fourier's Utopia had filled with new life."[60]

Unitary urbanism was a social project, then, but also an artistic project, the making of the *Gesamtkunstwerk.* "Integral art, which has been talked about so much, can only be realized at the level of urbanism," Debord loftily declared.[61] This revived a persistent trend in modern architecture, fashionable not least in CIAM circles.[62] Full-blown situationism, however, regarded previous attempts at unifying the arts as partial, because they had interpreted the process merely in terms of form. It was an approach Debord redressed when he argued that unitary urbanism should be "infinitely more far-reaching than the old domination of architecture over the traditional arts."[63] Under previous schemes, architecture had mustered the other arts

**Figure 3.6**

Victor Considérant, "Perspective of a phalanstery or palais sociétaire *dedicated to humanity,*" masthead of the late nineteenth-century Fourierist newspaper L'Avenir, depicting a massive building employing rues-galeries (street-galleries), long covered arcades uniting the building's facilities and spaces, and, it was hoped, the society that inhabited the building. Constant retained a copy of the picture in his archive.

for a specific aesthetic program. Under unitary urbanism, however, architecture would merge seamlessly with all other arts, assailing the senses not with a single aesthetic but with a panoply of changing ambiances. Conventional notions of building science could hardly survive such a program. Unitary urbanism, Debord pronounced, "must include the creation of new forms and the *détournement* of previous forms of architecture, urbanism, poetry and cinema," making ambient use even of food and drink.[64] "We do not recognize the existence of architecture," Jorn wrote. "Cologne Cathedral is nothing but an empty magic sculpture, whose aim is purely psychological—just like a glass of beer is architecture."[65]

If this mass assault upon the senses was to completely revolutionize the life of the city, unitary urbanism would have to orchestrate the city's constituent parts, its unities of ambiance. The unities of ambiance already discovered by drifting situationists were regarded as ruins of a mislaid and superior social space, urban fragments seemingly bypassed by spectacular urbanism and awaiting reunification. "All cities are geological," Chtcheglov claimed, conjuring up the idea of a city resistant to rationalization by the layering of its pasts. "We move within a closed landscape whose landmarks constantly draw us toward the past. Certain shifting angles, certain receding perspectives, allow us to glimpse original conceptions of space, but this vision remains fragmentary."[66] These urban fragments were intended to take hold of the reader's mind in rather the same way that *ekphrases* (descriptions of architecture from classical literature) had once taken hold of the imaginations of students of antiquity. The building of unitary urbanism could be deferred while its possibilities were constructed in the collective imagination, and in the meantime the fantasy of "détourning" certain *quartiers* of existing Paris was considered to be an exercise in planning, not an idle pastime. Cutting up maps of Paris, and their boring confirmation of the city's current formation, was the first step in the creation of a new order.[67] Unitary urbanism was an urban future that would recover the lost, mythic wholeness that had been shattered by capital and bureaucracy.

What, then, might be the nature of the new urban unity, composed out of fragments? The best-known precedents for a "unitary" city—Le Corbusier's Ville Contemporaine, for example—had tended to be idealizing, classicizing, and rationalizing. Situationist architects, however, projected a city based not on functional order but on purposeful disorder. Other than the urban picturesque, there had been precious few models for such a city since the Middle Ages.[68] And not even the picturesque had posited a plan quite so radically decentered as unitary urbanism. Like a biological body, unitary urbanism would be one organism, but with many organs, all with their own humors. The arrows on *The Naked City* had pointed the fragments both to separation and to unity, making them both independent from and interdependent upon each other (as in more recent exercises in

architectural deconstruction). Debord explained, "In each of its experimental cities unitary urbanism will act by way of a certain number of force fields, which we can temporarily designate by the classic term 'quarter.' Each quarter will tend toward a specific harmony, divided off from neighboring harmonies; or else will play on a maximum breaking up of internal harmony."[69] It was Chtcheglov who had first suggested the adaptation of the traditional quarter for synthetic psychological effect. He believed that the districts of the future city "could correspond to the whole spectrum of diverse feelings that one encounters by chance in everyday life. Bizarre Quarter—Happy Quarter (specially reserved for habitation)—Noble and Tragic Quarter (for good children)—Historical Quarter (museums, schools)—Useful Quarter (hospital, toolshops)—Sinister Quarter, etc."[70]

Unitary urbanism rejected the idealistic quest for fixed forms and permanent solutions that had been the basis of traditional town planning. Since situationism regarded art as a playful means of social organization, unitary urbanism would naturally envisage "the urban environment as the terrain of a game in which one participates."[71] The city would become a giant playground, its quarters acting as stations for a perpetual Revolutionary Festival. On this fundamental point situationists were agreed: the creation of the situationist city would pass from its avant-garde city fathers to its citizens. But as in all great revolutions, the nature of that transition was disputed. At what point should the situationist avant-garde disengage? When would situationist agitation give way to anarchic free play? What really would be the relationship between the architecture of the old city and that of the situationist city?

When Constant began work on his New Babylon project, it was in the belief that unitary urbanism would require situationists to somehow start building their new city, just as had utopians before them, like the Fourierists and Owenites and the garden city movement. "*The hacienda must be built*," Chtcheglov had emphatically declared, and Constant was prepared to rise to the challenge, seeing in the convergence of situationism and the latest structural technology the chance finally for architecture to escape the confines of rationalism.[72] He was tempted, perhaps, by Debord, who asked the preparatory conference of the SI to imagine the "most elementary unit of unitary urbanism" as being "the architectural complex, which combines all the factors conditioning an ambiance, or a series of clashing ambiances, on the scale of the constructed situation."[73]

In 1958 Debord and Constant could still find sufficient common ground to coauthor the "Declaration of Amsterdam," a brave attempt to summarize the principles of unitary urbanism, though for all the certainty of its tone it was a rather schizophrenic document. One can see the tenets by which Constant set most store—the ones about "striving for a perfect spatial art," coordinating "artistic and scientific means" to the point of "com-

plete fusion," and so on. Debord's emphasis was different; for him, unitary urbanism, "independent of all aesthetic considerations," was "the result of a new kind of collective creation," making revolutionary sociocultural activity the first step—"the immediate task of today's creatively active people."[74]

And over the next couple of years Debord and his allies within the SI began to feel that unitary urbanism should never abandon the existing city in favor of virgin territory. They would not be exiled to a New Babylon in the way that the Jews had been exiled to the old Babylon. It increasingly seemed to them that their role in the making of unitary urbanism was as propagandists, not architects: Kotányi and Vaneigem, who took over the situationist "Bureau of Unitary Urbanism" after Constant's resignation in 1960, described unitary urbanism as

**a living critique, fuelled by all the tensions of daily life. . . . Living critique means the setting up of bases for an experimental life. . . . Such bases cannot be reservations for "leisure" activities separated from society. . . . Situationist bases will exert pressure in the opposite direction, acting as bridgeheads for an invasion of the whole of daily life. U.U. [unitary urbanism] is the contrary of a specialized activity; to accept a separate urbanistic domain is already to accept the whole urbanistic lie.[75]**

*Internationale situationniste* even proposed building a situationist base that could populate, "through the example of the stations in the Antarctic," the

Allée des Cygnes, the long, narrow, uninhabited island on the Seine that connects the Pont de Bir-Hakein and Pont de Grenelle, whence situationists would make sorties into the inhabited city.[76]

### Constant's New Babylon

Absorbing his energies for more than a decade, New Babylon was Constant's masterwork, a means to realize his own and the situationists' architectural ambitions simultaneously. There was a conflict between these ambitions, since the spirit of situationism demanded that personal creative ambition and vision be subsumed to group will. As Debord had announced at the SI's founding conference, "It must be understood once and for all that something that is only a personal expression within a framework created by others cannot be termed a creation," and Constant's maquettes were always treated with a degree of caution by the Debordist faction, which greeted them in 1959 as "pre-situationist."[77]

Constant never failed to reiterate that ultimately New Babylon could only be a collective, social project, and that his work should be understood as nothing more than the projected framework for the construction of situations and the decor for a life of leisure. Yet in 1960 Constant was hounded out of the SI, accused of "plagiarizing two or three poorly understood fragments of Situationist

ideas."[78] Although he was a victim in part of the group's abandonment of any serious development of unitary urbanism, accusations of individualism were to be partly substantiated as Constant continued to work on New Babylon independently.

Constant introduced the label "New Babylon" to his works around 1958, drawing upon established comparisons of legendary old Babylon with the heady phenomenon of the modern city.[79] The metaphor of Babylon brought the architectural and cultural neatly together. Architecturally, modern cities have revived the fascination with elevation, engineering, and spectacle that made old Babylon famous. Culturally, Babylon and the building of its tower have survived as a fable of common effort giving way to fragmentation and finally to decadence.[80] So Babylon, once a parable of the godless modern city, was on the contrary revived by Constant as an exemplar for the modern city—technological, universal, and playful. In 1870 a German newspaper denounced Paris as a modern "Babylon," and the Commune that Paris collapsed into the following year was celebrated as a New Babylon in the classic 1929 Soviet film of the same name.[81] Babylonian decadence promised a spiral into social anarchy. "The Commune represents the only realization of a revolutionary urbanism to date—attacking on the spot the petrified signs of the dominant organization of life, understanding social space in political terms, refusing to accept the innocence of any monument," the situationists wrote.[82] The Communards' tactics were concentrated less upon the appropriation of economic wealth than of urban space, joyfully annexing private space into the public sphere, demolishing the monuments of the old order, and barricading the circulation of its troops.

Constant's interest in urbanism was a response to his observations as a *flâneur* in Paris and London in the early 1950s, where he had seen "people building, demolishing, removing. . . . The traffic increased, man disappeared . . . mechanized technological environments emerged."[83] Worried about the aloofness of the artist from the new industrial revolution engendered by postwar reconstruction, Constant took advantage of the dissolution of the raw expressionism of COBRA by giving his work a strongly architectonic flavor. Postwar construction work, permanently encrusted with scaffolding, crawling with people busied in building, and apparently in a perpetual state of becoming, had a continued resonance in Constant's architectural vision.

One curious piece of 1955 was suggestive of a sort of obstacle course across wasteland: in *Ambiance de jeu* (Ambiance of play), wooden shapes and copper rod, painted and mounted on a support, created a large geometric composition, designed to be hung rather than viewed flat, that fell in between hard-edge abstraction and architectural model-making (fig. 3.7). This transitory stage, like an El Lissitzky *proun* (fig. 3.8), was a "changing of trains" between art and architecture, or, according to a 1959 catalogue, "an experiment

with space."[84] Likewise, the 1958 *Model for a Gypsy Camp* seemed to be only slightly more functional than the various neoconstructivist sculptures that Constant had been working on, belying the relative stringency of the brief (fig. 1.15). Yet the exercises were absolutely sincere bids at unifying art, architecture, science, and environment, spinoffs from a "Spatiodynamic" project that Constant developed with the ex-COBRA sculptor Stephen Gilbert and architect Nicolas Schöffer between 1953 and 1956.[85]

Constant continued to address the problems of play, flexibility, and nomadism in New Babylon, but as the project advanced the mass of models and illustrations became more expansive rather than more detailed. In attempting to give visual form to unitary urbanism, Constant explained, New Babylon was "not primarily a town planning project. Equally, it is not intended as a work of art in the traditional sense nor as an example of architectonic structure . . . [but as] a creative game with an imaginary environment."[86] Constant had obviously learned the tactic of the situationist tract: inspire rather than prescribe. Constant's images were like visual equivalents for the situationist aphorism. The images could accordingly be found dropped casually into an editorial in *Internationale situationniste*,[87] while Constant's 1959 catalogue strangely juxtaposed his sculptures with quotations from Paul-Henri Chombart de Lauwe. "To what extent can we freely build the framework of a social life in which we can be guided by our aspirations and not by our instincts?," one

**Figure 3.7**

Constant, Ambiance de jeu, *1955–1956, wood and copper, Gemeentemuseum, The Hague. The piece, one of Constant's earliest excursions into abstract architectural model-* making, invoked Aldo van Eyck's Amsterdam children's playgrounds of the late 1940s, recognized at the time for making modernism feel more human and capricious.

**Figure 3.8**

El Lissitzky, Proun R.V.N.2, *1923, tempera and silver paint on canvas, Kunstmuseum Hannover mit Sammlung Sprengel, Hannover. Like Lissitzky's prouns, Constant's* Ambiance de jeu *was originally hung rather than viewed flat, and represented a transition from art to architecture.*

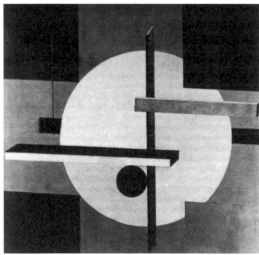

**Figure 3.9**

*Double-page spread from the catalogue* Constant *(Paris, 1959). Constant's abstract sculptures are juxtaposed with aphorisms on architecture and life. The catalogue was published by the situationist press, the Bibliothèque d'Alexandrie.*

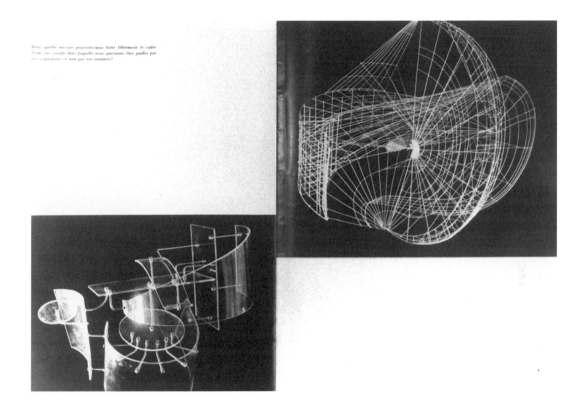

quotation asked. The elegant sculptures, presumably, were part of Constant's answer (fig. 3.9).[88]

Pragmatic readers disturbed by New Babylon's lack of detail might overcome their frustration if one day they could participate in the building of the new world envisaged by Constant. Even as this was endowed with an elaborate theoretical framework, the gap between Constant's texts and images remained to be filled by the imaginative reader, since Constant was intent upon explaining the context rather than the content of his work. Readers could more easily discover the position of New Babylon within the history of utopia and recent social theory than how New Babylon's movable partitions or atmospheric conditioning systems might actually work.[89] In the meantime the projections of New Babylon became ever more ambitious in design and site. Constant's celebration of building technology and of the great public building paid homage to the tradition of visionary

**Figure 3.11 (below)**

*Ivan Leonidov*, Design for the Lenin Institute, *1927, maquette.*

**Figure 3.10 (above)**

*Etienne-Louis Boullée*, Monument to Sir Isaac Newton, *c. 1785, engraving.*

**Figure 3.12 (facing page)**

*Constant*, Space Furrow with Base Plate, Concert Hall for Electronic Music, *1960, metal, perspex, and wood, Wilhelm Lehmbruck Museum, Duisburg. Constant's architecture drew upon a great utopian tradition of fantastic visionary public buildings, while consciously addressing the contemporary age: his maquettes were largely made from industrial waste, a fact announced by their rough-hewn finish. The space furrow was apparently formed from the windshields of an Iso Isetta bubble car, endowing the piece with connotations of smart engineering, fun, and mobility.*

design from Etienne-Louis Boullée to constructivism (figs. 3.10, 3.11, 3.12). New Babylon was shown precariously suspended over entire cities and countries, making literal Debord and Jorn's invocation in the pages of their *Mémoires* of "a floating city."[90]

### The structure of New Babylon

New Babylon was an important part of the boom in experimental design during the 1950s and 1960s, and may well have influenced other projects: the first maquettes for New Babylon were exhibited at the Stedelijk as early as 1959.[91] Experimental designers of the period were trying to drive beyond rationalism by advocating free forms, mixed use, and functional flexibility. They expected to create new senses of meaning and place in the city, sympathetic to human ludic and social need.

With his 1958 maquettes for New Babylon, Constant aligned himself with the vanguard of thought on megastructure, inasmuch as the structures that he proposed would house some of the multiple functions that the traditional city

accommodates individually.[92] By designing structures that could cut a tentacular swath through the existing landscape or cityscape, megastructuralists like Constant sought to supersede the constrictions imposed through the separation of function between buildings and between city districts. A typical New Babylon "sector," at 20–30 hectares "much bigger than . . . any present building," could handle leisure, transport, and shelter, and so could go some way toward addressing situationist worries about the separation of activities by rationalist urbanism.[93]

Within practice, New Babylon had overtones of "metabolism" (the design of long-term structures to support short-term components) but related specifically to what had become known by 1963 as spatial urbanism (*urbanisme spatiale*).[94] Constant's work was comparable to that of architect Yona Friedman (figs. 3.13, 3.14). Friedman, frustrated by the vagaries of Team 10's ideas about "mobility," "development," and "growth and change," had become the best-known advocate of spatial urbanism, founding his GEAM—Groupe d'Etudes d'Architecture Mobile (Mobile Architecture Study Group)—in

**Figure 3.14**

Yona Friedman, Urbanisme spatiale, New York, *1960–1962,
ink on paper. As colleagues in the Groupe d'Etudes
d'Architecture Mobile (Mobile Architecture Study Group),*       both Friedman and Constant envisaged the remaking of the
city as taking place in space frame structures suspended
over old cities and open land.

1957; as a participant in GEAM, Constant was immersed in the sophisticated spatialist theories of the likes of Eckhard Schulze-Fielitz and Frei Otto.[95] Friedman and Constant alike proposed supporting the city's systems within a space frame, raised on a *pilotis* (a grid of supporting columns) above nature and old cities, thus providing a clean sheet for "three-dimensional" urban planning and growth. "The ground remains free for motorized transport and agriculture, wild nature and historical monuments," Constant explained. New Babylon sectors, floating "16 metres above the ground," would "represent a sort of extension of the Earth's surface,

*Figure 3.15*

*Alex Moulton, Moulton Standard Bicycle, 1962, pictured on a brochure cover designed by Colin Banks with John Miles, 1964. The Moulton, with its small wheels and full suspension, was as conscious an attempt to reinvent the bike as New Babylon was to reinvent the city (and as the Austin Mini, which Moulton also helped engineer, was to reinvent the car); they were statements of faith in the boundless capacity of technology to mobilize everyday life. Reyner Banham, for instance, appreciated the sense of fun and mobility embodied in them all.*

a new skin that covers the earth and multiplies its living space."[96]

Here again, a situationist was adopting a solution that originated in the much-maligned Le Corbusier, pioneer of *pilotis* and deck structures.[97] Nonetheless, one would hardly mistake Constant's work for that of Le Corbusier. The spidery chaos of New Babylon eschewed Corbusian monumentalism, reviving instead an ambition long since shelved by mainstream modernism. A 1943 essay, "Nine Points on Monumentality," by Sigfried Giedion, José Luis Sert, and Fernand Léger, had foreseen the precepts of Constant's architecture: "Today modern architects know that buildings cannot be conceived as isolated units, that they have to be incorporated into vaster urban schemes. There are no frontiers between architecture and town planning," the authors declared. They went on,

**Modern materials and new techniques are at hand, light metal structures . . . panels of different textures, colors, and sizes; light elements like ceilings which can be suspended from big trusses covering practically unlimited spans. . . . Mobile elements, changing positions and casting different shadows when acted upon by wind or machinery, can be the source of new architectural effects. During night hours, color and forms can be projected on vast surfaces. . . . Man-made landscapes would be correlated with nature's landscapes and all elements combined in terms of the new and vast facade, sometimes extending for many miles, which has been revealed to us by the air view. This could be contemplated not only during a rapid flight but also from a helicopter stopping in mid-air.[98]**

Yet Giedion, Sert, and Léger's sentimental attachment to the traditional role of the master plan and the monument was anathema to Constant, who was attuned to a newer, postwar vision for design, one that preferred the transitory formations of technology to the permanence of "good form."[99] A nice set of juxtapositions was created when Constant's 1964 article about New Babylon was sandwiched by the British magazine *Architectural Design* between reviews of two very different design icons of the period, a Le Corbusier Unité d'Habitation at Briey-en-Forêt and an Alex Moulton small-wheeled bicycle, as championed by freewheeling Reyner Banham (fig. 3.15).[100] The "good form" of the Unité, however impressive and megastructural, was founded upon older ideas about materials, housing, and society,

**Figure 3.16**

Constant, Ambiance of a Future City, *maquette with model cars, 1958, illustration from the catalogue* Constant *(Paris, 1959). The "sector" sweeps over the traffic below,* permitting an ease of circulation beyond even the wildest dreams of mainstream modernism.

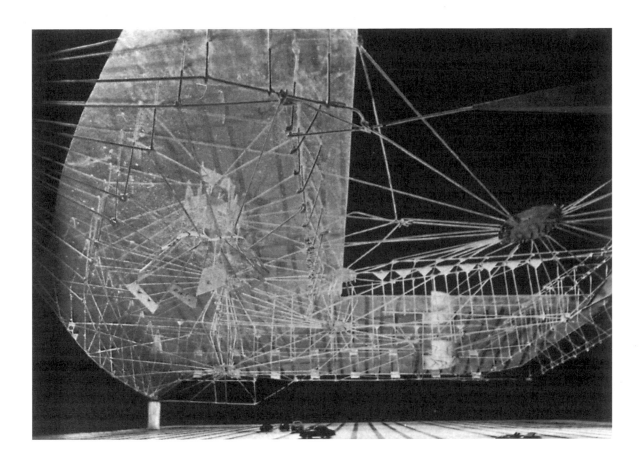

**Figure 3.17**

Konrad Wachsmann, prefabricated tubular space frame building system for airplane hangars, 1950–1953. Wachsmann's designs inspired a new wave of engineered architecture.

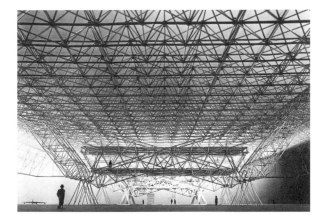

while the Moulton was, *Architectural Design* felt, "this radical rethinking of conventional . . . design," herald for a new era of choice and mobility.[101] New Babylon was like a specter bridging the two, monolithic and overengineered. It was as assertively collective as the Unité, yet it also promoted an individualist mobility like the bike, facilitated by joyriding in pedal vehicles, cars, and flying machines (fig. 3.16).

New Babylon's space frame was ideally suited to the creation of transitory, amorphous architecture, fantastic vistas and fecund space, ready for *homo ludens* to let his imagination run wild. Any city is artificial, but New Babylon would be an exquisitely fabricated environment where everything would truly sing of humanity. Constant, writing in *Internationale situationniste* against "the idea of the green city, which most modern architects have adopted," proposed that "far from being a return to nature, to the idea of living in a park, like the solitary aristocrats of times past, we can see in such immense structures [as New Babylon] the possibility of the conquest of nature."[102]

The anarchic possibilities of a building composed of movable partitions had been part of Chtcheglov's "Formulary," and was mentioned again by Debord, who admired the flexibility of a 1955 helicoidal ("snail shell") house about which he had read.[103] Constant embraced the idea, envisaging a system of movable partitions within a fixed framework, "a quite chaotic arrangement of small and bigger spaces that are constantly mounted and dismounted by means of standardised mobile construction elements, like walls, floors and staircases."[104] Suppleness would be achieved through the use of the lightweight products that were coming out of materials science: describing New Babylon's Yellow Sector in *Internationale situationniste* in 1960, Constant drew the reader's attention to its titanium floors and nylon pavements and partitions.[105] His claims for structural technology were not as maverick as they might have seemed. They simply pushed the *Zeitgeist* to its limits: in 1954 Konrad Wachsmann published his works on spatial building systems, his space frame structure for aircraft hangars emboldening a new generation of experimental architects (fig. 3.17).[106]

### New Babylon's utopian fun

Comparisons between Constant's situationist vision and the work of other avant-gardists are teasing, because although New Babylon shared many of its structural principles with other architectural experiments, its meaning was quite distinct. Britain's Archigram group, for instance, aired ideas of "situation" at their seminal 1963 "Living City" exhibition at the Institute of Contemporary Arts. *The Situationist Times*, doubtless

*Figure 3.18*

*Peter Cook for Archigram,* Plug-in City, Maximum Pressure Area, *1963–1964, section, ink. Thanks in part to their determinedly architectural rather than utopian solutions for modern living, Archigram's images gained a following among young architects that New Babylon did not.*

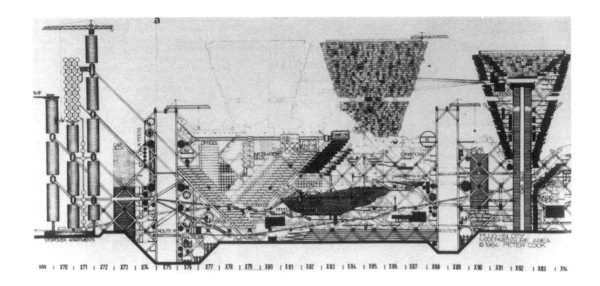

noticing that Archigram had even collaged a fragment of the *Guide psychogéographique de Paris* into its display, discovered that situationism had itself become victim to the plagiarism that it advocated.[107] For Archigram in its early days, "situation—the happenings within spaces in the city . . . —is as important, possibly more important, than the built demarcation of space. . . . This time/movement/situation thing is important in determining our whole future attitude to the visualisation and realisation of city."[108]

The Archigram group attended Constant's 1964 ICA lecture in London, read his lecture notes, and invited him to contribute to *Archigram* no. 5, the "Metropolis" issue of their increasingly influential newsletter.[109] Yet situationism was conspicuous by its absence from *Experimental Architecture,* the key retrospective account published in 1970 by Archigram's Peter Cook. Perhaps New Babylon did not sufficiently impress Constant's contemporaries. Through attention to detail, Archigram architects insisted on the buildability of their structures, however fantastic they might seem, evincing a rigor somewhat lacking in the work of Constant, artist-*provocateur* (fig. 3.18). The empiricism of Britain's "Meccano generation," in other words, was only partly compatible with Constant's continental existentialism. The detail and practicality of British experimental architecture almost invariably set it apart from Constant's work. The famous Fun Palace leisure center project (1962–1967), for example, planned for the Lea

Valley Regional Park in East London by architect Cedric Price (who was friends with Alexander Trocchi) and impresario Joan Littlewood, got as far as satisfying fire regulations, more than Constant and the SI had managed with their very much more modest installation proposed for the Stedelijk (fig. 3.19). And it was almost as ambitious as New Babylon, if not in scale then in its technical services, promising "charged static vapour zones, optical barriers, warm air curtains," and a "fog dispersal plant."[110]

Differences within the avant-garde, compounded by its raw competitiveness, were symptomatic of an ideological chasm between situationism and contemporary movements. So while the Frenchman Yona Friedman was inspired, like Constant, by Huizinga's notion of a "ludic" instinct in humanity and Roger Caillois's theories of play and leisure, he also stressed the essential rationality of his brand of spatial urbanism, referring to its adaptability not only to the existing city but to industry, business, and homes, sending appeals for endorsement to figures as diverse as Le Corbusier and Buckminster Fuller.[111] Constant, meanwhile, foresaw the need only for a few hotels servicing leisured nomads. Friedman sought the incorporation of convenience services: Constant preferred *disconvenience*.

Of all the megastructural projects, New Babylon was the most radically utopian, and Constant sought more than a structural reevaluation of the existing city. He introduced New Babylon to his British public by reminding them that "since the beginning of this century there has been constant discussion about the creative faculties of the human race, and more than one avant-garde movement has declared itself in favour of a *poésie fait par tous* [a poetry made by all, the key refrain that the situationists inherited from Lautréamont]. The realisation of such a mass-culture does obviously not depend on the intentions of artists only, and would demand thorough changes within society."[112] As the sixties wore on, New Babylon emerged as a utopian icon, a phalanstery for the love generation, as Constant tested the limits of the Dutch state's repressive tolerance with the help of his colleagues from Provo. New Babylon filled a 1965 issue of *Provo* magazine, and by 1967, when it was the focus for a rally in Amsterdam's Parkkerk, New Babylon served as a totem for the architectural empowerment of the people.[113] Constant's environmentalism and anticapitalism could hardly have been in starker contrast to Peter Cook's assertion that "it will often be part of the architect's brief . . . to exploit the maximum profit from a piece of land. In the past this would have been considered an immoral use of the talents of an artist. It is now simply part of the sophistication of the whole environmental and building process in which finance can be made a creative element in design."[114] Archigram's libertarianism seemed to take a rightward turn, its increasingly personalized "architectures" isolating the citizen from the

*Cedric Price,* Arriving by Helicopter, *rendering for the Fun Palace leisure center project, planned for the Lea Valley Regional Park by Cedric Price and Joan Littlewood, 1962–1967. The Fun Palace project probably came closest to making the dream of a spontaneous leisure architecture for the 1960s into a reality.*

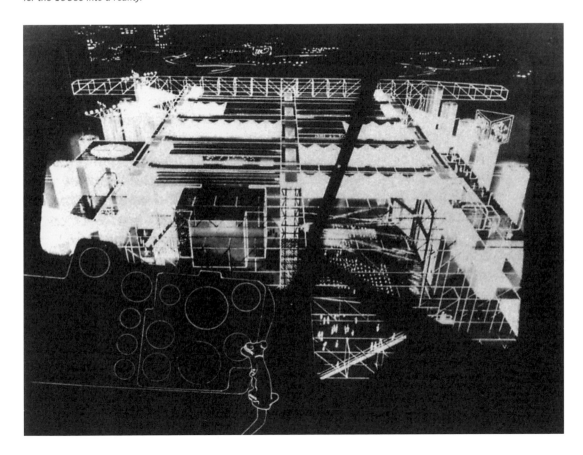

festive crowd with inventions like Michael Webb's Cushicle and Suitaloon, bubbles of individual freedom (fig. 3.20).[115]

In fact, New Babylon was so far removed from conventional concerns with profit and loss that its economy remained something of a mystery. Constant joined Thomas More, Henri de Saint-Simon, Charles Fourier, Karl Marx, and the like to investigate the possibility of a noncommodity socialism, a scientific utopia where scarcity and suffering were confined to history.[116] He calmly asserted, "The effects of machine-production are leading slowly to a reduction in human labour, and we can state

**Figure 3.20**

*Michael Webb for Archigram,* Cushicle Fully Opened Out and in Use, *1966–1967. "The Cushicle is an invention that enables a man to carry a complete environment on his back," Archigram announced. But, as with Banham's Environment Bubble (fig. 1.16), the individualism of this sort of "complete nomadic unit" was at odds with the collectivist notions underpinning the situationist utopia.*

**Figure 3.21**

*Michael Webb (later of Archigram),* Sin Centre, *1958–1962, metal and Plexiglas. Often aimed at the burgeoning leisure industry, Archigram's "fun" architecture was actually based upon far less radical notions of leisure than those motivating the situationists.*

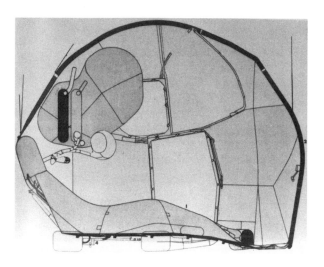

already with certainty, that we will enter a new era, in which production-labour will be automatic. For the first time in history, mankind will be able to establish an affluent society in which nobody will have to waste his forces, and in which everybody will be able to use his entire energy for the development of his creative capacities." Questions about fiscal economy were no longer valid. "The question," Constant insisted, "is how the free man of the future will use his unlimited energies."[117]

Chtcheglov's confident words echoed through the New Babylonian sectors: "The economic obstacles are only apparent. . . . This is demonstrated by the immense prestige of Monaco and Las Vegas—and Reno, that caricature of free love—although they are mere gambling places. Our first experimental city would live largely off tolerated and controlled tourism. Future avant-garde activities and productions would naturally tend to gravitate there. In a few years it would become the intellectual capital of the world and would be universally recognized as such." Chtcheglov thought of fun culture as a historical necessity: "The appearance of the notion of relativity in the modern mind allows one to surmise the EXPERIMENTAL aspect of the next civilization (although I'm not satisfied with that word; say, more supple, more 'fun')."[118] For Constant as well, the introduction of "fun" onto the agenda of experimental architecture was not something to be treated as a sinful diversion from labor. Nor should fun be a commodity peddled in specialized leisure centers like Price and Littlewood's Fun Palace, or the Sin Centre planned by Archigram's

**Figure 3.22**

Constant, "View approaching sectors G and E" ("A high level of
a typical structure, showing its surface divided by ever-changing
mobile elements"), illustration from Constant, "Description de
la zone jaune," Internationale situationniste, no. 4 (1960),
reprinted (cropped) in "New Babylon/An Urbanism of the
Future," Architectural Design, June 1964. This detail of
Constant's maquette for sectors G and E in New Babylon represented the situationist city as a sort of pinball machine.

Michael Webb for London's entertainment area of
Leicester Square (fig. 3.21). Even Reyner
Banham (the best-known apologist for Archigram)
admitted that the group's preoccupations with
leisure "prove, in the last analysis, to be so trivial
as to drive a serious historian to despair."[119] For
the New Babylonian, fun would not be a break
from work and social normalcy. "The new *homo
ludens* . . . on the contrary, will rather be the normal type of man."[120]

The elevated utopianism of New Babylon
condemned it to the limbo occupied by those
ideas that could be either abstract critical principle or serious practical proposition. This, in the

end, may be the reason why commentators kept New Babylon at arm's length. When it ran its feature on New Babylon, the editors of *Architectural Design* politely avoided interpreting the photographs of Constant's bizarre work in any detail, fluctuating between the giddiness of Constant's own claims and the secure ground of structure and material: "The lines indicate trajectories of movements actually taking place or past. All of Constant's models are made out of coloured elements of Perspex and metal" (fig. 3.22).[121] Constant himself struggled to negotiate the tricky utopianism of New Babylon, downplaying the "situationist teams" that would have been necessary to the running of New Babylon, yet which would have been a little out of keeping with the anarchic ideologies of situationism.[122] It was an anomaly present also in other contemporary leisure architectures. Littlewood and Price confined their army of technical assistants to quarters in the Fun Palace's service basement, and, more sinister, Disney built a police station beneath Main Street USA, Disneyland. Constant specifically separated "technical services" from the rest of the New Babylon sector, so that New Babylonians would have been as ignorant of the mechanical workings of their environment as Ludwig II of Bavaria was indifferent to the weary electrician and workmen stoking the furnaces at his Linderhof grotto. "I don't want to know how it works," Ludwig is reputed to have said. "I just want to see the effects."[123]

## Disorientation

The sovereignty of fun and leisure generated the plan of New Babylon. It was a clear attempt to model the drift, to build passages and unities of ambiance and *plaques tournantes* in the style of those opened up by the Lettrist International through Paris (see chapter 2). "The principal activity of the inhabitants will be the CONTINUOUS DRIFT," Chtcheglov had predicted for the situationist city. "The changing of landscapes from one hour to the next will result in complete disorientation."[124] Debord had reiterated the idea: "Within architecture itself, the taste for drift tends to promote all sorts of new forms of labyrinths made possible by modern techniques of production."[125]

Adapting the 1958 Alison and Peter Smithson project for a pedestrian net suspended over the old street pattern of Berlin, the projected sectors of New Babylon tiptoed over selected European cities, echoing old street patterns, hovering above certain districts and streets, keeping a respectful distance from historic city cores.[126] This "open-city" thesis treated the modern city as necessarily permanently "ruined," "in the sense that accelerated movement and change in the 20th century were incapable of relating to the pattern of a preexisting fabric."[127] It was a concept that the situationists exaggerated when they described how, in their city, "the new neighborhoods . . . could be constructed increasingly towards the west . . . while to the same extent the east would be abandoned to

**Figure 3.23**

Constant, "New Babylon, overhead view," from the New Babylon Atlas, *1964, ink on paper, Gemeentemuseum, The Hague. New Babylon had the capacity for almost infinite expansion or contraction, its sectors leaving the landscape* *below apparently unaffected. In this rendering, strangely reminiscent of Le Corbusier, note the provision of air transportation bequeathed by a long line of modern utopias and science fiction cities.*

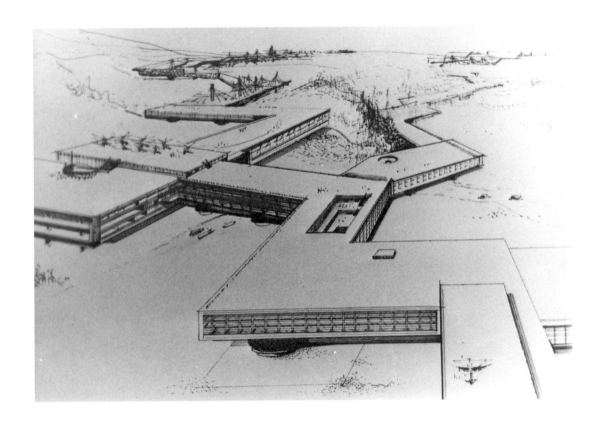

the overgrowth of tropical vegetation" (fig. 3.23).[128] New Babylon's overhead streets were like a revival of the "lateral piercing" developed, of necessity, in the Paris Commune, when new and elevated routes were opened up by knocking through as many adjoining houses as possible (fig. 3.24).[129]

New Babylon sectors could be imagined as "abstractions" of the unities of ambiance discovered by psychogeographers in existing cities.

Chtcheglov had originally proposed that the quarters of the situationist city might correspond to the "Happy," the "Bizarre," the "Sinister," and so forth, but Constant tended to abandon attempts to prescribe ambiances so rigidly, preferring to identify his sectors by their physical features—"Hanging Sector," "Red Sector," "Yellow Sector" (fig. 3.25). The predominantly "abstract" facilities of New Babylon ("spatial color" and "movable elements")

## Figure 3.24

*Constant,* New Babylonian Sectors Superimposed upon a Map of Amsterdam, *c. 1963. In a series of projections covering European cities and regions, Constant paid careful attention to the ways in which New Babylon related to the topographies that it was superimposed upon. At Amsterdam, for instance, New Babylon respected the historic core, while at Rotterdam it had no hesitation in flying low over a city center almost completely destroyed by Second World War bombing—and partially reconstructed by Team 10's Jacob Bakema.*

## Figure 3.25 (facing page)

*View of Constant's maquette for New Babylon's Yellow Sector, 1958–1961, wood, metal, and Plexiglas, Gemeentemuseum, The Hague, photograph by Victor Nieuwenhuys. Many of New Babylon's sectors derived their ambiance from a key sensory stimulation, here yellow light. Victor Nieuwenhuys's stunning photographs of Constant's maquettes almost gave the impression of New Babylon as real architecture.*

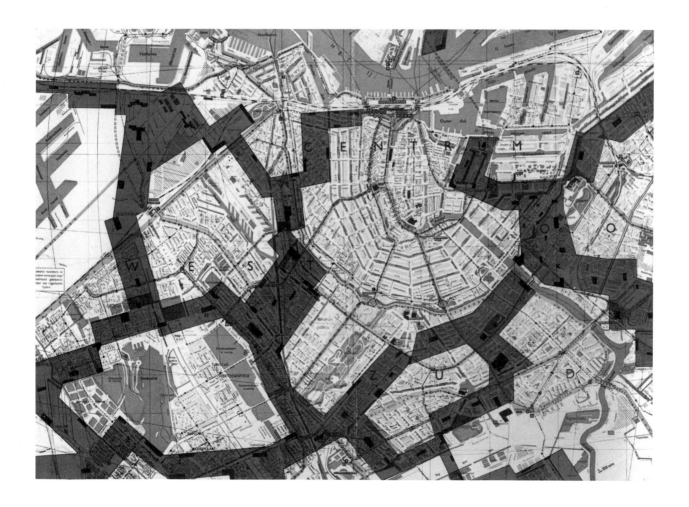

were in pointed contrast to the exemplars of deterministic, "figurative" entertainment architecture found at Disneyland.[130] "Every definition of form restricts . . . the suggestion it projects," Constant wrote in 1948; "the more perfectly defined the form, the less active is the onlooker."[131] New Babylon's labyrinths provided for endless constructed situations. "The inner spaces [of New Babylon] are for collective use," Constant wrote, "and are for no other function than to be an 'artistic medium.'"[132] Life in New Babylon would be an endless chain of encounters between mind, body, space, and architecture. New Babylon was one vast site for an extraordinarily pure sort of drift. "Drifters" in the traditional city traversed their passages through relatively fixed surroundings in the constant hope of encountering a situation, but in New Babylon the passage need not be something traveled

through: New Babylonians could physically rearrange the "street" they stood in.

When the architect Victor Considérant produced his treatise for the Fourierist phalanstery, he emphasized the importance of circulation along "street-galleries" (*rues-galeries*) running through the entire complex, unifying every wing of the giant structure, and symbolizing association founded upon "passionate attraction" (fig. 3.6).[133] Constant's New Babylon would be a global phalanstery for the twentieth century, its sectors joined "in all directions," a "comprehensive metropolis girding the earth like a network," a unitary urbanism of hallucinatory dimensions.[134] The fantastic spaces and vistas of New Babylon would be truly reminiscent of the sublime visions of Piranesi and John Martin (figs. 3.26, 3.27, 2.10). Some corridors within New Babylon would

**Figure 3.26**

*Constant,* Ode à l'Odéon, *1969, oil on canvas, Gemeentemuseum, The Hague. Constant's drawings, prints, and paintings consistently depicted ambiguous and infinite spaces articulated by multilevel, minimalist structures, evocative of scaffolding or modern set design. The ladder was a motif that tied New Babylon back to COBRA's iconography of aspiration (compare fig. 0.2).*

John Martin, Belshazzar's Feast, *1821, engraving after the painting of 1820 (private collection). Depicting the downfall of Belshazzar, King of Babylon, offered Martin a fine pretext for imagining the "baroque" splendor of the ancient city—its massive buildings, its towers, its gold and silver, and its decadence—in one of the most popular pictures of the day. Constant wrested such sublime atmospheric and spatial conditions from fine art into the "real world" of New Babylon.*

even have lenses instead of windows to increase the panoptical qualities of the views over other sectors or, in old cities, across streets and waterways.[135] Occupants of those sectors built over the ground-level access routes would enjoy views of speeding traffic; citizens taking advantage of the air transport available could meditate upon a city of infinite dimensions.[136]

These sublime experiences were another "pleasure" provided by New Babylon, a reminder of the forbidding degree of commitment demanded from participants in situationist fun. To enter into the New Babylon labyrinth was to submit to what Constant called its "principle of disorientation": "New Babylon is one immeasurable labyrinth. Every space is temporary, nothing is recognisable, everything is discovery, everything changes, nothing can serve as a landmark. Thus psychologically a space is created which is many times larger than the actual space."[137] In other words,

**Figure 3.28**

Constant, New Babylon on an Historic Map of Middlesex, 1967, ink on photograph, Gemeentemuseum, The Hague. The image wittily alluded to New Babylon as a transhistorical architecture, perpetually renovated by its occupants, and binding together the conservative commuter belts to the west of London.

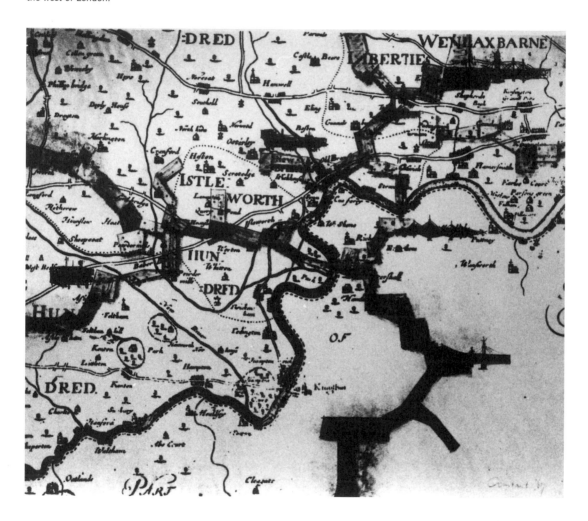

Constant was engineering into architecture the "trippy" qualities that the Lettrist International had noted as occurring naturally during the drift. In New Babylon, "time is valueless."[138] Existence would be marked out not through the abstraction of time but through the mutation of situations; decisions about what to do next would be made not through the tyranny of the clock but through

**Figure 3.29**

*Superstudio,* A Journey from A to B, *1969, pencil on photomontage. Superstudio pushed situationist aspirations for
the transcendence of the commodity to ironic lengths.*

instinct, as at a party or carnival. In 1967
Constant superimposed New Babylon over an
antique map, creating a metaphor for atemporali-
ty that had parallels with Marshall McLuhan's
commentary on the city: in *Understanding Media*
(1964) McLuhan noted how, by comparing the
city to the unchanging functions of the human
body, James Joyce had established a "parallel
between ancient Ithaca and modern Dublin, creating a sense of human unity in depth, transcend-
ing history" (fig. 3.28).[139]

Here in New Babylon was an architecture so
powerful that it was working directly on the body.
Occurring outside nature, the sensations of nature
were being replaced by their synthetic amplifica-
tion, the logical outcome of art's perfection of
nature. New Babylonians would cross "cool and
dark spaces, hot, noisy, chequered, wet," and,
occasionally, "windy spaces under the bare sky."[140]
Like gamblers in windowless casinos, occupants of
the sectors could choose to be undistracted by the
passing of the days and the seasons, enjoying
instead an intensification and disruption of nature's
cycles (as today visitors to Caesar's Palace in Las
Vegas can experience sunset every half-hour).

Viewers unfamiliar with situationist fun may
well have wondered whether New Babylon was an
ironic comment on the megalomaniac ambitions of
utopia, or whether it was simply ill conceived. The
issues became stark when Italy's Superstudio group
drew its own "Endless City" in the late 1960s,
partly in homage to the work of Constant and the
situationists (fig. 3.29). "The destruction of
objects, the elimination of the city, and the disappearance of work are closely connected events,"
Superstudio explained. "When design as an
inducement to consume ceases to exist, an empty
area is created."[141] Superstudio left its bearded,
possessionless wanderers to explore a city without
spectacle and without architecture as well.

Certainly, the sublime disorientation of New
Babylon came at a practical and ideological price.
There were risks, for instance, in the practice of
continual drift, as Chtcheglov eventually admitted.
"Yes, continual like the poker game in Las Vegas,
but continual for a certain period," he warned; "the
continual drift is dangerous to the extent that the
individual, having gone too far . . . without defenses, is threatened with explosion, dissolution, disso-
ciation, disintegration. And thence the relapse into
what is termed 'ordinary life.'"[142] Recognizing this,
Constant scattered the sectors with hotels as places
for rest, so that the endless play and absorption
into place could be suspended, at least for a while.
For the drunkard, or for children playing blind

man's buff, disorientation is temporarily amusing, but in the long term it is profoundly distressing. New Babylon struggled to maintain a balance between the deprivation and enhancement of its citizens' faculties. Both the overorientation imposed by the rational city and the disorientation imposed by the interrogation wing of the prison are instruments of power over the subject. Potential clients might be forgiven for wanting to decline Constant's invitation to visit his "deaf rooms, lined with insulating materials, the screaming room decorated with bright colors and overwhelming sounds," and "the echo room (with radio-speaker games)." "A long stay in one of these houses has the beneficial effect of a washing of the brain," he cheerily claimed, "and it is practiced frequently to erase the habits of nature."[143] Not unlike participants in acts of bondage, New Babylonians had to trust implicitly that power still ultimately resided with the self. Only then could the Babylonian live out the Nietzschean ideal of labyrinthian wanderings, free from subjugation.[144]

The labyrinthian plan itself offered some reassurance, making the effective governance of New Babylon something of an impossibility. Like Piranesi's *Carceri*, the plan of New Babylon was absolutely decentered: "In [the *Carceri*] etchings," Manfredo Tafuri has noted, "the space of the building . . . is an infinite space. What has been destroyed is the center of that space, signifying the correspondence between the collapse of ancient values, of the ancient order, and the 'totality' of the

disorder."[145] The mobile internal guts of New Babylon offered the citizen infinite possibilities for cover, something withheld by the open spaces and transparency of mainstream modernism.

Above all Constant wanted to emphasize that the labyrinth could work supremely well as social space, contrasting his so-called "dynamic labyrinth" with the "classical" or "static" labyrinth. The disadvantage of the latter, he argued, was that the subject can potentially come into every space that the labyrinth offers, and is distracted by the fact that there is a destination—the center (in much the same way that the drift would have been destroyed by flow toward a specific destination). The flow of the dynamic labyrinth, however, would work centrifugally. Moreover, it would be determined by the users of the labyrinth, since they could choose their trajectories at the macrolevel (between sectors), while retaining the option to reshape the labyrinth at the microlevel (using the "mobile elements" provided within each sector). Constant argued that no matter how impressive the classical labyrinth may be, it could never match this "creative" use of space.[146] In the dynamic labyrinth activities would not be constrained by spatial form.

That there was no tradition of dynamic labyrinths was simply an indictment of social organization, Constant argued, since the dynamic labyrinth could only be designed collectively, as an ongoing product founded upon degrees of social freedom and creativity unimaginable in utilitarian society. The postcapitalist abundance that characterized New Babylon would, ironically, be achieved in part by its ingenious spatial economy. As Constant pointed out, the spaces of New Babylon's dynamic labyrinth could be constantly reused, and the subjects of the labyrinth were in any case too disoriented to notice whether they had already encountered a space or not. For the first time in history, the spatial boundaries of a utopian community would seem to dissolve.

It is tempting to think of Constant's dynamic labyrinth as an anticipation through real architecture of the possibilities offered by computerized cyberspace a few decades later.[147] The comparison cannot be taken very far, of course; unlike the utopian impulses motivating situationist architecture, the development of cyberspace was distinctly pragmatic. Most seriously, cyberspace represented a retreat into a virtual rather than a real space, and, therefore, an impoverishment of situationist aspiration. Cyberspace has nonetheless enjoyed a suitably subcultural and even political cachet, and the rapid growth of Internet subscription has indicated the technology's social potential. Though history denied us the opportunity to spend our leisure time wandering around situationist space, we have been offered the chance to while away our free time in cyberspace, with its potential to produce a version of social space with even greater finesse than New Babylon. Cyberspace has lacked a destination, a center, with just as much piquancy; despite its vigilant origins as a military and information technolo-gy, cyberspace has proven to be exceptionally disorienting, as short on reliable directories as New Babylon lacked road signs.

But in assessing the impact of electronic technology, it was Archigram rather than Constant that had the most prescience, such that their 1963 commentary on their own "Living City" exhibition ended up questioning megastructural ambition itself:

**this thing's come a long way since we started this exhibition**
**wasn't it a great floating city to begin with—a Europe city that spanned the channel**
**why did we give that idea up?**
**perhaps because of the purely visionary nature of the idea it'll be years before there's a political set-up sufficient for this thing to come into being and anyway with communications, closed circuit TV we may not want to live in cities any more**
**yeah, I think that's where Kiesler and Schulze-Fielitz with his space frame city fall down**
**as liberators of ideas they are tremendous but their technology can only answer today's problems**[148]

### A cybernetic architecture

Constant created New Babylon at something of an intersection for avant-garde ideas about the possibilities of art and architecture. Binding the cities of the world together, New Babylon would literally have been the "global village," that umbrella concept for ideas about the impact of media that were earning Marshall McLuhan cult status in the years that Constant was working on New Babylon.[149]

McLuhan's 1964 book *Understanding Media* epitomized the futurology of which Constant's work was also a part, however differently it may have been motivated ideologically. The key intellectual maneuver was to think of architecture as a medium rather than as the art of shelter. Architecture mediated between the individual body, the social body, artificial sensations, and nature.[150] Writing on architecture, McLuhan outlined concerns that were highly pertinent to psychogeography, and renewed, albeit idiosyncratically, the traditional metaphors that link architecture to the human body—"Cities are an . . . extension of bodily organs to accommodate the needs of large groups."[151]

This way of thinking about architecture was clarified and detailed by the conjunction of Constant with the likes of McLuhan. "Clothing and housing," McLuhan wrote, "as extensions of the skin and heat-control mechanisms, are media of communication, first of all, in the sense that they shape and rearrange the patterns of human association and community."[152] Constant and McLuhan were influenced by a discourse on cybernetics that feels as quaint today as our own euphoria about cyberspace will seem in the future.[153] Cybernetics was defined in 1947 by the MIT mathematician Norbert Wiener as the comparative scientific study

of "control and communication in the animal and the machine," and the extraordinary ramifications of Wiener's ideas were noted by Constant.[154] Wiener's indication that the principles of control are common to both organic and inorganic systems suggested an intimacy between man and machine that was the very stuff of technophilia. Much of the theory and practice pumped out by Banham, his Independent Group colleagues, and Archigram were by-products of cybernetic culture, but as a giant machine working directly with and upon its citizens' emotions Constant's New Babylon architecture was pretty much unparalleled in its fraternization with the human body.

By the situationists' own admission, their work heralded the "science fiction of urbanism,"[155] and cybernetic agendas served as a high-tech, quasi-science-fictional stick with which to beat the sensibilities of mainstream modernism. Running against the version of modernism that promoted natural air, light, and volume, Constant promised "the total suppression of volume," claiming that this would facilitate the creation of "ambiances."[156] Constant even boasted that the metallic construction of the Yellow Sector "frees" its interior from the sun.

The stress placed by cybernetics upon the role of information was particularly appealing to the avant-garde. Cybernetics identified the feedback of information as the determinant for correcting or controlling the future behavior of the system. The extreme refinement of the control systems of New

Babylon would permit a symbiotic, ever-evolving relationship between people and architecture. And the derivation of the word *cybernetics,* from the Greek for "steersman," augured well for the governance of New Babylon, implying that adaptive control would be more like steersmanship by all than dictatorship by the situationist few. New Babylon came as near as any other contemporary piece of experimental architecture to meeting McLuhan's pseudo-cybernetic agenda: "An immediate simulation of consciousness would by-pass speech in a kind of massive extra-sensory perception, just as global thermostats could by-pass those extensions of skin and body that we call houses. Such an extension of the process of consciousness by electric stimulation may easily occur in the 1960s."[157] Constant's ambitions for a cybernetic architecture were never more explicit than when he provided a chart that broke architecture down, via "architectonics," "climatology," and "psychology," into its relations with the five senses.[158] As an experiment in the Rotterdam Building Centre in 1966, Constant and his team built a labyrinth that would fully test the body and its senses, with rooms that exposed their occupants to sounds, colors, and smells, as well as rooms that compressed them so that they had to crawl their way through (fig. 3.30). Constant welcomed the resultant disorientation as an instrument for lateral experience and thinking (though, having wired the labyrinth with telephones as a way of canvassing visitors' reactions, he was dis-

appointed to find that behavior remained "conditioned" and "rational").[159]

Working the body and senses, Constant's architecture tended to bully as well as encourage—some New Babylon maquettes seemed to refer to the Lettrist International's analogy of the ambient city as a pinball machine, pushing its disoriented inhabitants from one obstacle to another (fig. 3.22).[160] But other studies set up more positive tests for the body, a sort of gym lesson, as figures clambered across frameworks and through passageways (fig. 3.31). For better or worse, this was an architecture that celebrated the able body. And occasionally, at least, New Babylonians would be reminded of their freedom by the way in which the built environment yielded to their will.[161]

More to the point, architecture would become a medium for social contact, providing New Babylonians with something to do together. That might even have turned architecture into an alternative to verbal language, in much the same way as inflatables in a swimming pool or balloons at a party become the media for play and interaction. The competition for space that alienates individuals forced together in the commuter crowd would be superseded by a willing association through objects. One historian has rightly been concerned that Constant's work "fell far short of the flexible, festive space he imagined," but while it was convenient (and doubtless disappointing) for Constant that New Babylon remained untested, there seems no absolute reason why his intentions could not

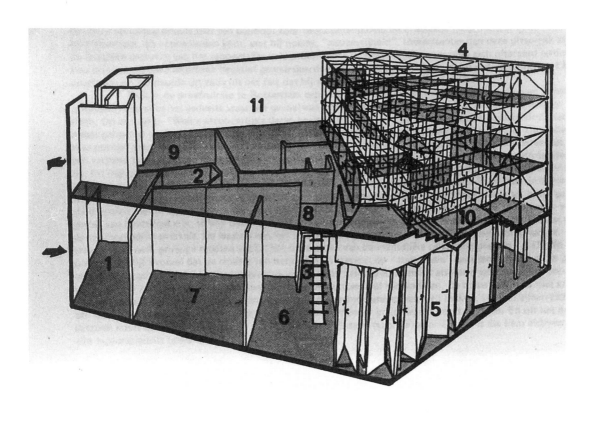

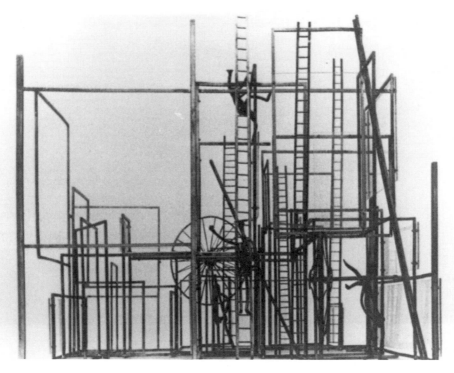

**Figure 3.30 (facing page, top)**

*Constant, plan for Experiment Studio Rotterdam, 1966, reprinted in Constant,* New Babylon *(1974). The construction of the Experiment Studio was the nearest that Constant came to testing his theories of direct sensory stimulation through architecture. The areas were designated 1, documentation room, 2, sound room, 3, bending-over room, 4, metal space structure, 5, door labyrinth, 6, canary floor, 7, mirror room, 8, crawling hallway, 9, smelling room, 10, module hallway, 11, workshop.*

**Figure 3.31 (facing page, bottom)**

*Constant,* Ladder-Labyrinth, *1967, wood, brass, and Plexiglas, Wilhelm Lehmbruck Museum, Duisburg. Living in New Babylon would have demanded extraordinary energy.*

have succeeded under the right social and technical conditions.[162] The superficially brutal appearance of New Babylon was no more a hindrance to festivity than the raw look of a warehouse is an impairment to the mood of a warehouse party.

Indeed, at present a burgeoning club culture represents the best analogue (and, arguably, a partial vindication) of Constant's precepts.[163] Could Constant's systems have been engineered, his architecture would have had a level of tactility and sensory stimulation sufficient for the most restless consumer of the drug Ecstasy. "The situationist considers his environment and himself as plastic," the Situationist International announced in 1960.[164] McLuhan claimed that modern engineering, which offered exactly such wonders as "large buildings with inside walls and floors that can be moved at will," created a "flexibility [which] naturally tends toward the organic. Human sensitivity seems once more to be attuned to the universal currents that made of tribal man a cosmic skin-diver."[165] In this, both Constant and McLuhan were in harmony with an epoch much concerned with the liberation of the mind and body. New Babylon's promises of glass grottoes, cinematographic plays, water games, erotic sports and dances added up to a hedonism truly evocative of a latter-day Cockaigne and anticipative of the 1960s rock festival, making "the body an instrument of pleasure rather than of labour," as Herbert Marcuse was to demand.[166] By the 1960s Marcuse, Wilhelm Reich, and Erich Fromm had successfully inflected leftist thinking

with hopes for a modern "eupsychia," or psychological utopia, hopes anticipated in the situationist city: Chtcheglov promised that it would include "rooms more conducive to dreams than any drug, and houses where one cannot help but love."[167]

### The debate over technocracy

"New Babylon is the product of the non-utilitarian, creative technocracy," Constant admitted, unashamedly.[168] The swing away from the essential "primitivism" and expressionist individualism of COBRA to an embrace of the machine became a subject of heated debate in early issues of *Internationale situationniste*, which came to a head by the journal's fifth issue at the end of 1960. Constant, who wasted no time in getting technology onto the situationist agenda, seemed to conceive of situationism as a new forum for the sort of socialist, material experimentation once associated with the Dessau Bauhaus.[169] Situationists had long realized that "when freedom is practiced in a closed circle, it fades into a dream, becomes a mere representation of itself,"[170] and Constant argued that the seizure of industrial culture and its technologies was the only means by which situationism could meet the demands of the masses. "Without it the integration of art into the construction of human habitat remains as chimerical as the propositions of Gilles Ivain [the pseudonym of Ivan Chtcheglov]," Constant claimed.[171] Giuseppe Pinot-Gallizio was still more wildly in favor of a technology turned over to "the people." "The planet will be transformed into a Luna-Park without frontiers, producing new emotions and passions," he foresaw, conjuring up a quasi-futurist vision of a civilization that at its least ambitious painted its motorways, at its most ambitious supplanted architecture with synesthetic communications technology. "There in the future are our works without surface and without volume. We are near to the fourth dimension of pure poetry."[172]

Constant's implicit criticism was that the activities at the Imaginist Bauhaus, despite Jorn's demands that artistic research "be carried out by artists with the assistance of scientists," were more nostalgic for craft than responsive to the technologies of the "situationist frontier."[173] Initially, the Situationist International's official line, set by Jorn, was one of compromise. Real social change would have to put the brakes on a headlong rush into the machine world. But as Constant and the Dutch section became more dogged, the SI's reaction began to bear a severity more characteristic of Debord. When Constant claimed that, in the absence of conditions for revolution, an evolutionary struggle against suppressive material conditions was better than no struggle at all, Debord accused him of a naive reformism that failed to comprehend the "recuperative" capacities of capitalism. Constant's proposals, it was true, had a whiff of

reformism about them. By 1964 he would be announcing that his scheme "reckons with facts like the rapid spread of the world population, the perpetual growth of traffic, the cultivation of the whole planet, and total urbanization. Thus the project takes account of the purely functional problems of current town planning, traffic and housing and strives for extreme solutions."[174] Debord's faction instead demanded that unitary urbanism be understood as "not a doctrine of urbanism but a critique of urbanism."[175]

If Constant was not paying proper regard to the critical principles of unitary urbanism, it was also true that Debord and his allies were tinkering with them. Throughout the 1950s they had written as if the construction of the situation and of unitary urbanism was a realizable proposition, that utopia could indeed be built. *Internationale situationniste* retreated from this modern, socialist, and technological ambition to a notion of utopia much closer to its sixteenth-century origins in Sir Thomas More, who conceived of utopia as the perfect society that is nowhere, a critical, political, and moral standard by which to judge the institutions of actual European societies.[176] This fastidious attitude was persistently, hypnotically reiterated by the SI after 1961. "It is not a matter of . . . suppressing a few deviationist seeds that have since blossomed into gross results (e.g., Constant's technocratic concept of a situationist profession . . . ) but of correcting and improving the most important of our theses," *Internationale situationniste* declared.[177] It was now easier to pretend that situationism was an analytical metaphor than to promote it as an ongoing experiment in living; *Internationale situationniste* admitted in 1963 that experiments "in matters of behavior" had "barely begun," blaming a "considerable absence of means."[178]

The best that *Internationale situationniste* could suggest for those wishing to carry on envisaging the situationist city was that they return to the principles of *détournement*. It was more a matter of colonizing the material fabric of history than of creating new structures. "The employment of *détournement* in an architecture for the construction of situations marks the reinvestment of products that it is necessary to shield from the actual socioeconomic system, and the rupture with the formalist concern of abstractly creating the unknown." Situationists would have to feel their own way around the situationist frontier. "We know of no desirable form or guarantee of happiness," *Internationale situationniste* courageously admitted.[179] And by the later sixties, even Constant privately expressed doubts about the possibility of building the situationist city. "I see the danger of a new idealism that may arise in intellectual circles," Constant told performance artist Sean Wellesley-Miller in 1966. "I am very much aware of the fact that New Babylon can not be realised now, that a way of life the New Babylon project is based on depends on new conditions in the field of economy. Automation now does not mean freedom from slavery and toiling, but poverty and boredom for the workers."[180] "You are the techno-social guilty conscience of our time," an exasperated Pierre Restany, founder of French *nouveau réaliste* pop art, informed Constant in 1967, "and I hope you stay that way."[181]

In June 1962 situationists opened the leading French architectural journal *L'Architecture d'aujourd'hui* to find a little bit of New Babylon tucked cozily into the corner of page seventy-seven, alongside its GEAM stablemates.[182] Those situationists who had repudiated Constant's work were philosophical. "The S.I.'s element of failure," *Internationale situationniste* noted, "is what is commonly considered success—the artistic value that is beginning to be appreciated in us; the fact that certain of our theses have come to be sociologically or urbanistically fashionable."[183] Card-carrying members of the SI comforted themselves that it was they, not the "technician" Constant, who "held the key" to the effective use of those situationist ideas merely *represented* in New Babylon.[184] After he left the SI, which now boasted an "anti-public relations service," the group denounced Constant as a "public relations man . . . integrating the masses into capitalist technological civilization" with his "models of factories" (fig. 3.32).[185]

Its assimilation into a *L'Architecture d'aujourd'hui* spread certainly proved New Babylon's resonance with trends from outside situationism. As Reyner Banham put it, "In one sense they [the later SI] were right; once you begin to clothe the naked concept of homo ludens in usable equipment, and

**Figure 3.32**

*Constant,* Collage View of a New Babylonian Sector, *1971, watercolor and pencil on photomontage, Gemeentemuseum, The Hague. The drama of such images was double-edged, anticipating high tech and deconstructivist architecture on the one hand, on the other alienating those situationists seeking a less brutal and more ineffable vision of the future.*

to connect the constructed situations to the power mains, the result is liable to look remarkably like a swinging affluent society and its mobile, leisure-seeking citizens."[186] Which was a shame, because New Babylon was a sincere and heroic reaction to the *Existenzminimum* standards that had dominated so much rationalist thinking about domestic space, and which seemed manifest again in the new mass housing developments of Europe and America. New Babylon, which even looked forward to being sited in outer space, was an attempt to deliver on Chtcheglov's promise that "everyone will live in his own personal 'cathedral,' so to speak," and situationist urbanism, like the "pop" projects of Archigram, could not help being a by-product of the atmosphere of postwar boom and leisure.[187]

In any case, by the mid-sixties progressive architectural culture generally was submitting to some situationist demands of its own accord. Christopher Alexander's key 1965 essay "A City Is Not a Tree" showed that even a logician had to admit to the poverty of rationalism. "The city is not only a series of incidents but a network of incidence," Archigram's Peter Cook wrote.

**Christopher Alexander . . . in his cool mathematician's logical way, said what we had all been trying to think. Is it a coincidence that [Archigram's] Plug-in City, [Yona] Friedman's scheme and the Japanese [Metabolist] helicoidal scheme were all concerned with the potential of the multilayer cage and the diagonal to respond to situations rather than to incarcerate events in flat, defined boxes? And now McLuhan. . . . No, Professor, we didn't say it first or anything, but it's more than coincidental. We are subject to the same pressures as the rest, after all.[188]**

The absorption of the situationist city into architectural fashion was its death.

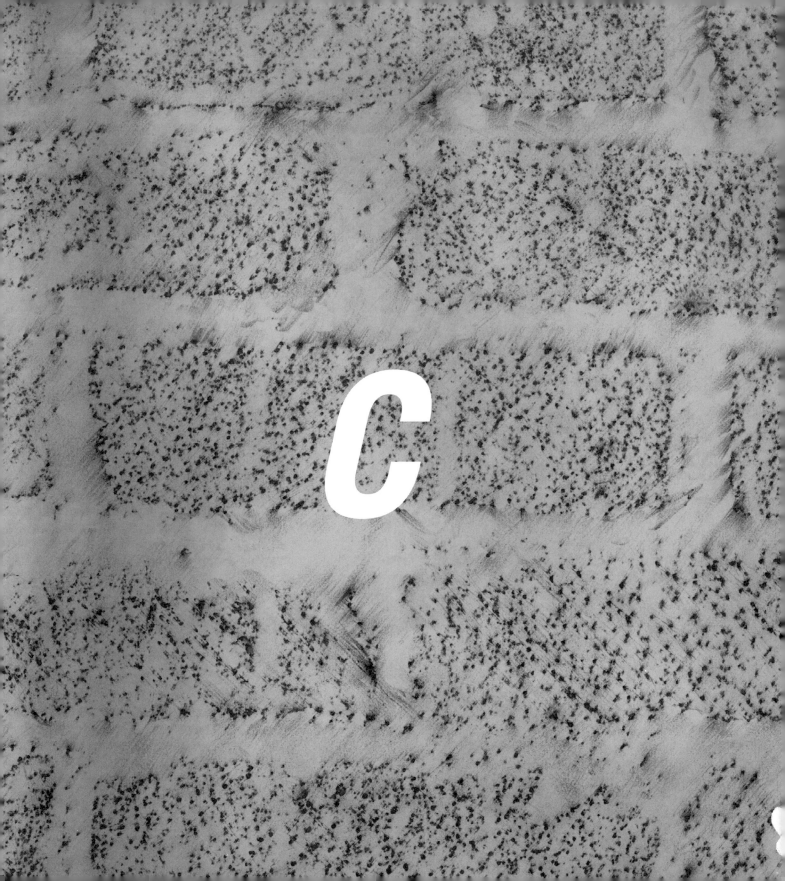

# CONCLUSIONS

The sorts of doubt about planning and modernism expressed by situationists have since met with spectacular consensus. The celebrated demolition in 1972 of the Pruitt-Igoe estate in St. Louis, Missouri, built along Athens Charter principles, was spectacle itself, broadcast on television, and emulated by municipal authorities around the world.[1] Orthodox modernism came to be regarded as practically inhuman. Strict zoning lost favor to mixed use, and many city centers became dominated by leisure use. It was of course a commercial rather than an anarchic leisure, since larger situationist demands remained marginalized by capitalism— which always seemed likely to be the case, except perhaps for a few heady days in May 1968.

But for all the propagandist brilliance of situationist critique, virtual incomprehensibility was an inherent feature of the situationist architectural project. Situationists were nearer the mark than they realized when they said that "situationism" did not exist.[2] At the center of the project was a methodological vacuum, a groping for the nonspectacular, some kind of everyday "other." The situationist critique of existing society was made up of givens in an apparently comprehensible relationship to one another: a functionalist environment, it seemed, bred functionalist behavior, and vice versa, through the grand anti-situation constructed by the state and its agents. But no such neat formulation was available by which to constitute "situationism" itself.

Situationists were certain that they had a set of revolutionary devices—psychogeography, drift, *détournement*, situations, and unitary urbanism— but were unable to arrange them into a coherent program (fig. 4.1). It was never made clear, for instance, whether unitary urbanism was a project for the here-and-now or for postrevolutionary society, nor indeed whether it was simply a metaphor for a better world. The same sorts of questions hung over the *situation*, caught in a troubling ellipsis, constructed situations creating the revolutionary situation which in turn produces the world in which the creation of situations is possible.

The open-endedness of situationism might have been its great strength, but this was belied by the Situationist International's posturing as a tightly organized revolutionary group, characterized less by free play than by a pattern of expulsions. Through their experiences of the city, of art, and of revolutionary, collective social activity situationists believed that they shared the same fragments of a single revolutionary consciousness, and that this consciousness extended to the population at large. This was at best only partially true. Debord, for instance, strikes one as a leftist theorist attracted

**Figure 4.1**

French Section of the Situationist International, New Theater of Operations within Culture, 1958, leaflet showing the nexus linking the "construction of situations" to "unitary urbanism," "experimental behavior," "drift," "psychogeography," "situationist architecture," "permanent play," and the "détournement of prefabricated aesthetic elements."

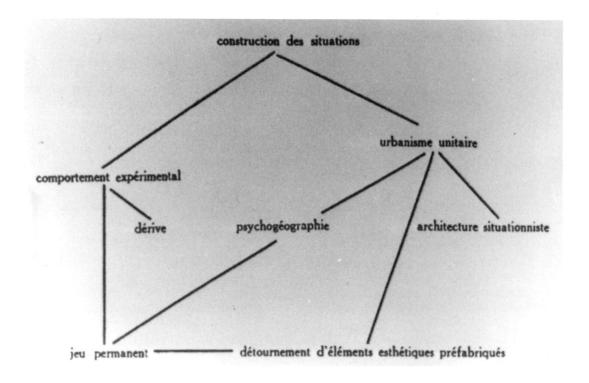

through his romanticism to the cachet of the avant-garde; Constant strikes one as the opposite, an avant-gardist attracted by the fervor of the left. That there should eventually have been a split between such differing revolutionary perspectives is hardly surprising.

Differences were not merely ideological but probably personal as well, and one has the impression that Debord and Debordists, with an increasing stranglehold on the movement, conflated personal-

ity with ideology, expelling people that were not considered to have the correct attitude. The struggle to prioritize various elements of the situationist program—art versus politics, technology versus expressionism versus the conceptual, corporatism versus specialization—cut at strange lines across situationist loyalties. Debord expelled Wolman; both had expelled Chtcheglov, though Debord later rehabilitated him; Jorn and Debord, with wildly differing priorities, remained friends, when Constant and Debord could not; Constant rounded upon Jorn, a long-standing associate, but did not offer his resignation as his colleagues from the SI's Dutch section were being expelled.[3]

Contestation over the direction of situationism was most likely permitted merely in order to find *any* direction at all for the movement. "It is too late for the making of art; a little too early for the concrete construction of situations of some magnitude," the penultimate edition of *Potlatch* lamented.[4] This helps to explain the otherwise curious decision, made by Bernstein and Debord, to take the remnants of the Lettrist International into a broadly based, art-oriented movement like the early Situationist International, even though concerns were being expressed in the same breath about the role within lettrism of "deviationist" artistic and mystical elements. The exclusions of Gil J. Wolman and Jacques Fillon were announced, schizophrenically, alongside Debord's defense of a certain liberalism—"we must reunite specialists of very diverse techniques; know the latest autonomous developments of these techniques . . . experiment with a unitary employment of means that are actually scattered."[5] He was desperately casting around for a way out of the impasse of five years of lettrist activity. And about five years after *that* he was instrumental in escaping another impasse, redefining situationism as a "non-art" movement.

Most of the architecture and spaces that were endorsed by situationists existed by chance rather than by design: back streets, urban fabric layered over time, ghettos. Perhaps situationist exemplars could not adequately be synthesized, abstracted, or even "détourned"—only preserved, the passing of time itself being an architectural agent, the fourth-dimensional attribute of use, weathering, and legend that psychogeographers keenly noted. Probably most situationists realized the near-impossibility of constructing truly situationist architecture.[6] Asger Jorn apparently concentrated upon the production of situationist theory rather than of genuinely situationist works, and hopelessly ambitious situationist projects rarely went much further than the written idea.[7] Debord left his maps fractured and uncertain without proceeding to depict a unitary urbanism proper, so it is unsurprising that he considered Constant's projections of an uncontested future space to be highly improbable. Significantly, perhaps, it is difficult to trace anything that Jørgen Nash's Second Situationist International might have produced toward the construction of situations or of a unitary urbanism.

In relating their visions the situationists relied, of course, on a sympathetic relationship with one another and with their audience. Situationist exemplars like de Chirico, or the sublime magic of the lonely city street at night, could be neither explained lucidly to a skeptical public nor converted into a situationist method for the construction of situations. Whereas the effects of alienation, itself a highly subjective condition, could at least be demonstrated through sociological data or theorized within a model of commodity capitalism, the main attempt to explain its obverse was preposterous: psychogeography sits uncomfortably with the air of rigor that the situationists wished to project. Psychogeography comprehended buildings through their use, their history, and their collective and associative generation of meaning and mood, like words in poetry; it inferred a poetic rather than analytic response to the environment. The romantic tradition of urban contemplation found in De Quincey, Baudelaire, Dickens, and Benjamin could proffer few techniques for detailed architectural analysis, and even fewer for the establishment of a new urban structure.[8] In the effort to keep situationism as something distinctive and radical, situationists also avoided directly invoking disciplines that might have had a bearing upon their work—psychological and psychoanalytic analyses of art and architecture, for instance, or sociology, or structuralism.

Anyone who has really lived understands psychogeography, it was assumed, and anyone will understand it once they have experienced *real life*. This simply assumed that we all want the same things from the city, and that our experience and knowledge are homogeneous; in short, that we are the sort of person who was attracted to the SI or, more to the point, that we *should* be that sort of person. Situationist writing was full of such assumptions, audacious considering the situationists' failure even to agree among themselves. *Potlatch* openly admired a bit of Nietzschean determination and "absolutist enterprise": "Ferdinand

Cheval and Ludwig of Bavaria built the castles that they wanted, to the size of a new human condition."[9] More than anything this high-mindedness revealed the social descent of the situationists—from the avant-garde, the *flâneur*, and the connoisseur—which they combined with the tiresome cockiness of youth.

Non-situationists may have wished to argue against the extension of urban "ambiances" in favor of a more ecological use of city space, for instance. The creation as well of personal senses of place, sheltered from the endless energy of the public domain, was almost entirely refused by situationist collectivist dogma (a private use of space need not of course be synonymous with the capitalized use of space). Constant only allowed places for temporary privacy and rest in New Babylon, denying us space for permanent private habitation and ritual. Early situationism did indeed threaten to replace the totalitarian ideologies of capitalism and communism with a new totalitarian ideology of situationist play, enforced by peer pressure and the situationist appropriation of space. (One is reminded of Jean-Jacques Rousseau's opinion that we should be "forced to be free.")

Viewed like this, the artworks produced and projected by early situationism seemed to further the closure against a complex or contested revolutionary project. A voluntary mass defection to a world constructed from Pinot-Gallizio's industrial painting was, frankly, unlikely. Ironically Debord, virtually the inventor of the constructed situation, obstructed most maneuvers to construct one, as if he suspected that it was of little revolutionary value: that its realization would, indeed, be faintly ridiculous. Jens-Jørgen Thorsen at the Second Situationist International certainly thought so: "The Guy Debord theory stated that by rapidly passing through completely unknown surroundings of labyrinthine character, people should be forced into a . . . situation [of] wanting to express new wishes for a new urbanism. . . . To me this theory always seemed nonsense."[10] Constant's early neoconstructivist sculptures were a charming escape into the "aesthetic dimension," and many of his sketches depicted an unstable space and indefinite architecture into which viewers could imaginatively project themselves; but his detailing of New Babylon only confirmed that the revolutionary vision of one situationist could be very different from that of another.

The response of Debordists was not to question directly the universalizing assumptions of the situationist project but to strike out the most visible reminder of its fracture: the continued production of art. The Debordist justification for narrowing the agenda of situationism by the expulsion of fellow-travelers and visionaries must constitute one of the most satisfying and anarchic statements ever issued by an avant-garde: "the SI can only be a Conspiracy of Equals, a general staff that *does not want troops*. It is a matter of finding, of opening up, the 'Northwest Passage' toward . . . the conquest of everyday life. *We will only organize the detonation*: the free explosion must escape us and any other control forever."[11] SI hard-liners, no longer interested in designing a unitary urbanism or the constructed situation, now regarded the *situation* purely as a revolutionary consciousness regardless of its spatial location and decor, and the forms of the postrevolutionary world could, technically, be contested by its inhabitants (fig. 4.2). But the denunciation of the role of art and architecture had barely clarified the revolutionary processes of situationism. Nostalgic references to the old devices persisted (the "Northwest Passage" and "free explosion"), and many of the theoretical problems of early situationism were still present. Foremost among these was the avant-garde role of the SI, the group maintaining its unquestioning trust in the existence of a common revolutionary consciousness that would automatically take a "Northwesterly" (i.e., situationist) trajectory.

With the abandonment of early situationism, the SI abandoned its *imagining* of utopia—a devastating decision, surely unprecedented in the history of the avant-garde, and yet at the same time surely the situationists' greatest contribution to that history: the recognition that in changing the world, avant-garde art cannot be a substitute for the popular redistribution of power. Marx himself had dismissed calls for a detailed portrait of a future society: "I write no recipes for the cookshops of the future."[12] In 1961 Kotányi and Vaneigem explained that they and their colleagues had "invented the architecture and urbanism that cannot be realized without the revolution of everyday life."[13]

**Figure 4.2**

*"Critique of urbanism (supermarket in Los Angeles, August 1965)," illustration from anon., "The Decline and Fall of the Spectacle-Commodity Economy,"* Internationale situationniste, *no. 10 (1966). Direct action, the later Situationist International argued, was the true expression of the situationist city.*

Perhaps they realized that their interests in revolution and in art and architecture might be only complementary, informing one another but by no means mechanically linked. Later situationism confirmed the steady slide of the "situation" from a revolutionary art project to a metaphor for a more fully lived life—confirmed, because early situationism had always been a powerfully abstract and utopian set of concepts. Situationists would of course have vigorously attacked such a suggestion. It undermined the sense of revolutionary urgency they wished to project, and indeed utopianism has had pejorative connotations within both the left and right. From the left, for example, Stewart Home has noted that "although the L.I., and later the situationists, planned a *total transformation* of the urban environment, they never advanced a workable plan of how to maintain a sense of human community during and after this transformation."[14] From the new right, the art critic Peter Fuller has polemicized against new left "utopianism" generally: "There were of course those who, after 1956, continued to promote the dream of socialism detached from Stalinism (and indeed, from any other instance embarrassing enough to be 'actually existing'). . . . In other words, they pursued socialism as an abstract or psychological ideal."[15]

Needless to say, it is too easy to be dismissive of utopianism in general and of situationism in particular, challenges from which we can find ourselves running scared. Krishan Kumar, the historian of utopias, explains: "Utopia has been a

subversive form: that is perhaps the first point to make in 'mapping' utopia. The very uncertainty over the intention of the author—is this satire? is it wish-fulfilment? is it a call to action?—has provoked authorities to blanket suppression."[16] The way that situationism flickered between deadly seriousness and an embrace of play made an effective cover for the ultimate situationist aim of real social and cultural revolution. To its enemies it seemed flippant and facetious, while it appealed to those jaded with rationalism and the preaching of the traditional left. *Internationale situationniste* put it this way: "We are not completely devoid of humor; but our humor is of a rather new kind. If someone wants to know how to approach our theses, leaving aside the fine points and subtleties, the simplest and most appropriate attitude is to take us completely seriously and literally."[17]

Utopianism soars over the entrenched minutiae of the here-and-now, and the thrill of the flight may explain why the situationist fallout scattered so widely, and so thinly: onto Team 10; onto Ralph Rumney's "Place" exhibition at the ICA in 1959; onto Italian radical design; onto the environments and happenings movement; onto Archigram, thence to the Architectural Association in London, and so onto, for example, Richard Rogers, Bernard Tschumi, Nigel Coates, and the NATO Group; and even into the art-historical syllabus itself, through the agency of British situationist-turned-historian T. J. Clark.[18] At best utopianism provides a critical benchmark, and even if the situationist vision of a unitary revolution was flawed, it nevertheless maintained an indefatigable belief in the possibility of a better organization of everyday life. Only the hardest-hearted readers of *Potlatch* could have failed to be touched by the lettrist justification for "drifting":

**We want to believe that those people who sought the Grail weren't dupes. We have to see their DRIFT, their arbitrary promenades, and their unbridled passion as resembling our own. The religious make-up doesn't matter. Those cavaliers of a mythical Western had everything for pleasure: a great faculty for getting lost as a game; for the wonder-filled journey; for the love of speed; for a relative geography. . . . The Romance of the Quest for the Grail prefigures in several ways a very modern behavior.[19]**

Architecture was the key to this situationist consciousness: whether discovered in the city or the mind, architecture mapped out revolutionary desire.

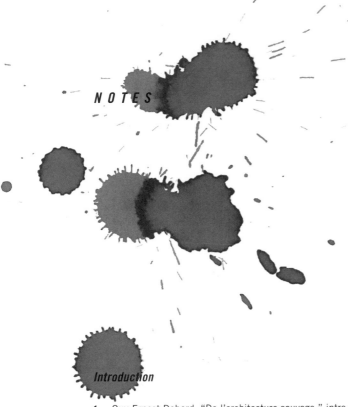

# NOTES

## Introduction

1  Guy-Ernest Debord, "De l'architecture sauvage," introduction to Asger Jorn, *Le jardin d'Albisola* (Turin: Pozzo, 1974), trans. Thomas Y. Levin as "On Wild Architecture," in Elisabeth Sussman, ed., *On the Passage of a Few People through a Rather Brief Moment in Time: The Situationist International, 1957–1972* (Cambridge, Mass.: MIT Press/ Institute of Contemporary Arts, Boston, 1989), pp. 174–175.

2  P. Bourdieu and A. Darbel, *L'amour de l'art: les musées d'art européens et leur public* (Paris: Minuit, 1966), pp. 93–94, trans. in Brian Rigby, *Popular Culture in Modern France: A Study of Cultural Discourse* (London and New York: Routledge, 1991), p. 99.

3  Mike Peters, "A Posthumous Fame?," in *Here and Now Guy Debord Supplement*, pp. iii–iv, issued with *Here and Now*, no. 16/17 (Glasgow and Leeds, Winter 1995/1996). It should be stressed, however, that this sort of dogmatism is by no means shared by all contributors to *Here and Now*. Some anti-academic polemic is also better-humored: a satirical 1996 Pro-situ leaflet, "On the Recuperation of the Situationist Revolt," recommended that academics try out the following workshops: "Unitary Suburbanism," "Psychogeography and Buying Your Own Home," "Détournement and Home Decorating."

4  Simon Ford, *The Realization and Suppression of the Situationist International: An Annotated Bibliography 1972–1992* (Edinburgh and San Francisco: AK Press, 1995), p. xiv.

5  Anon., "Définitions," *Internationale situationniste*, no. 1 (Paris, June 1958), pp. 13–14, trans. Ken Knabb as "Definitions," in *Situationist International Anthology* (Berkeley: Bureau of Public Secrets, 1981), pp. 45–46.

6  See Stewart Home, *The Assault on Culture: Utopian Currents from Lettrisme to Class War* (London: Aporia Press and Unpopular Books, 1988), p. 30.

7  The London Psychogeographical Association (LPA) was relaunched in 1992, celebrating "thirty-five years of non-existence," although its interests seemed to fuse Scandinavian situationism with postwar Bretonist surrealism rather than align with Rumney's Paris-derived psychogeography. At a conference convened by Manchester University on the "Legacy of the Situationist International," January 1996, Rumney was moved to despatch "Some Remarks Concerning the Indigence of Post-Situationists in Their Attempts to Recuperate the Past," dismissing the latter-day LPA's preoccupation with "new age" geography. But in *Sucked*, a dry LPA polemic issued in the wake of the Manchester conference, the group offered a frank insight into its thinking. "We offer no attempt to 'justify' or 'rationalize' the rôle of magic in the development of our theories. It is sufficient that it renders our theories *completely unacceptable*. But our task of reconciling this with the need to offer a fundamental explanation of society has not proved easy" (LPA's emphasis). A few months on, the LPA seemed to be finding its theoretical feet, but only by defining itself against "academia": for the LPA apologist writing as "Dusty Bin" (in a quasi-academic journal), "There's nothing more entertaining than watching the reaction of situationist historians and academic recuperators to the activities of the magico-Marxists of the . . . LPA. . . . The literal brains that dominate 'critical theory' start melting at this point. They want to know whether the LPA 'really believes' in ley-lines and the occult powers of the ruling class," but, Bin claims with a

triumphal note, "I'm afraid that their suffering will continue as long as they remain wedded to scientific metaphors of, and approaches to, radical critique." The LPA "is engaged in the excavation of the imagination of the ruling class." It remains to be seen whether the ruling class survives the LPA exposé. Though doubtless inspired by the LPA, other new psychogeographical groups—the Manchester Area Psychogeographic (MAP) and Associazione Psicogeografica di Bologna—"tend to draw on more traditional situationist and historical sources than the LPA," notably popular radical history. See "Reviews," *Transgressions: A Journal of Urban Exploration*, nos. 2/3 (London and Newcastle, August 1996), pp. 120–121.

**8**   For more on lettrism, see Stephen C. Foster, ed., "Lettrisme: Into the Present," *Visible Language* 3, no. 17 (Summer 1983).

**9**   In effect, COBRA negotiated between the ideas of Asger Jorn's Host group from Denmark, Christian Dotremont's Revolutionary Surrealist Group from Belgium, and Constant's Reflex Group from Holland. For a discussion of this process, see, for instance, Graham Birtwistle, "Old Gotland, New Babylon: Peoples and Places in the Work of Jorn and Constant," *Transgressions,* no. 2/3 (August 1996), pp. 55–67.

**10**   See Home, *Assault on Culture,* pp. 25, 28. Sottsass resigned in protest at the insulting tone of a letter in which the IMIB and LI accused the organizers of the Milan Triennale of allowing IMIB/LI plans for an experimental pavilion to gather dust. The silence of Sottsass biographies concerning his involvement with situationism may be due to the acrimony of the split.

**11**   Reprinted in *Potlatch,* no. 28 (Paris, May 1957), unpaginated, and in *Potlatch 1954–1957* (Paris: Editions Gérard Lebovici, 1985), p. 232.

**12**   Guy-Ernest Debord, "Rapport sur la construction des situations et sur les conditions de l'organisation et de l'action de la tendance situationniste internationale," preparatory text for the Cosio d'Arroscia conference, July 1957, reprinted in Gérard Berreby, ed., *Documents relatifs à la fondation de l'Internationale situationniste: 1948–1957* (Paris: Editions Allia, 1985), pp. 607–619, trans. as "Report on the Construction of Situations and on the International Situationist Tendency's Conditions of Organization and Action" (excerpts), in Knabb, *Anthology,* pp. 17–25. The ideas of Debord et al. about the future of the avant-garde were largely developed prior to the foundation of the Internationale situationniste, in the pages of *Potlatch.* See especially *Potlatch* nos. 6, 16, and 27.

**13**   See Debord, "Rapport sur la construction des situations"; Guy-Ernest Debord and Gil J. Wolman, "Mode d'emploi du détournement," *Les lèvres nues,* no. 8 (Brussels, 1956), reprinted in Berreby, *Documents,* pp. 302–309, trans. as "Methods of Détournement," in Knabb, *Anthology,* pp. 8–14 ("Since the negation of the bourgeois conception of art and artistic genius has become pretty much old hat, [Duchamp's] drawing of a moustache on the *Mona Lisa* is no more interesting than the original version of that painting"); Constant, "Reflex Manifesto," *Reflex* (Amsterdam, 1948), trans. Leonard Bright in Willemijn Stokvis, *Cobra* (New York: Rizzoli, 1988), pp. 29–31; and Jorn's arguments in favor of a "materialist" art (that is, an art that could have real impact in everyday life), for instance "Discours aux pingouins," in *Cobra, no.* 1 (Brussels, 1948), pp. 8–9. The issues of *Cobra* are reprinted in facsimile in one volume as *COBRA 1948–1951: bulletin pour la coordination des investigations artistiques* (Amsterdam: Van Gennep, 1980).

**14**   Anon., "L'urbanisme unitaire à la fin des années 50," *Internationale situationniste,* no. 3 (Paris, December 1959), pp. 11–16, trans. T. Y. Levin as "Unitary Urbanism at the End of the 1950s," in Sussman, *On the Passage of a Few People,* pp. 143–147.

**15**   Constant, "Reflex Manifesto"; Christian Dotremont, writing on the abstract artists of the Salons des Réalités Nouvelles, "Nous irons dans les bois et nous laisserons les lauriers," in the catalogue of the *Salon Octobre* (Brussels, 1953), quoted in Jean-Clarence Lambert, *COBRA* (New York: Abbeville Press, 1985), p. 204.

**16**  Michel Colle, "Vers une architecture symbolique," in *Cobra,* no. 1 (Brussels, 1948), pp. 21–23.

**17**  Colle, "Vers une architecture symbolique." The relationship between modern architecture and the "man in the street" was taken up the following year at the seventh CIAM congress (Bergamo, 1949), with uncompromising results. "CIAM cannot accept class distinctions nor a lowering of artistic standards for sentimental or political reasons. On the contrary we believe that anyone not perverted by false education is capable of appreciating true values in art" (quoted in Joan Ockman with Edward Eigen, eds., *Architecture Culture 1943–1968: A Documentary Anthology* [New York: Columbia Books of Architecture/Rizzoli, 1993], p. 120). Colle treated the economic rationale for rationalism with contempt, writing off the increased cost of a "symbolic" architecture as simply "the price of poetry and dream . . . in a socialist world."

**18**  Günther Feuerstein, "Thesen über inzidente Architektur," in *Spur,* no. 5, "Spezialnummer über den unitären Urbanismus" (Munich, June 1961).

**19**  Quoted in Anthony Vidler, *The Architectural Uncanny: Essays on the Modern Unhomely* (Cambridge, Mass.: MIT Press, 1992), p. 150.

**20**  Henry-Russell Hitchcock and Philip Johnson, *The International Style: Architecture since 1922* (New York: Museum of Modern Art, 1932; reprinted, New York: Norton, 1966).

**21**  Le Corbusier and Pierre Jeanneret, *Oeuvre complète 1934–1938* (Zurich: Girsberger, 1939), with an introduction by Max Bill.

**22**  See "Contre le fonctionalisme," in Asger Jorn, *Pour la forme: ébauche d'une méthodologie des arts* (Paris: Internationale situationniste, 1958), reprinted in Berreby, *Documents,* pp. 425–431. Max Bill's reply to Asger Jorn at the 1954 Triennale is reprinted in Mirella Bandini, *L'estetico il politico: da COBRA all'Internazionale situazionista, 1948–1957* (Rome: Officina Edizioni, 1977), p. 243.

**23**  Asger Jorn, "Argomenti a proposito del Movimento internazionale per un Bauhaus immaginista contro un Bauhaus immaginario e sua ragione attuale," *Immagine e forma,* no. 1 (Milan, 1954), trans. as "Arguments à propos du Mouvement international pour un Bauhaus imaginiste contre un Bauhaus imaginaire, et sa raison actuelle," in "Image et forme," in Jorn, *Pour la forme,* reprinted in Berreby, *Documents,* pp. 417–419; English trans. in Ockman and Eigen, *Architecture Culture,* pp. 172–175.

**24**  See Asger Jorn, "Notes sur la formation d'un Bauhaus imaginiste" (1957), in "Contre le fonctionalisme," in Jorn, *Pour la forme,* reprinted in Berreby, *Documents,* pp. 428–429, trans. as "Notes on the Formation of an Imaginist Bauhaus," in Knabb, *Anthology,* pp. 16–17. See also Guy Atkins, *Asger Jorn: The Crucial Years* (London: Lund Humphries, 1977). In a series of articles for the Swedish review *Byggnastaren,* published in Stockholm ("The Life Content of the Language of Form," no. 12, 1946 and "Apollo and Dionysus," no. 17, 1947), Jorn dissociated himself from Le Corbusier and from rationalism. For an early review of the consequences of Jorn's ideas for architecture, see Michael Ventris, "Function and Arabesque," *Plan* (Journal of the Architectural Students' Association), no. 1 (London, 1948), reprinted in *Cobra,* no. 1 (1948), p. 18.

**25**  Mohamed Dahou for the Lettrist International, "La première pierre qui s'en va," *Potlatch,* no. 26 (Paris, May 1956), reprinted in *Potlatch 1954–1957,* pp. 204–205. Extracts from "Image et forme" were published as "Une architecture de la vie," *Potlatch,* no. 15 (Paris, December 1954, reprinted in *Potlatch 1954–1957,* pp. 84–86. The extracts cut out Jorn's wider theories of art in order to concentrate on architecture and rationalism, in accordance with the LI's own interests. See also Debord, "De l'architecture sauvage": "At one point he [Jorn] was one of the first to undertake a contemporary critique of that most recent form of repressive architecture, a form that to this day is like oil stains on 'the frozen waters of egotistical calculation,' and whose tenants and supporters can thus be judged everywhere case by case."

**26** *Potlatch* conveniently overlooked Ulm's slide into an even more orthodox functionalism under Bill's successor, Tomás Maldonado, who was to remain unchallenged until the first edition of *Internationale situationniste*, in Jorn's article "Les situationnistes et l'automation" (*Internationale situationniste*, no. 1 [Paris, 1958], pp. 22–25).

**27** Jane Jacobs, *The Death and Life of Great American Cities* (New York: Random House, 1961).

**28** On the back cover of Asger Jorn and Guy-Ernest Debord, *Fin de Copenhague* (Copenhagen: Permild and Rosengreen, 1957), unpaginated.

**29** Rumney's project was partially published in *ARK: The Journal of the Royal College of Art*, no. 24 (London, 1958), and is reprinted in Iwona Blazwick, ed., *An Endless Adventure, an Endless Passion, an Endless Banquet: A Situationist Scrapbook* (London: Institute of Contemporary Arts/Verso, 1989), pp. 45–49, and in Tom Vague, ed., *Vague*, no. 22 (London, 1989), pp. 33–35.

**30** See, for instance, James Stirling, "Garches to Jaoul—Le Corbusier as Domestic Architect in 1927 and 1953," *Architectural Review* 118 (September 1955), pp. 145–151, in which the author confronted the fact that rationalism had been an applied style in architecture. Stirling's mentor was the historian Colin Rowe, among the first to openly discuss the stylization and historification of modern architecture. Stirling's Independent Group colleague, the historian Reyner Banham, was writing his Ph.D. dissertation on the expressive rather than determinist roles of rationalism and technology in modern architecture, a study eventually published as the seminal *Theory and Design in the First Machine Age* (London: Architectural Press, 1960).

**31** Internationale lettriste, "Les gratte-ciel par la racine," *Potlatch*, no. 5 (Paris, July 1954), reprinted in *Potlatch 1954–1957*, pp. 34–36. The phrase used is "croûtes néocubistes."

**32** Anon., "Les barbouilleurs," *Potlatch*, no. 8 (Paris, August 1954), reprinted in *Potlatch 1954–1957*, pp. 51–53.

**33** See Jorn, "Image et forme," p. 412.

**34** The *béton brut* (raw concrete) styling of Le Corbusier's 1947–1952 Unité d'Habitation near Marseilles, widely regarded as the first major modern building since the war, was far too relaxed and "organic" to be considered rationalist in the old, interwar sense; the "brutal" textures of his 1952–1956 Maisons Jaoul at Neuilly-sur-Seine, Paris, seemed to own up to the fact that the smoothness of Garches was indeed a surface treatment rather than a necessity; and his 1950–1954 Pilgrimage Chapel at Ronchamp, France, might almost have found a place alongside the wild thumbnail sketches, reminiscent of the expressionism of Bruno Taut and Erich Mendelsohn, that Colle had used in his critique of Le Corbusier only a few years earlier in *Cobra* magazine. On *art autre*, see the trends brought together by Michel Tapié for his book *Un art autre* (Paris: Gabriel-Giraud, 1952).

**35** Jorn, "Image et forme," p. 413; Alison and Peter Smithson, "The New Brutalism," *Architectural Design*, April 1957, quoted in Reyner Banham, *The New Brutalism: Ethic or Aesthetic?* (London: Architectural Press, 1966), p. 66.

**36** Anon., "La plate-forme d'Alba," *Potlatch*, no. 27 (Paris, November 1956), reprinted in *Potlatch 1954–1957*, pp. 213–216.

**37** Henry de Béarn, André-Frank Conord, Mohamed Dahou, Guy-Ernest Debord, Jacques Fillon, Patrick Straram, and Gil J. Wolman, "Sans commune mesure," *Potlatch*, no. 2 (Paris, June 1954), reprinted in *Potlatch 1954–1957*, pp. 16–17.

**38** *Psychogéographie* was first mentioned in *Potlatch*, no. 1 (June 1954); *détournement* in *Potlatch*, no. 2 (June 1954); *dérive* in *Potlatch*, no. 9–10–11 (August 1954); *situation* in *Potlatch*, no. 14 (November 1954) (and in Debord's film *Hurlements en faveur de Sade*, 1952); and *urbanisme unitaire* in *Potlatch*, no. 27 (November 1956).

**39** "Maintenant, l'I.S.," *Internationale situationniste,* no. 9 (Paris, August 1964), pp. 3–5, trans. as "Now, the S.I.," in Knabb, *Anthology,* pp. 135–138.

**40** Raoul Vaneigem, "La cinquième conférence de l'I.S. à Göteborg," *Internationale situationniste,* no. 7 (Paris, April 1962), trans. as "The Fifth S.I. Conference," in Knabb, *Anthology,* p. 88.

**41** See Home, *Assault on Culture,* p. 39.

**42** Michèle Bernstein, M. Dahou, Véra, and Gil J. Wolman, "La ligne générale," *Potlatch,* no. 14 (Paris, November 1954), reprinted in *Potlatch 1954–1957,* pp. 76–77.

**43** *Guy Debord: son art et son temps,* 1994, dir. Brigitte Cornand and Guy Debord for Canal+ Télévision, Paris.

**44** See, for instance, Jérôme Garcin, "L'insituable Guy Debord," *L'Express,* 8 December 1994, pp. 83–84. Debord's apparent suicide on 1 December 1994 has naturally been linked to the supposedly "copycat" suicides of his friends, the publisher Gérard Voitey on 3 December 1994 and the writer and *provocateur* Roger Stéphane on 4 December 1994. Certainly there was an air of finality about Debord's Canal+ film, which had just been completed. Nonetheless this chain of deaths was disturbing, following as it did the murder in 1984 of Debord's friend, publisher, and patron, the filmmaker Gérard Lebovici.

### Chapter 1

**1** For a complete definition of the spectacle, see Guy-Ernest Debord, *La société du spectacle* (Paris: Buchet-Chastel, 1967; reprinted, Paris: Editions Champ Libre, 1971), trans. as *The Society of the Spectacle* (London: Rebel Press and Aim Publications, 1987).

**2** Lawrence Alloway, "City Notes," *Architectural Design,* no. 29 (January 1959), pp. 34–35, part reprinted in David Robbins, ed., *The Independent Group: Postwar Britain and the Aesthetics of Plenty* (Cambridge, Mass.: MIT Press, 1990), p. 167. Alloway's approving citation of John Rannells, *The Core of the City* (New York: Columbia University Press, 1956), gives a sense of the widespread attention being paid to the "heart" of the city.

**3** Alloway, "City Notes."

**4** Guy-Ernest Debord, "Perspectives de modifications conscientes dans la vie quotidienne," *Internationale situationniste,* no. 6 (Paris, August 1961), pp. 20–27, trans. as "Perspectives for Conscious Alterations in Everyday Life," in Ken Knabb, ed., *Situationist International Anthology* (Berkeley: Bureau of Public Secrets, 1981), p. 71.

**5** Guy-Ernest Debord, "Introduction à une critique de la géographie urbaine," *Les lèvres nues,* no. 6 (Brussels, 1955), reprinted in Gérard Berreby, ed., *Documents relatifs à la fondation de l'Internationale situationniste: 1948–1957* (Paris: Editions Allia, 1985), pp. 288–292, and trans. as "Introduction to a Critique of Urban Geography," in Knabb, *Anthology,* pp. 5–8. Cf. William Shakespeare, *Macbeth* V.v.23–28: "Life's but a walking shadow, a poor player, That struts and frets his hour upon the stage, And then is heard no more; it is a tale Told by an idiot, full of sound and fury, Signifying nothing."

**6** Attila Kotányi and Raoul Vaneigem, "Programme élémentaire du bureau d'urbanisme unitaire," *Internationale situationniste,* no. 6 (Paris, August 1961), pp. 16–19, trans. as "Elementary Program of the Bureau of Unitary Urbanism," in Knabb, *Anthology,* pp. 65–67.

**7** Anon., "Géopolitique de l'hibernation," *Internationale situationniste,* no. 7 (Paris, April 1962), pp. 3–10, trans. as "Geopolitics of Hibernation," in Knabb, *Anthology,* pp. 76–82.

**8** Anon., "Critique de l'urbanisme," *Internationale situationniste,* no. 6 (Paris, August 1961), pp. 5–11.

**9** Raoul Vaneigem, "Commentaires contre l'urbanisme," *Internationale situationniste,* no. 6 (Paris, August 1961), pp. 33–37.

**10** Mark Shipway reports: "The real purchasing power of the average French worker's wage rose by 170% between 1950 and 1975, and overall consumption rose by 174% during the same period. Personal expenditure on 'leisure activities' quadrupled in real terms between 1950 & 1977. . . . In 1956 French workers won the legal right to three weeks holiday per year, extended to four weeks in 1965." Mark Shipway, "Situationism," in Maximilien Rubel and John Crump, eds., *Non-Market Socialism in the Nineteenth and Twentieth Centuries* (Basingstoke: Macmillan, 1987), pp. 151–172.

**11** Asger Jorn and Guy-Ernest Debord, *Fin de Copenhague* (Copenhagen: Permild and Rosengreen, 1957), unpaginated. See also Greil Marcus, "Guy Debord's *Mémoires*: A Situationist Primer," in Elisabeth Sussman, ed., *On the Passage of a Few People through a Rather Brief Moment in Time: The Situationist International, 1957–1972* (Cambridge, Mass.: MIT Press/Institute of Contemporary Arts, 1989), pp. 125–131.

**12** Anon., "Définitions," *Internationale situationniste,* no. 1 (Paris, June 1958), pp. 13–14, trans. as "Definitions," in Knabb, *Anthology,* pp. 45–46.

**13** Debord and Jorn, *Fin de Copenhague*, unpaginated. Note, however, that the typography of the last line quoted looks suspiciously like the IMIB's own.

**14** J. V. Martin, J. Strijbosch, R. Vaneigem, and R. Viénet, "Réponse à une enquête du Centre d'art socio-expérimental," *Internationale situationniste,* no. 9 (Paris, August 1964), pp. 40–44, trans. as "Response to a Questionnaire from the Centre for Socio-Experimental Art," in Knabb, *Anthology,* pp. 143–147.

**15** Alison and Peter Smithson, "But Today We Collect Ads," *ARK: The Journal of the Royal College of Art,* no. 18 (November 1956), pp. 49–52, reprinted in Robbins, *The Independent Group,* pp. 185–186.

**16** For an excellent survey of the formations of French popular culture, see Brian Rigby, *Popular Culture in Modern France: A Study of Cultural Discourse* (London: Routledge, 1991).

**17** Introduction to Angus Calder, ed., *Britain by Mass Observation* (London: Cresset, 1986), p. xiii (my thanks to Mike Harrison for bringing this quotation to my attention). The Independent Group photographer Nigel Henderson was married to Judith Stephen, a Cambridge anthropologist who, assisted and encouraged by Tom Harrisson, a founder of Mass Observation, ran a course called "Discover Your Neighbour." See James Lingwood, "Nigel Henderson," and David Robbins, "The Independent Group: Forerunners of Postmodernism?," in Robbins, *The Independent Group,* pp. 76–77, 237–248.

**18** See Stewart Home, *The Assault on Culture: Utopian Currents from Lettrisme to Class War* (London: Aporia Press and Unpopular Books, 1988), pp. 8, 31. In 1957–1958 Debord and Vaneigem attended Lefebvre's sociology course at the University of Nanterre. Debord reciprocated by contributing a tape-recorded talk to Lefebvre's Group for Research on Everyday Life in 1961. See Debord, "Perspectives for Conscious Alterations in Everyday Life."

**19** See the Smithsons' *CIAM Grille* (1953), reproduced in Robbins, *The Independent Group,* p. 114. Henderson's pictures were reproduced in Theo Crosby, ed., *Uppercase 3* (London: Whitefriars Press, 1961), and in "Patterns of Association and Identity," in Alison Smithson, ed., *Team 10 Primer* (London: Studio Vista, 1968).

**20** See, for instance, Alison and Peter Smithson, "Cluster City: A New Shape for the Community," *Architectural Review* 122 (November 1957), pp. 333–336. The idea of the cluster seems to have derived from the American urbanist Kevin Lynch, who wrote about it in *Scientific American*, April 1954, and to have passed into architectural use through Denys Lasdun, who built his (in)famous cluster blocks in Bethnal Green, London, in the 1950s and 1960s. See Reyner Banham, *The New Brutalism: Ethic or Aesthetic?* (London: Architectural Press, 1966), p. 72.

21   Reyner Banham, "CIAM," in Vittorio Magnago Lampugnani, ed., *The Thames and Hudson Encyclopaedia of 20th-Century Architecture* (London: Thames and Hudson, 1986), pp. 68–70.

22   For a summary of the proceedings of CIAM 8 (Hoddesdon, 1951), see E. N. Rogers, J. L. Sert, and J. Tyrwhitt, eds., *The Heart of the City: Towards the Humanisation of Urban Life* (New York: Pelligrini and Cudahy, 1952).

23   "Principles of the Fourth Congress" (1933), published anonymously by Le Corbusier as *Urbanisme des CIAM, la Charte d'Athènes* (Paris: Plon, 1943), reprinted 1957, and trans. in Ulrich Conrads, *Programmes and Manifestoes on Twentieth Century Architecture* (London: Lund Humphries, 1970), pp. 137–147.

24   Guy-Ernest Debord, "Positions situationnistes sur la circulation," *Internationale situationniste,* no. 3 (December 1959), pp. 36–37, trans. as "Situationist Theses on Traffic," in Knabb, *Anthology,* pp. 56–59.

25   Ibid.

26   See Constant, *New Babylon Bulletin*, no. 1 (Amsterdam, n.d. [c. 1963]).

27   Debord, "Positions situationnistes sur la circulation."

28   Anon., "Urbanisme comme volonté et représentation," *Internationale situationniste,* no. 9 (Paris, August 1964), pp. 12–13, trans. Thomas Y. Levin as "Urbanism as Will and Representation," in Sussman, *On the Passage of a Few People,* p. 162.

29   See Pierre Couperie, "The War, the 4th and 5th Republics," in *Paris au fil de temps* (Paris: Joël Cuénot, 1968), trans. as *Paris through the Ages: An Illustrated Historical Atlas of Urbanism and Architecture* (London: Barrie and Jenkins, 1970); and Kristin Ross, *Fast Cars, Clean Bodies: Decolonization and the Reordering of French Culture* (Cambridge, Mass.: MIT Press, 1995), p. 54.

30   Couperie, "The War, the 4th and 5th Republics."

31   Ibid.

32   For brief introductions to the impact of Provo, see, for instance, Home, *Assault on Culture,* pp. 65–68, or "History of Amsterdam," in Martin Dunford and Jack Holland, *Amsterdam: The Rough Guide* (London: Rough Guides, 1994), pp. 233–241, which also discusses the Nieuwmarkt clearances.

33   Anon., "Urbanisme comme volonté et représentation."

34   Le Corbusier, *Urbanisme des CIAM, la Charte d'Athènes.*

35   Debord, "Positions situationnistes sur la circulation."

36   For more on van Eyck and COBRA, see Jean-Clarence Lambert, *COBRA* (New York: Abbeville Press, 1985), especially pp. 138–139. For a comprehensive survey of van Eyck's work, see Francis Strauven, *Aldo van Eyck relativiteit en verbeelding* (Amsterdam: Meulenhoff, 1994).

37   Aldo van Eyck, "Statement against Rationalism," paper read at CIAM, Bridgwater, 1947, reprinted in Sigfried Giedion, *A Decade of Modern Architecture* (Zurich: Girsberger, 1954), pp. 43–44.

38   Giedion, *A Decade of Modern Architecture,* pp. 83–84, 236–237.

39   Rogers, Sert, and Tyrwhitt, *The Heart of the City,* p. 167.

40   Ibid.

41   Giancarlo De Carlo, cited in Kenneth Frampton, *Modern Architecture: A Critical History* (London: Thames and Hudson, 1985), p. 279.

42   See Ian McCullum, "Spontaneity at the Core," in Rogers, Sert, and Tyrwhitt, *The Heart of the City,* pp. 64–65.

43   Reyner Banham, "City as Scrambled Egg," *Cambridge Opinion*, no. 17, "Living with the 60s" issue (Cambridge, 1959), pp. 18–23.

44   Ibid., p. 19.

45   Ibid., insert, pp. 22–23.

46   See also van Eyck's 1966 Arnheim Pavilion, the labyrinthine effect of which the architect described as "Bump!—sorry. What's this? Oh hello!" Quoted in Charles Jencks,

*Modern Movements in Architecture* (Harmondsworth: Penguin, 1973), p. 316.

**47** The tract "Man and House" is reprinted in Berreby, *Documents,* pp. 182–183. Spatial colorism later reemerged in essence in parts of the Children's Home, and in the Red and Yellow sectors of Constant's New Babylon.

**48** Aldo van Eyck, "Knots and Labyrinths," in Jacqueline de Jong, ed., *Situationist Times*, no. 4 (Paris, 1963). The *Situationist Times*, published outside the Parisian SI and associated more with the Second Situationist International, was a lavish "artistic" spinoff from situationist activity.

**49** See Vittorio Magnago Lampugnani, "Structuralism," in Magnago Lampugnani, *Thames and Hudson Encyclopaedia,* pp. 322–323.

**50** Quoted in Alison Smithson, *Team 10 Primer*, p. 15, and in Jencks, *Modern Movements in Architecture,* p. 311.

**51** Although American, Shadrach Woods was based in France.

**52** Cited in Frampton, *Modern Architecture,* p. 278.

**53** Giancarlo De Carlo, *Legitimizing Architecture* (1968), quoted in Frampton, *Modern Architecture,* p. 278.

**54** For typical instances of contemporary modernist antipathy toward popular culture and design, see Clement Greenberg, "Avant Garde and Kitsch," *Partisan Review* 6, no. 5 (New York, Fall 1939), pp. 34–39, reprinted in Charles Harrison and Paul Wood, eds., *Art in Theory 1900–1990: An Anthology of Changing Ideas* (Oxford: Blackwell, 1992), pp. 529–542; Ernö Goldfinger and Edward Carter, *The County of London Plan* (Harmondsworth: Penguin, 1945); Edgar Kaufmann, "Borax, or the Chromium-Plated Calf," *Architectural Review* 103–104 (August 1948), pp. 88–92; and *Architectural Review* 108, "Man Made America" issue (December 1950).

**55** For positive reassessments of popular industrial design, see, for example, Reyner Banham, "Machine Aesthetic," *Architectural Review* 117 (April 1955), pp. 225–228, reprinted in Reyner Banham, *Design by Choice*, ed. Penny Sparke

(London: Academy Editions, 1981), pp. 44–47; and Asger Jorn, "Image et forme," in Asger Jorn, *Pour la forme: ébauche d'une méthodologie des arts* (Paris: Internationale situationniste, 1958), reprinted in Berreby, *Documents,* pp. 411–419.

**56** See "Forme et structure," in Jorn, *Pour la forme*, reprinted in Berreby, *Documents,* pp. 437–469.

**57** Constant, "C'est notre desir qui fait la revolution," *Cobra,* no. 4 (1948).

**58** See *Eristica*, journal of the IMIB, July 1956, reprinted in Berreby, *Documents,* pp. 371–400; and see Home, *Assault on Culture,* p. 24.

**59** Reyner Banham, "Pop and the Body Critical," *New Society*, no. 16 (December 1965), p. 25, quoted in Barry Curtis, "From Ivory Tower to Control Tower," in Robbins, *The Independent Group,* pp. 221–227. Until 1944, English education was separated into state (elementary), church, and private (prep and public school) sectors. My thanks to Brian Bench at Hungerford School, London, for discussing with me the history of English education.

**60** Guy-Ernest Debord, "Rapport sur la construction des situations et sur les conditions de l'organisation et de l'action de la tendance situationniste internationale," preparatory text for the Cosio d'Arroscia conference, July 1957, reprinted in Berreby, *Documents,* pp. 607–619, and trans. as "Report on the Construction of Situations and on the International Situationist Tendency's Conditions of Organization and Action" (excerpts), in Knabb, *Anthology,* pp. 17–25.

**61** Asger Jorn, "Les situationnistes et l'automation," *Internationale situationniste*, no. 1 (Paris, June 1958), pp. 22–25, trans. as "The Situationists and Automation" (excerpts), in Knabb, *Anthology,* pp. 46–47.

**62** Asger Jorn, "Image et forme," in Berreby, *Documents,* p. 413; anon., "Problèmes préliminaires à la construction d'une situation," *Internationale situationniste*, no. 1 (Paris, June 1958), pp. 11–13, trans. as "Preliminary Problems in Constructing a Situation," in Knabb, *Anthology,* pp. 43–45.

**63**  Anon., "Problèmes préliminaires à la construction d'une situation."

**64**  See Marcel Mauss, "Essai sur le don," *Année sociologique*, n.s. 1 (1925), trans. as *The Gift* (London, 1925).

**65**  Walter Benjamin, "The Author as Producer" (1934), trans. Edmund Jephcott in *Reflections*, and reprinted in Francis Frascina and Charles Harrison, eds., *Modern Art and Modernism: A Critical Anthology* (London: Harper and Row, 1982), pp. 213–216.

**66**  "Industrial painting" in fact used various craft processes, pressing, spraying, and painting oil and resin onto canvas: semi-mechanical treatments devised not by industry but by Pinot-Gallizio himself. The procedure might also be perceived as a continuation of the artists' interest in action painting (for a short time Italy's nuclear art movement had a close association with the Imaginist Bauhaus), and it may have been this feature that attracted the interest of galleries. For further discussion of industrial painting and situationist art in general, see Peter Wollen, "Bitter Victory: The Art and Politics of the Situationist International," in Sussman, *On the Passage of a Few People,* pp. 20–61, and Mirella Bandini, *L'estetico il politico: da Cobra all'Internazionale situazionista, 1948–1957* (Rome: Officina Edizioni, 1977).

**67**  Namely the Notizie Gallery, Turin (May-June 1958), the Montenapoleone Gallery, Milan (July 1958), the Van de Loo Gallery, Munich (April 1959), and René Drouin Gallery, Paris (May 1959), and the Stedelijk Museum, Amsterdam, and Notizie Gallery, Turin (June 1960). See Home, *Assault on Culture,* pp. 33–36.

**68**  See Giuseppe Pinot-Gallizio, "Discours sur la peinture industrielle et sur un art unitaire applicable," *Internationale situationniste,* no. 3 (Paris, December 1959), pp. 31–34.

**69**  See, for instance, "A Note on 'une architecture autre,'" in Banham, *The New Brutalism*, pp. 68–69.

**70**  Reyner Banham and François Dallegret, "A Home Is Not a House," *Art in America*, no. 53 (April 1965), pp. 70–77,

reprinted with commentary in Charles Jencks and George Baird, eds., *Meaning in Architecture* (New York: Braziller, 1969), pp. 109–118, and in Joan Ockman and Edward Eigen, eds., *Architecture Culture 1943–1968: A Documentary Anthology* (New York: Columbia Books of Architecture/Rizzoli, 1993), pp. 370–378.

**71**  Alain Touraine, "Travail, loisirs et société," *Esprit*, special number on leisure, June 1959, p. 986, cited in Rigby, *Popular Culture in Modern France*, p. 81. Touraine went on to write *La société post-industrielle* (Paris: Denoël, 1969).

**72**  See Lawrence Alloway, "The Long Front of Culture," *Cambridge Opinion,* no. 17 (Cambridge, 1959), pp. 25–26, reprinted in John Russell and Suzi Gablik, eds., *Pop Art Redefined* (London: Thames and Hudson, 1969), pp. 41–43, and excerpted in Robbins, *The Independent Group,* pp. 165–166.

**73**  Anon., "Manifeste," *Internationale situationniste*, no. 4 (Paris, June 1960), pp. 36–38, trans. as "'Situationists': International Manifesto," in Conrads, *Programmes and Manifestoes,* pp. 172–174.

**74**  Sottsass's Memphis style has since become archetypal of postmodern design.

**75**  Guy Atkins, *Asger Jorn* (London: Methuen, 1964), reprinted in Iwona Blazwick, ed., *An Endless Adventure, an Endless Passion, an Endless Banquet: A Situationist Scrapbook* (London: Institute of Contemporary Arts/Verso, 1989), p. 59. A few months before this meeting, the ICA had screened Debord's LI film *Hurlements en faveur de Sade* (1952). The screening ended in mayhem—"People stood around making angry speeches. One man threatened to resign from the ICA unless the money for his ticket was refunded" (ibid.).

**76**  Christian Dotremont eventually became disenchanted with politics altogether and began to take the first steps toward depoliticizing COBRA. When the 1949 COBRA exhibition at the Stedelijk became something of a political *cause célèbre*, Constant and Jorn resisted even Dotremont's defense of COBRA as being free from any fixed ideological position (see Lambert, *COBRA,* pp. 138–139). Debord criticized COBRA in his "Rapport sur la construction des situations": "Their lack of ideological rigor, the limitation of their pursuits to largely plastic experimentation, and above all the absence of a comprehensive theory of the conditions and perspectives of their experience led to their breaking up." The second issue of *Internationale situationniste* (1958) also led with an unsolicited critique of COBRA.

**77**   For more on the cultural impact of the Algerian war, see Ross, *Fast Cars, Clean Bodies,* passim.

**78**   Quoted in Reyner Banham, "The Atavism of the Short Distance Mini-Cyclist," *Living Arts,* no. 3 (1963), pp. 91–97, reprinted in Banham, *Design by Choice,* pp. 84–89, and excerpted in Robbins, *The Independent Group,* pp. 176–177. The article, a transcript of the Terry Hamilton Memorial Lecture, delivered at the ICA in November 1963, offers the best insight into the politics of the Independent Group.

**79**   This notion of autonomy was, ironically, similar to Greenberg's, except that the Situtionist cultural sphere would be one that celebrated the "everyday" rather than the abstract.

**80**   Anon., "Critique de l'urbanisme," pp. 8–9.

**81**   Ibid.

**82**   Anon., "Poésie," *Potlatch,* no. 24 (Paris, November 1955), unpaginated, reprinted in *Potlatch 1954–1957* (Paris: Editions Gérard Lebovici, 1985), pp. 182–183.

**83**   Guy-Ernest Debord and Gil J. Wolman, "Mode d'emploi du détournement," *Les lèvres nues,* no. 8 (Brussels, 1956), reprinted in Berreby, *Documents,* pp. 302–309, trans. as "Methods of Détournement," in Knabb, *Anthology,* pp. 8–14. It should be noted that situationist theories of partisan cultural appropriation revived debates about revolutionary art previously encountered in the Soviet Union in the 1920s. On Guy Debord's personal tastes, see Lucy Forsyth, "The

Sup(e)r(s)ession of Art," unpublished paper delivered at the Manchester University conference "The Hacienda Must Be Built: On the Legacy of the Situationist Revolt," Manchester, January 1996.

**84**   Guy Debord, *Commentaires sur la société du spectacle* (Paris: Editions Champ Libre, 1988), quoted by Phil Edwards, "Debord: The Aesthetic, the Political and the Passage of Time," in *Here and Now Guy Debord Supplement,* p. xvi, issued with *Here and Now,* no. 16/17 (Glasgow and Leeds, Winter 1995/1996).

**85**   Debord and Wolman, "Methods of Détournement," p. 11.

**86**   Eleonore Kofman and Elizabeth Lebas are correct in their opinion that "the relationship between Lefebvrian and Situationist concepts awaits a serious study" (Henri Lefebvre, *Writings on Cities,* ed. and trans. Eleonore Kofman and Elizabeth Lebas [Oxford: Blackwell, 1996], p. 13, note 6), and it will doubtless be forthcoming.

**87**   See Henri Lefebvre, *Le retour de la dialectique. 12 mots clés* (Paris: Messidor/Editions Sociales, 1986), p. 13, and *Le temps des méprises* (Paris: Editions Stock, 1975), p. 110, both cited in Lefebvre, *Writings on Cities,* pp. 12–13.

**88**   David Harvey, "Afterword," in Henri Lefebvre, *The Production of Space,* trans. Donald Nicholson-Smith (Oxford: Blackwell, 1991), pp. 425–434. Lefebvre advanced the concept of the "moment" in *La somme et la reste,* 2 vols. (Paris, 1959).

**89**   Guy-Ernest Debord, Attila Kotányi, and Raoul Vaneigem, "Theses on the Paris Commune" (Paris, March 1962), trans. in Knabb, *Anthology,* pp. 314–316. The essay was used by Lefebvre in *La proclamation de la Commune* (Paris: Gallimard, 1965); see Lefebvre, *Writings on Cities,* p. 13, citing Rémi Hess, *Henri Lefebvre et l'aventure du siècle* (Paris: A. M. Métaille, 1988), p. 228.

**90**   See Guy-Ernest Debord, "Perspectives de modifications conscientes dans la vie quotidienne," presented on tape, 17 May 1961, at a conference of the Group for Research on

Everyday Life, convened by Henri Lefebvre in the Center of Sociological Studies of the CNRS, published in *Internationale situationniste,* no. 6 (Paris, August 1961), pp. 20–27, and trans. as "Perspectives for Conscious Alterations in Everyday Life," in Knabb, *Anthology,* pp. 68–75. Note that the Sorbonne and several other major educational institutions appeared on Debord and Jorn's *Guide psychogéographique de Paris* (1956) but not on their map of *The Naked City* (1957), suggesting an increasing disillusionment with the spaces of higher education. But after the Strasbourg University scandal of 1966 (when student radicals took over the student union and used its funds to produce situationist propaganda, publishing *On the Poverty of Student Life*), the SI reappraised the potential of academia as revolutionary territory, and held places on the Sorbonne Occupation Committee in May 1968.

**91**  David Harvey, "Afterword," pp. 429–430.

**92**  For discussions of the sources of the *situation*, see Peter Wollen, "Bitter Victory," and Sadie Plant, *The Most Radical Gesture: The Situationist International in a Postmodern Age* (London: Routledge, 1992).

**93**  Guy-Ernest Debord, "Report on the Construction of Situations," p. 24. This tremendous assertion of the possibilities of the here-and-now of everyday life renewed the optimism of revolutionary surrealism. André Breton had argued that Sigmund Freud's pioneering work in psychoanalysis alerted us to the fact that we act out our desires and fantasies as compensation for the unsatisfactory nature of our everyday lives. It was perfectly possible, Breton argued, to go a stage further by sublimating desire into artistic creation, putting two supposedly distinct realms—desire and everyday life—into communication. See André Breton, *Les vases communicants* (Paris: Gallimard, 1933).

**94**  See Ockman and Eigen, *Architecture Culture*, p. 427. Within Marxist philosophy, meanwhile, Lefebvre's main adversary was the structuralist Marxist Louis Althusser.

**95**  Asger Jorn, "Contre le fonctionalisme," in *Pour la forme*, reprinted in Berreby, *Documents,* pp. 425–431. For the assertion of the value of amateurism, see also Constant, "Reflex Manifesto," *Reflex* (Amsterdam, 1948), trans. Leonard Bright in Willemijn Stokvis, *Cobra* (New York: Rizzoli, 1988).

**96**  Thesis 179, "The Organisation of Territory," in Debord, *The Society of the Spectacle*, unpaginated.

**97**  Anon., "Critique de l'urbanisme," p. 7, reviewing Henri Lefebvre, "Utopie expérimentale: pour un nouvel urbanisme," *Revue française de sociologie,* no. 3 (Paris, July-September 1961).

**98**  The German section of the SI, Spur, published a lengthy pamphlet on situationist architectural theory, collecting relevant texts and translating them into German. See Gruppe Spur, *Spur,* no. 5, "Spezialnummer über den unitären Urbanismus" (Munich, June 1961). The piece was criticized in anon., "Critique de l'urbanisme."

**99**  It is heartening to find the legacies of situationism and Lefebvre still valued. So-called "postmodern geographers," for instance, look to Lefebvre and the situationists as sources, citing their transference of sociological attention from time to space as a major ontological change. We have nonetheless to be alert to the fact that postmodern tendencies to celebrate social difference and partial transgressions of the dominant cultural order for their own sake, or to regard power as highly diffuse, are somewhat alien to the original precepts of the situationists and Lefebvre. For a summary of the aims of postmodern geography, see Edward W. Soja, "Preface and Postscript," in *Postmodern Geographies: The Reassertion of Space in Critical Social Theory* (London: Verso, 1989), p. 1: "For at least the past century, time and history have occupied a privileged position in the practical and theoretical consciousness of Western Marxism and critical social science. . . . Today, however, it may be . . . the 'making of geography' rather than the 'making of history' that provides the most revealing tactical and theoretical world." On this tension between space and time, see Véra, "Quelques formes que prendra LA DÉRIVE," *Potlatch,* no. 17 (Paris, February 1955), reprinted in *Potlatch 1954–1957*, p. 108, where it was insisted that situationist drift "must be a) through time—constant, lucid; influential and above all enormously fugitive b) through space—disinterested, social, always passionate."

**100**   Harvey, "Afterword," p. 430. The superiority of the spatio-temporality of the "situation" over the pure temporality of Lefebvre's "moment" was insisted upon in anon., "Théorie des moments et construction des situations," *Internationale situationniste,* no. 4 (Paris, June 1960), pp. 10–11.

**101**   See Ockman and Eigen, *Architecture Culture,* p. 427. Utopie's "interdisciplinary membership included urban historian Hubert Tonka, theorist Jean Baudrillard, feminist Isabelle Auricoste, and architects Jean Aubert, Jean-Paul Jungmann, and Antoine Stinco. . . . The group published two issues of *Utopie: Revue de la sociologie de l'urbain,* a journal dedicated to a revolutionary critique of the city, culture, and power, illustrated with comic strip satires and 'detourned' images," very much in the vein of *Internationale situationniste.*

**102**   Ockman and Eigen, *Architecture Culture,* p. 427.

**103**   Kotányi and Vaneigem, "Elementary Program of the Bureau of Unitary Urbanism," p. 67.

**104**   Asger Jorn, "Une architecture de la vie," *Potlatch,* no. 15 (Paris, December 1954), reprinted in *Potlatch 1954–1957,* pp. 84–86, trans. and extracted from *Immagine e forma,* no. 1 (Milan, 1954), later trans. as "Image et forme," in Jorn, *Pour la forme.*

**105**   Anon., "Critique de l'urbanisme," p. 9.

**106**   See Ockman and Eigen, *Architecture Culture,* p. 427.

**107**   Even a critic as sensitive as Lewis Mumford was tempted to pillory Le Corbusier. See, for instance, Mumford's classic *The City in History: Its Origins, Its Transformations, and Its Prospects* (New York: Harcourt Brace, 1961), as read by Debord in Thesis 172 of *The Society of the Spectacle.*

**108**   See anon., "Echec des manifestations de Marseille," *Potlatch,* no. 27 (Paris, November 1956), reprinted in *Potlatch 1954–1957,* pp. 211–213. The event was variously referred to as the "Festival de l'Art d'avant-garde" and "Festival de la Cité radieuse." In fact, Le Corbusier's *La ville radieuse* (1935, trans. as *The Radiant City* [London and New York: Orion Press, 1967]) was something of a humanistic revision of his more austere visions of the future.

**109**   Le Corbusier, *Vers une architecture* (Paris: Editions Crès, 1923), trans. Frederick Etchells as *Towards a New Architecture* (London, 1927; reprinted, London: Butterworth, 1987), pp. 269, 284.

**110**   Guy-Ernest Debord and Asger Jorn, *Mémoires* (Copenhagen: Permild and Rosengreen, 1959), unpaginated. This collage book was assembled in 1957. The phrase, like several others from *Mémoires,* is reiterated by Vaneigem in "Commentaires contre l'urbanisme."

**111**   Ballanche's city fitted into a history of Platonic and theocratic urban utopias, from Vitruvius to St. Augustine, Alberti, Campanella, and Calvin.

**112**   Internationale lettriste, "Les gratte-ciel par la racine," *Potlatch,* no. 5 (Paris, July 1954), reprinted in *Potlatch 1954–1957,* pp. 34–36; see Le Corbusier, *Le modulor* (Paris, 1948; reprinted, Boulogne: Editions de l'Architecture d'Aujourd'hui), trans. as *The Modulor* (London: Faber and Faber, 1954). Similar arguments relating the grid to the Protestant spirit have reemerged in Richard Sennett, *The Conscience of the Eye: The Design and Social Life of Cities* (London: Faber and Faber, 1990).

**113**   Internationale lettriste, "Les gratte-ciel par la racine." Lefebvre's and de Certeau's preferred term for this effect was "quadrillage," i.e., a tight military or police control of an area; it also refers to checkered material or paper, and by extension to the grid pattern of streets. See Rigby, *Popular Culture in Modern France,* p. 36.

**114**   See also the illustration for "La fin de l'économie et la réalisation de l'art," *Internationale situationniste,* no. 4 (Paris, June 1960), p. 21, apparently depicting a monastery. The motif of the prison seems to have gained a certain currency: in 1962 it closed a documentary made by Chris Marker about everyday life in Paris, *Le joli mai*. See Ross, *Fast Cars, Clean Bodies*, p. 89.

**115**   Anon., "Ariane en chômage," *Potlatch*, no. 9–10–11 (Paris, August 1954), reprinted in *Potlatch 1954–1957*, p. 63. See also Gilles Ivain [pseudonym of Ivan Chtcheglov], "Formulaire pour un urbanisme nouveau," 1953, reprinted in *Internationale situationniste*, no. 1 (Paris, June 1958), pp. 15–20, trans. as "Formulary for a New Urbanism," in Knabb, *Anthology,* pp. 1–4, for use of the Jardin des Plantes labyrinth as a motif.

**116**   Clipping from *Le Monde*, 22 August 1963, reprinted in anon., "Urbanisme comme volonté et représentation." It turns out that the situationists were closer to the truth than even they realized: apparently meetings between the planners of the postwar municipal council of Paris and the prefect of police were routine. See Philippe Nivet, "Le Conseil municipal face aux rénovations (1945–1977)," in Jacques Lucan, *Eau et gaz à tous les étages. Paris, 100 ans de logement* (Paris: Pavillon de l'Arsenal/Picard Editeur, 1992).

**117**   The 6.6 million residents of greater Paris in 1946 were swelled by a further 700,000 within four years. Note also the impact of an increasing birthrate.

**118**   A.-F. Conord, "Construction de taudis," *Potlatch*, no. 3 (Paris, July 1954), reprinted in *Potlatch 1954–1957*, p. 23.

**119**   Anon., "Les colonies les plus solides . . . ," *Potlatch*, no. 12 (Paris, September 1954), reprinted in *Potlatch 1954–1957*, pp. 65–66. Le Corbusier had himself devised a massive scheme for Algiers in 1930.

**120**   See anon., "Critique de l'urbanisme," p. 8. For further discussion of Sarcelles and the crisis of French architecture, see Ockman and Eigen, *Architecture Culture*, p. 456.

**121**   Eleonore Kofman and Elizabeth Lebas, "Introduction: Lost in Transposition—Time, Space and the City," in Lefebvre, *Writings on Cities*, p. 14.

**122**   See anon., "Géopolitique de l'hibernation," *Internationale situationniste,* no. 7 (Paris, April 1962), pp. 3–10,

trans. as "The Geopolitics of Hibernation," in Knabb, *Anthology*, pp. 76–82. The following year the situationists attempted to create "the atmosphere of an atomic fallout shelter as the first site meant to provoke one to think" at the exhibition "Destruktion af RSG–6" held at the Galerie EXI, Odense, Denmark. See Guy Debord, "Les situationnistes et les nouvelles formes d'action dans la politique ou l'art," *Destruktion af RSG–6: En kollektiv manifestation af Situationistisk International* (Odense, 1963), pp. 18–22, trans. Thomas Y. Levin as "The Situationists and the New Forms of Action in Politics or Art," in Sussman, *On the Passage of a Few People,* pp. 148–153.

**123**   Thesis 172 in Debord, *The Society of the Spectacle*, unpaginated.

**124**   Constant, "Une autre ville pour une autre vie," *Internationale situationniste,* no. 3 (Paris, December 1959), pp. 37–39.

**125**   The claims for the importance of street life would soon find a popular following in the wake of Jane Jacobs's 1961 attack on "the Radiant Garden City Beautiful"—her satirical compound of the planning principles of Le Corbusier, Ebenezer Howard, and Daniel Burnham in *The Death and Life of Great American Cities* (New York: Random House, 1961), cited in "Editors' Introduction: Jane Jacobs, 'The Uses of Sidewalks: Safety,'" in Richard T. LeGates and Frederic Stout, eds., *The City Reader* (London: Routledge, 1996), pp. 103–104.

**126**   Constant, "Une autre ville pour une autre vie."

**127**   Debord, "Positions situationnistes sur la circulation."

**128**   See, for instance, Walter Benjamin, *Charles Baudelaire: A Lyric Poet in an Era of High Capitalism*, trans. Harry Zohn (London: New Left Books, 1973, reprinted London: Verso, 1983).

**129**   Anon., "Urbanism as Will and Representation," p. 161.

**130**   See Claude Eveno and Pascale de Mezamat, eds., *Paris perdu: quarante ans de bouleversements de la ville* (Paris:

Editions Carré, 1991), p. 159, cited in Ross, *Fast Cars, Clean Bodies*, p. 151.

**131**   Michèle Bernstein, Guy-Ernest Debord, and Gil J. Wolman, "Intervention lettriste: protestation auprès de la rédaction du *Times*," *Potlatch*, no. 23 (Paris, October 1955), reprinted in *Potlatch 1954–1957*, pp. 171–173. The group had unproblematically borrowed the phrase from Jorn's debate with Max Bill—"The aim of all production must be to satisfy the needs and the aspirations of man"—to talk about ghettos rather than consumer goods (see Jorn, "Contre le fonctionalisme").

**132**   Jacques Fillon, "Description raisonée de Paris," *Les lèvres nues*, no. 7 (Brussels, December 1955), reprinted in Berreby, *Documents*, p. 300.

**133**   See, for instance, Guy-Ernest Debord, "Deux comptes rendus de dérive," appendixes to "Théorie de la dérive," *Les lèvres nues*, no. 9 (Brussels, November 1956), reprinted in Berreby, *Documents*, pp. 316–319, trans. Thomas Y. Levin as "Two Accounts of the Dérive," in Sussman, *On the Passage of a Few People*, pp. 135–139.

**134**   Anon., "'La forme d'une ville change plus vite . . . ,'" *Potlatch*, no. 25 (Paris, January 1956), reprinted in *Potlatch 1954–1957*, p. 196.

**135**   Bernstein, Debord, and Wolman, "Intervention lettriste."

**136**   The slogan was illustrated in *Internationale situationniste*, no. 8 (Paris, January 1963). Cf. R. Hausmann and R. Huelsenbeck's dadaist manifesto, 1918: "Only by unemployment does it become possible for the individual to achieve certainty as to the truth of life and finally become accustomed to experience," cited in Greil Marcus, *Lipstick Traces: A Secret History of the Twentieth Century* (London: Secker and Warburg, 1989), p. 232.

**137**   Anon., "On détruit la rue Sauvage," *Potlatch*, no. 7 (Paris, August 1954), reprinted in *Potlatch 1954–1957*, p. 49.

**138**   See Lopez's plan, "Îlots a rénover" (Blocks for renovation), 1957, reprinted in *Construction et urbanisme dans la Région parisienne* (Paris: Ministère de Construction, 1958), and another version in Nivet, "Le Conseil municipal face aux rénovations," pp. 146–147.

**139**   Couperie, "The War, the 4th and 5th Republics." In the *grand ensemble* of Grigny, for instance, 450 lodgings were declared to be *insalubre* a mere five years after predominantly working-class and immigrant Parisians were relocated there (Ross, *Fast Cars, Clean Bodies*, p. 155).

**140**   The *Guide psychogéographique de Paris: discours sur les passions de l'amour* measures 60 x 74 cm; *The Naked City: illustration de l'hypothése* [sic] *des plaques tournantes en psychogeographique* [sic] measures 33 x 47.5 cm. The making of a psychogeographic map was announced in anon., "La carte forcée," *Potlatch*, no. 23 (Paris, October 1955), reprinted in *Potlatch 1954–1957*, p. 174.

**141**   M. Christine Boyer, "Twice-Told Stories: The Double Erasure of Times Square," in Iain Borden, Joe Kerr, Alicia Pivaro, and Jane Rendell, eds., *Strangely Familiar: Narratives of Architecture in the City* (London: Routledge, 1996), pp. 77–81.

**142**   The plan was led by the De Gaulle–appointed delegate to the district of Paris, later prefect for the Seine, Paul Delouvrier, between 1961 and 1963. See Anthony Sutcliffe, *Paris: An Architectural History* (New Haven: Yale University Press, 1993), p. 164.

**143**   For one of the most passionate invectives on Parisian planning, see Louis Chevalier, *L'assassinat de Paris* (Paris: Calmann-Levy, 1977), trans. David P. Jordan as *The Assassination of Paris* (Chicago: University of Chicago Press, 1994).

**144**   Scrofula is a term, no longer in medical use, for tuberculosis of the lymphatic glands.

**145**   Alex Moscovitch, "Rénovation, aménagement, urbanisme . . . les taudis de Paris sont-ils sacrés?," *Conférence des ambassadeurs* n.s., no. 14 (11 March 1965), pp. 6–7, quoted in Nivet, "Le Conseil municipal face aux rénovations," p. 129. For more on urbanism and hygiene, see Ross, *Fast Cars, Clean Bodies*, passim.

**146**   Bernstein and Debord had moved to the Marais by 1961 (see Marcus, *Lipstick Traces*, p. 359).

**147**   Anon., "Urbanism as Will and Representation," p. 161.

**148**   For more on the development of Halles and Beaubourg, see Sutcliffe, *Paris: An Architectural History*, pp. 177–183, and Norma Evenson, *Paris: A Century of Change* (New Haven: Yale University Press, 1979), passim.

**149**   See Abdelhafid Khatib, "Essai de description psychogéographique des Halles," *Internationale situationniste,* no. 2 (Paris, December 1958), pp. 13–17; Guy-Ernest Debord, dir., *Sur le passage de quelques personnes à travers une assez courte unité de temps* (1959), reprinted in *Oeuvres cinématographiques complètes, 1952–1978* (Paris: Editions Champ Libre, 1978), trans. as "On the Passage of a Few Persons through a Rather Brief Period of Time," in Knabb, *Anthology,* pp. 29–33.

**150**   Sutcliffe, *Paris: An Architectural History,* p. 178, and "Les Halles," special issue of *Architectural Design*, no. 9–10 (1980), passim.

**151**   See Bryan Appleyard, *Richard Rogers—a Biography* (London: Faber and Faber, 1986), p. 159.

**152**   Ibid., p. 138.

**153**   Ibid., p. 163.

**154**   Ibid., p. 162.

**155**   Jean Baudrillard, *L'effet Beaubourg: implosion et dissuasion* (Paris: Galilée, 1977), pp. 22–24, cited in Rigby, *Popular Culture in Modern France*, p. 187. See also the BBC Television program "The Pompidou Centre," made for the Open University course A315, *Modern Art and Modernism*, 1982, in which Michael Baldwin (from the conceptual art group Art & Language) launched an attack on the Centre of such ferocity that the BBC prefixed screenings with a disclaimer.

**156**   Many of the Centre's designers, managers, and apologists started out in the intellectual milieu of sixties student radicalism and ended up as administrators of the pluralist cultural policies of seventies Gaullism and eighties Jack Lang socialism. Claude Mollard was well aware of the criticisms of the Centre, for which he was secretary-general, but could not find anything remotely sinister about bringing an "anti-authoritarian" architecture to a working-class district in order to make culture an everyday practice. Jacques Rigaud defended such a policy of cultural democratization, claiming that "it is not Beaubourg which has imploded, but the ideas of those who challenged Beaubourg in the name of some kind of spontaneist culture." Jacques Rigaud, "L'effet," in P. Ory, ed., *Mots de passe 1945–1985: petit abécédaire des modes de vie* (Paris: Autrement, 1985), pp. 43–44, cited in Rigby, *Popular Culture in Modern France*, p. 189.

### Chapter 2

**1**   Gilles Ivain [pseudonym of Ivan Chtcheglov], "Formulaire pour un urbanisme nouveau," 1953, reprinted in *Internationale situationniste*, no. 1 (Paris, June 1958), pp. 15–20, trans. as "Formulary for a New Urbanism," in Ken Knabb, ed., *Situationist International Anthology* (Berkeley: Bureau of Public Secrets, 1981), pp. 1–4, reprinted in Joan Ockman and Edward Eigen, eds., *Architecture Culture 1943–1968: A Documentary Anthology* (New York: Columbia Books of Architecture/Rizzoli, 1993), pp. 167–171. The "Formulary" was adopted by the LI in October 1953, yet curiously its author was expelled from the group in June 1954, accused of "mythomania, delirium of interpretation, and lack of revolutionary consciousness" (Gil J. Wolman, "A la porte," *Potlatch*, no. 2 [Paris, June 1954], unpaginated, reprinted in *Potlatch 1954–1957* [Paris: Editions Gérard Lebovici, 1985], p. 19), and the essay remained unpublished until 1958, by which time it must have been distributed privately.

**2** Guy-Ernest Debord, "Rapport sur la construction des situations et sur les conditions de l'organisation et de l'action de la tendance situationniste internationale," preparatory text for the Cosio d'Arroscia conference, July 1957, reprinted in Gerard Berreby, ed., *Documents relatifs à la fondation de l'Internationale situationniste: 1948–1957* (Paris: Editions Allia, 1985), pp. 607–619, and trans. as "Report on the Construction of Situations and on the International Situationist Tendency's Conditions of Organization and Action" (excerpts), in Knabb, *Anthology,* pp. 17–25.

**3** Brian Rigby, *Popular Culture in Modern France: A Study of Cultural Discourse* (London: Routledge, 1991), p. 20.

**4** A "unity" implied a sizable area of the city, and situationists would sometimes break it down, discussing subsidiary *zones d'ambiance.*

**5** Poète's urban geography was cited by Aldo Rossi in *L'architettura della città* (Padua: Marsilio, 1966), trans. Diane Ghirardo and Joan Ockman as *The Architecture of the City* (Cambridge, Mass.: MIT Press, 1982); see Ockman and Eigen, *Architecture Culture,* p. 392.

**6** Guy-Ernest Debord, "Introduction à une critique de la géographie urbaine," *Les lèvres nues,* no. 6 (Brussels, September 1955), reprinted in Berreby, *Documents,* pp. 288–292, and trans. as "Introduction to a Critique of Urban Geography," in Knabb, *Anthology,* pp. 5–8.

**7** Abdelhafid Khatib, "Essai de description psychogéographique des Halles," *Internationale situationniste,* no. 2 (Paris, December 1958), pp. 13–17. Khatib's survey of Halles may not have properly identified the agents of ambiance, but insofar as he plotted the main flows of the psychogeographer drifting through Halles, along its "internal runs and exterior communications," he fulfilled the situationist undertaking to "study the specific effects of the geographical environment . . . on the emotions and behavior of individuals."

**8** Michèle Bernstein, "Le Square des Missions Etrangères," *Potlatch,* no. 16 (January 1955), reprinted in *Potlatch 1954–1957,* pp. 97–98.

**9** Ibid.

**10** Ibid.

**11** See Guy-Ernest Debord, "Deux comptes rendus de dérive," appendices to "Théorie de la dérive," *Les lèvres nues,* no. 9 (Brussels, November 1956), pp. 10–13, reprinted in Berreby, *Documents,* pp. 316–319, trans. Thomas Y. Levin as "Two Accounts of the Dérive," in Elisabeth Sussman, ed., *On the Passage of a Few People through a Rather Brief Moment in Time: The Situationist International, 1957–1972* (Cambridge, Mass.: MIT Press/Institute of Contemporary Arts, Boston, 1989), pp. 135–139.

**12** The two paintings also featured in Debord's 1973 film *La société du spectacle.*

**13** Guy-Ernest Debord, "Two Accounts of the Dérive," p. 139. The Rotunda has since been restored.

**14** See, for instance, Ian Nairn, "Outrage," special number of the *Architectural Review* 117 (June 1955), reprinted in *Outrage* (London: Architectural Press, 1956).

**15** Asger Jorn, "Origine utopique de nos idées sur l'architecture," in "Forme et structure," in Asger Jorn, *Pour la forme* (Paris: Internationale situationniste, 1957), reprinted in Berreby, *Documents,* pp. 438–439.

**16** Anon., "Projet d'embellissements rationnels de la ville de Paris," *Potlatch,* no. 23 (Paris, October 1955), reprinted in *Potlatch 1954–1957,* pp. 177–180; Debord, "Deux comptes rendus de dérive."

**17** Michèle Bernstein, "Le Square des Missions Etrangères."

**18** Diana Ketcham, *Le Désert de Retz: A Late Eighteenth-Century French Folly Garden, the Artful Landscape of Monsieur de Monville* (Cambridge, Mass.: MIT Press, 1994), p. 3, citing C. H. Watelet, *Essai sur les jardins* (Paris, 1774).

**19** See Anon., "La carte forcée," *Potlatch,* no. 23 (Paris, October 1955), reprinted in *Potlatch 1954–1957,* p. 174, and anon., "Urbanisme," *Potlatch,* no. 24 (Paris, November 1955), reprinted in *Potlatch 1954–1957,* p. 181. The gardens of the Désert de Retz and Parc Monceau were created on the eve of the 1789 French Revolution.

**20**   Guy-Ernest Debord, "Exercice de la psychogéographie," *Potlatch,* no. 2 (Paris, June 1954), reprinted in *Potlatch 1954–1957,* p. 18.

**21**   Ibid. The article also cited the New York dadaist Arthur Cravan as "psychogeography in the rushed drift."

**22**   Guy-Ernest Debord, "Théorie de la dérive," *Les lèvres nues,* no. 9 (Brussels, November 1956), reprinted in *Internationale situationniste,* no. 2 (Paris, December 1958), pp. 19–23, trans. as "Theory of the Dérive," in Knabb, *Anthology,* pp. 50–54.

**23**   Ibid.

**24**   Ibid.

**25**   Ibid.

**26**   Ibid.

**27**   Lacan cited in Anthony Vidler, *The Architectural Uncanny: Essays on the Modern Unhomely* (Cambridge, Mass.: MIT Press, 1992), p. 144.

**28**   Debord, "Two Accounts of the Dérive." Even though Debord claimed that drift could be aimed either at "studying a terrain or at emotional disorientation," he straightaway admitted that it was "impossible to isolate one of them in a pure state." The assumption, though, was that pedestrians who "let go" of their habitual uses of the city would find themselves subject to a more organic, symbiotic relationship with it.

**29**   See, for instance, Debord, "Theory of the Dérive," p. 52: "The exploration of a fixed spatial field . . . presupposes the determining of bases and the calculation of directions of penetration," and so on. See also Khatib, "Essai de description psychogéographique des Halles," and Groupe de Recherche psychogéographique de l'Internationale lettriste, "Position du Continent Contrescarpe," *Les lèvres nues,* no. 9 (Brussels, November 1956), reprinted in Berreby, *Documents,* pp. 324–326—meticulous inventories of the propulsive effects upon *dérive* of certain streets.

**30**   Guy-Ernest Debord, "L'architecture et le jeu," *Potlatch,* no. 20 (Paris, May 1955), reprinted in *Potlatch 1954–1957,* pp. 137–140.

**31**   Ralph Rumney, *The Leaning Tower of Venice* (1957), published (abridged) in *ARK: The Journal of the Royal College of Art,* no. 24 (London, 1958), pp. vi–ix; Iwona Blazwick, ed., *An Endless Adventure, an Endless Passion, an Endless Banquet* (London: Institute of Contemporary Arts/Verso, 1989), pp. 45–49; and Tom Vague, ed., *Vague,* no. 22 (London, 1989), pp. 33–35. See also David Mellor, *The Sixties Art Scene in London* (London: Barbican Art Gallery/Phaidon, 1993), p. 59. Mellor proposes that the famous "Place" exhibition, coorganized by Rumney at the ICA in September 1959—where a degree of audience participation in the show was induced by a hanging that created a maze—was a retrospective invocation of situationism.

**32**   Anon., "Venise a vaincu Ralph Rumney," *Internationale situationniste,* no. 1 (Paris, June 1958), p. 28. Rumney was expelled for returning his project after the deadline set by the Situationist International in Paris; his marital commitments and the recent birth of his son were not accepted as an excuse. See Stewart Home, *The Assault on Culture: Utopian Currents from Lettrisme to Class War* (London: Aporia Press and Unpopular Books, 1988), p. 32.

**33**   Anon., "Poésie," *Potlatch,* no. 24 (Paris, November 1955), reprinted in *Potlatch 1954–1957,* p. 183. Situationists were prepared to acknowledge a less certain world. "Fixed forms . . . if they are to continue to be practicable," the LI wondered, "might be *momentary*: the verbal process of drift, the rendering of ambiance, the plan of situation."

**34**   Guy Debord and Asger Jorn, *Mémoires* (Copenhagen: Permild and Rosengreen, 1959), unpaginated.

**35**   Guy-Ernest Debord, dir., *Critique de la séparation,* 1961, reprinted in Guy-Ernest Debord, *Oeuvres cinématographiques complètes: 1952–1978* (Paris: Editions Champ Libre, 1978), trans. as "Critique of Separation," in Knabb, *Anthology,* pp. 34–37, and also cited (translation modified) in David Pindar,

"Subverting Cartography: The Situationists and Maps of the City," in *Environment and Planning A* 28 (March 1996), pp. 405–427.

**36**  Guy-Ernest Debord, dir., *Sur le passage de quelques personnes à travers une assez courte unité de temps* (1959), reprinted in Debord, *Oeuvres cinématographiques complètes*, p. 17; quoted in Thomas Y. Levin, "Dismantling the Spectacle: The Cinema of Guy Debord," in Sussman, *On the Passage of a Few People,* p. 89; Debord and Jorn, *Mémoires.* Arguably, this skepticism with the visual was consistent with the critique of spectacle. See Martin Jay, *Downcast Eyes: The Denigration of Vision in Twentieth-Century French Thought* (Berkeley: University of California Press, 1993), and a review of the book, Mark Durden, "Story of the Eye," *Art History* 18, no. 1 (March 1995), pp. 119–123. Note, however, that some situationists regarded the metaphor of trompe l'oeil as creative—Chtcheglov decided that the future situationist architecture "could be compared with trompe l'oeil Chinese and Japanese gardens." See Ivain [Chtcheglov], "Formulary for a New Urbanism," p. 2.

**37**  Anon., "Contradictions de l'activité lettriste-internationaliste," *Potlatch,* no. 25 (Paris, January 1956), reprinted in *Potlatch 1954–1957,* pp. 197–199.

**38**  Anon., "La frontière situationniste," *Internationale situationniste,* no. 5 (Paris, December 1960), pp. 7–9.

**39**  Debord and Jorn, *Mémoires.*

**40**  Guy-Ernest Debord, "Exercice de la psychogéographie," *Potlatch,* no. 2 (Paris, June 1954), reprinted in *Potlatch 1954–1957,* p. 18.

**41**  Quoted in Sadie Plant, *The Most Radical Gesture: The Situationist International in a Postmodern Age* (London: Routledge, 1992), p. 103, citing Walter Lewino, *L'imagination au pouvoir* (Paris: Le Terrain Vague, 1968).

**42**  Ivan Chtcheglov, "Lettres de loin," *Internationale situationniste,* no. 9 (Paris, August 1964), pp. 38–40, trans. as "Letters from Afar," in Knabb, *Anthology,* p. 372, note 53.

**43**  See Home, *Assault on Culture,* p. 34.

**44**  The matter-of-fact style adopted by many situationist reports seemingly emulated the official tone of the *Rapports* (Reports) put out by the planners of the Conseil Municipal.

**45**  Michel de Certeau, *The Practice of Everyday Life*, trans. Steven Rendall (Berkeley: University of California Press, 1984), pp. 36–37.

**46**  Ibid.; Karl von Clausewitz, *On War*, trans. M. Howard and P. Paret (Princeton: Princeton University Press, 1976), n.p., cited in Thomas F. McDonough, "Situationist Space," *October,* no. 67 (Winter 1994), note 45.

**47**  Debord, "Report on the Construction of Situations," p. 29.

**48**  The prospectus for the "First Exposition of Psychogeography," held at the Galerie Taptoe, Brussels, in February 1957, promised three "Plans psychogéographiques de Paris," tantalizingly entitled *Paris sous la neige (Relevé des principaux courants psychogéographiques de Paris), Axe d'exploration et échec dans la recherche d'un Grand Passage situationniste,* and *The Most Dangerous Game (Pistes psychogéographiques, vraies ou fausses).* According to Roberto Ohrt, Debord's plans were not exhibited.

**49**  Jacques Gomboust, quoted in L. Marin, *Portrait of a King* (Minneapolis: University of Minnesota Press, 1988), p. 170, and cited in Pindar, "Subverting Cartography," p. 407.

**50**  Anon., "Eloge en prose détournée," *Potlatch,* no. 26 (Paris, May 1956), reprinted in *Potlatch 1954–1957,* pp. 202–203.

**51**  *The Naked City* (1948), screenplay by Albert Maltz and Malvin Wald, cited in M. Christine Boyer, "Twice-Told Stories: The Double Erasure of Times Square," in Iain Borden, Joe Kerr, Alicia Pivaro, and Jane Rendell, eds., *Strangely Familiar: Narratives of Architecture in the City* (London: Routledge, 1996), pp. 77–81.

**52**  The sort of "cognitive mapping" represented by situationism has since been adopted enthusiastically by postmodern geography, attracted by the way it overthrows traditional cartography's pretensions to objectivity. See, for instance, Fredric Jameson, *Postmodernism, or, the Cultural Logic of*

*Late Capitalism* (London: Verso, 1991), and the discussion in McDonough, "Situationist Space." For further discussions of situationist mapping in the context of cartography and urbanism generally, see Daniel Soutif, *Topes et tropes, le plan de ville et la référence*, in Centre Pompidou, *La ville: art et architecture en Europe, 1870–1993* (Paris: Editions du Centre Pompidou, 1994), pp. 392–394; Jean-Hubert Martin, *Dérvives, Itinéraires surréalistes, dérive et autres parcours*, in Centre Pompidou, *Cartes et figures de la terre* (Paris: Editions du Centre Pompidou, 1980), pp. 197–202; and Christel Hollevoet, *Wandering in the City,* Flânerie *to* Dérive *and After: The Cognitive Mapping of Urban Space*, in Whitney Museum of American Art, *The Power of the City: The City of Power* (New York: Whitney Museum of American Art, 1992), pp. 25–55.

**53**  Debord, "Theory of the Dérive," p. 53.

**54**  The *Guide psychogéographique* is based upon the *Plan Blondel Paris et banlieue*, verso: *Plan de Paris à vol d'oiseau*, drawn by G. Peltier (Paris: Blondel la Rougery, 1956). The map comes with a booklet, and p. 7, ironically, lists "Les Spectacles." *The Naked City* accords with the *Guide Taride par arrondissement* (Paris: Taride, 1951). McDonough, "Situationist Space," incorrectly gives the Blondel *Plan de Paris* as the source of *The Naked City*.

**55**  Debord, "Theory of the Dérive," p. 53.

**56**  Ibid., p. 50.

**57**  See Paul-Henri Chombart de Lauwe, "Introduction à l'étude de l'espace social dans un arrondissement et un secteur de Paris . . . ," *Paris et l'agglomération parisienne*, vol. 1 (Paris: Presses Universitaires de France, 1952), pp. 130–131. The map is discussed in McDonough, "Situationist Space," p. 67.

**58**  For Chombart de Lauwe the *quartier* was "a group of streets, or even of houses, with more or less clearly defined borders, including a commercial center of variable size and, usually, other sorts of points of attraction. The borders of a neighborhood are usually marginal (dangerous) frontier areas." Chombart de Lauwe, *Paris et l'agglomération parisienne*, p. 67, cited in McDonough, "Situationist Space," p. 67.

**59**  Khatib, "Essai de description psychogéographique des Halles," p. 13.

**60**  Anon., "L'urbanisme unitaire à la fin des années 50," *Internationale situationniste,* no. 3 (Paris, December 1959), pp. 11–16, trans. Thomas Y. Levin as "Unitary Urbanism at the End of the 1950s," in Sussman, *On the Passage of a Few People,* pp. 143–147. For discussion of the *Carte de pays de Tendre,* see Claude Filteau, "Tendre," in Centre Pompidou, *Cartes et figures de la terre,* pp. 205–207. The *Carte* was created in 1653 and was published in 1654 in Madeleine de Scudéry's *Clélie: histoire romaine* (Geneva: Slatkine Reprints, 1973). The map of Feeling had been produced by the "Précieux," members of the salon of Madame de Scudéry, and in the formation of the practice of *dérive* the LI had been alert to "the capital contribution of *préciosité*" in validating "conversation and promenade as privileged activities." See Guy-Ernest Debord and Gil J. Wolman, "Pourquoi le lettrisme?," *Potlatch,* no. 22 (Paris, September 1955), reprinted in *Potlatch 1954–1957,* pp. 152–163. The fragmented situationist maps eschewed any master reading in favor of a "conversational" series of pleasing "comings-together." Similarly, the map of Feeling did not attempt to reconcile *précieux* debate but to show it as dialogical, a demonstration of the art of pleasing which took feminine conversation as a model. See also McDonough, "Situationist Space," pp. 60–61.

**61**  See André Breton, *Nadja* (Paris: Editions Gallimard, 1928, trans. New York: Grove Press, 1960).

**62**  See Debord, "Introduction to a Critique of Urban Geography," p. 7.

**63**  Debord, "Theory of the Dérive," p. 52.

**64**  Thomas De Quincey, *Confessions of an English Opium-Eater,* ed. Grevel Lindop (Oxford: Oxford University Press, 1985), pp. 47–48.

**65**   Guy-Ernest Debord and Asger Jorn, *The Naked City,* 1957, verso, bound into Jorn, *Pour la forme.*

**66**   Compare, for instance, the guides to the 1951 Festival of Britain, covered in little arrows which recommended, but did not dictate (for Britain is a free country, as the accompanying text reminded the visitor), certain routes through the Festival pavilions.

**67**   Debord, "Theory of the Dérive," pp. 50, 53.

**68**   Khatib, "Essai de description psychogéographique des Halles," p. 17.

**69**   Debord, "Theory of the Dérive," p. 53. There seems to have been a determination between the making of the *Guide psychogéographique* and that of *The Naked City* to institute a psychogeographic economy and simplify the maps: for instance, the area alongside the Jardin des Plantes and the Place Jusseau was trimmed. Areas like this had originally been included as "frontier zones," distinct from the *unité* but necessary to it and providing bridges to other *unités.* See Groupe de Recherche psychogéographique de l'Internationale lettriste, "Position du Continent Contrescarpe."

**70**   See, for instance, anon., "Urbanisme," *Potlatch,* no. 24 (Paris, November 1955), n.p., reprinted in *Potlatch 1954–1957,* p. 181, which suggests that the inclusion of the area around Rue de la Butte-aux-Cailles in the 13th Arrondissement might have greatly increased the surprisingly compact area covered by Debord and Jorn's maps.

**71**   Anon., "On détruit la rue Sauvage," *Potlatch,* no. 7 (Paris, August 1954), reprinted in *Potlatch 1954–1957,* p. 49.

**72**   Anon., "La forme d'une ville change plus vite . . . ," *Potlatch,* no. 25 (Paris, January 1956), reprinted in *Potlatch 1954–1957,* p. 196, cf. Groupe de Recherche psychogéographique de l'Internationale lettriste, "Position du Continent Contrescarpe."

**73**   On the right flank of *The Naked City* the Gare de Lyon and Place de la Bastille were kneaded into a smooth line by rotating the Arsenal chunk through forty-five degrees and totally suppressing a gap of almost a kilometer.

**74**   Debord, "Introduction to a Critique of Urban Geography," pp. 6–7.

**75**   Ibid.; Debord, "Theory of the Dérive," p. 50.

**76**   Guy-Ernest Debord and Gil J. Wolman, "Mode d'emploi du détournement," *Les lèvres nues,* no. 8 (Brussels, 1956), reprinted in Berreby, *Documents,* pp. 302–309, trans. as "Methods of Détournement," in Knabb, *Anthology,* pp. 8–14. The abandonment of the pinball machine project, which was conceived as a "metagraphic-spatial composition," was due to a lack of funds, the article claimed.

**77**   Debord and Jorn, *Mémoires.* The page in question features maps of Panthéon, Val de Grâce, etc.

**78**   The so-called Continent Contrescarpe around its headquarters survived, the LI observed, thanks to its relative isolation from the great arteries of Paris, and they lamented its steady encroachment through the opening of the Rue Calvin and the efforts to "populate" the area. See Groupe de Recherche psychogéographique de l'Internationale lettriste, "Position du Continent Contrescarpe."

**79**   One senses this rhythm, for instance, as one enters and exits the Jardin de Luxembourg as directed by *The Naked City,* descending through the northern area, a traditional site of promenade, to the southern stretches, often curiously deserted. The so-called Continent Contrescarpe, meanwhile, was divided by the LI into two subzones: the more chaotic one east of the Rue Mouffetard, and the western one designated as "desert." See Debord and Jorn, *Guide psychgéographique de Paris,* and Groupe de Recherche psychogéographique de l'Internationale lettriste, "Position du Continent Contrescarpe."

**80**   Debord, "Introduction to a Critique of Urban Geography," p. 7.

**81**   Debord, "Two Accounts of the Dérive," p. 138.

**82**   Anon., "Ne travaillez jamais," *Internationale situationniste,* no. 8 (Paris, January 1963), p. 42; Reyner Banham,

"City as Scrambled Egg," *Cambridge Opinion*, no. 17, "Living With the 60s" issue (Cambridge, 1959), pp. 18–23; Reclus cited and translated in Kristin Ross, *The Emergence of Social Space: Rimbaud and the Paris Commune* (Basingstoke: Macmillan, 1988), p. 19.

**83**   See, for instance, Debord, *Sur le passage de quelques personnes à travers une assez courte unité de temps.*

**84**   See Ross, *The Emergence of Social Space*, p. 85.

**85**   Elisée Reclus cited in ibid., pp. 90–91.

**86**   Henri Lefebvre, *The Production of Space*, trans. D. Nicholson-Smith (Oxford: Blackwell, 1991), pp. 355–356, and cited in McDonough, "Situationist Space," p. 65.

**87**   Elisée Reclus, *L'homme et la terre*, vol. 1 (n.d.; reprinted Paris, 1982), p. 71, cited in Ross, *The Emergence of Social Space*, p. 101.

**88**   Anon., "Définitions," *Internationale situationniste*, no. 1 (Paris, June 1958), pp. 13–14, trans. as "Definitions," in Knabb, *Anthology*, pp. 45–46.

**89**   Ross, *The Emergence of Social Space*, p. 54. Anthony Vidler draws on Ross's work and on the example of the situationists to illuminate the meaning of John Hejduk's "Vagabond Architecture": "Vagabonds . . . were guilty of no crime but that of vagabondage; *potential* criminals, outside the law not for a crime committed but for what might be committed in the future as the product of a wayward life. [Vagabonds] construct 'situations' from the part-random, part-preconceived intersection of objects and subjects, insistent provocateurs of the urban unconscious." Anthony Vidler, *The Architectural Uncanny*, p. 210.

**90**   Chtcheglov, "Lettres de loin."

**91**   Debord, "Theory of the Dérive," pp. 51–52.

**92**   Ivain [Chtcheglov], "Formulary for a New Urbanism," p. 4.

**93**   "One can drift alone," Debord felt, "but all indications are that the most fruitful numerical arrangement consists of several small groups of two or three people who have reached the same awakening of consciousness, since the cross-checking of these different groups' impressions makes it possible to arrive at objective conclusions. . . . In any case it is impossible for there to be more than ten or twelve people without the drift fragmenting into several simultaneous drifts." Debord, "Theory of the Dérive," p. 51. For evidence of drifts being conducted in this way, see anon., "Die Welt als Labyrinth," *Internationale situationniste,* no. 6 (Paris, June 1960), pp. 5–12.

**94**   Debord, "Theory of the Dérive," p. 53.

**95**   Ibid.

**96**   Ibid., p. 50, discussing Chombart de Lauwe, *Paris et l'agglomération parisienne*, p. 106.

**97**   Debord, "Theory of the Dérive," p. 50; cf. Charles Baudelaire, "The Salon of 1846: On the Heroism of Modern Life," trans. in J. Mayne, *Art in Paris* (London: Phaidon, 1965), pp. 116–120, reprinted in Francis Frascina and Charles Harrison, eds., *Modern Art and Modernism: A Critical Anthology* (London: Harper and Row, 1982), pp. 17–18.

**98**   De Quincey, *Confessions of an English Opium-Eater*, pp. 47–48.

**99**   See, for instance, "Shy Neighbourhoods," "Night Walks," and "Some Recollections of Mortality," reprinted in Charles Dickens, *The Uncommercial Traveller*, ed. Peter Ackroyd (London: Mandarin, 1991); and Charles Baudelaire, "The Salon of 1846: On the Heroism of Modern Life."

**100**   Walter Benjamin, *Charles Baudelaire: A Lyric Poet in the Era of High Capitalism*, trans. Harry Zohn (London: New Left Books, 1973, reprinted London: Verso, 1983), p. 69, also cited in Home, *Assault on Culture*, p. 21. For a useful summary of Benjamin's work on the city, see Christoph Asendorf, "Walter Benjamin and the Utopia of the 'New Architecture,'" in Jeannine Fiedler, ed., *Social Utopias of the Twenties: Bauhaus, Kibbutz and the Dream of the New Man* (Wuppertal: Müller and Busmann Press, 1995), pp. 23–29.

**101**   Aragon bemoaned "the great American passion for city planning, imported into Paris by a prefect of police during the

Second Empire and now being applied to the task of redrawing the map of capital in straight lines" (Louis Aragon, *Paris Peasant,* trans. Simon Watson-Taylor [London: Pan, 1978], p. 28).

**102** Ivain [Chtcheglov], "Formulary for a New Urbanism," p. 1.

**103** Greil Marcus, *Lipstick Traces: A Secret History of the Twentieth Century* (London: Secker and Warburg, 1989), p. 253.

**104** Internationale lettriste, "Réponse a une enquête du groupe surréaliste belge," *Potlatch,* no. 5 (Paris, July 1954), reprinted in *Potlatch 1954–1957,* pp. 37–38.

**105** For an exceptional visual record of the Left Bank in the 1950s, see Ed van der Elsken, *Love on the Left Bank* (London: André Deutsch, 1957).

**106** Social semiotics did not generally reemerge until the 1970s.

**107** Notably V. N. Vološinov and Mikhail Bakhtin.

**108** See V. N. Vološinov (Mikhail Bakhtin?), extract from *Marxism and the Philosophy of Language,* 1929, trans. Ladislaw Matejka and I. R. Titunik, reprinted in Charles Harrison and Paul Wood, eds., *Art in Theory 1900–1990: An Anthology of Changing Ideas* (Oxford: Blackwell, 1992), pp. 467–474.

**109** Internationale lettriste, "Les gratte-ciel par la racine," *Potlatch,* no. 5 (Paris, July 1954), reprinted in *Potlatch 1954–1957,* pp. 34–36.

**110** Anon., "Du rôle de l'écriture," *Potlatch,* no. 23 (Paris, October 1955), reprinted in *Potlatch 1954–1957,* pp. 176–177.

**111** A photograph published in *Cobra,* without supporting text and almost emblematic of the powerful creative potential of humans working upon their environment, showed "Constant at work," carving playful figures into a wall. See *Cobra,* no. 4 (Brussels, 1948).

**112** Constant, "Reflex Manifesto," *Reflex* (Amsterdam, 1948), trans. Leonard Bright in Willemijn Stokvis, *Cobra* (New York: Rizzoli, 1988), pp. 29–31. Asger Jorn advocated the study of "vandalism" through history, founding the so-called

"Institute of Comparative Vandalism" for the documentation of Viking art.

**113** Raoul Vaneigem, "Commentaires contre l'urbanisme," *Internationale situationniste,* no. 6 (Paris, 1961), pp. 33–37.

**114** Anon., "Du rôle de l'écriture."

**115** See Gil J. Wolman, "Vous prenez la première rue," in *Potlatch,* no. 9–10–11 (Paris, August 1954), reprinted in *Potlatch 1954–1957,* p. 58.

**116** Debord, "Critique of Separation," p. 35.

**117** See Bernstein, "Le Square des Missions Etrangères."

**118** See Khatib, "Essai de description psychogéographique des Halles."

**119** Interview with Alexander Trocchi, cited in Marcus, *Lipstick Traces,* p. 388.

**120** Chtcheglov, "Letters from Afar."

**121** Benjamin, *Charles Baudelaire,* p. 69.

**122** See Gaston Bachelard, *La dialectique de la durée* (Paris: Presses Universitaires de France, 1950, reprinted 1993), cited in Eleonore Kofman and Elizabeth Lebas, introduction to Henri Lefebvre, *Writings on Cities,* ed. and trans. Eleonore Kofman and Elizabeth Lebas (Oxford: Blackwell, 1996), pp. 28–29. Bachelard's philosophy of the poetics of space and time was also a definite influence upon the thought of the COBRA group.

**123** See de Certeau, *The Practice of Everyday Life,* p. 97. In "Part III: Spatial Practices" of this book, first published in 1974, de Certeau fully theorized the analogy between language and city living—"the act of walking," he claimed, "is to the urban system what the speech act is to language" (ibid.). De Certeau's ability to vastly expand upon and make explicit what was only inferred in situationism has helped make him preeminent in academic discussions of everyday life and the city. The tender, almost poetic tone of this former Jesuit is perhaps more palatable to academe, as well, than the belligerent class-consciousness of situationism. For the reasoning behind this "depoliticization" of urban ethnography, see Rigby, *Popular Culture in Modern France.*

**124**   See Frances A. Yates, *The Art of Memory* (London: Routledge, 1966).

**125**   Anon., "Unitary Urbanism at the End of the 1950s," p. 144.

**126**   Anon., "Projet d'embellissements rationnels de la ville de Paris," *Potlatch,* no. 23 (Paris, October 1955), reprinted in *Potlatch 1954–1957*, pp. 177–180, and part translated by Adam Cornford in Marcus, *Lipstick Traces,* pp. 410–412.

**127**   Ibid.

**128**   Anon., "Unitary Urbanism at the End of the 1950s," p. 144.

**129**   Anon., "En attendant la fermature des églises," *Potlatch,* no. 9–10–11 (Paris, August 1954), reprinted in *Potlatch 1954–1957*, p. 61. Christian place names survived the Revolutionary calendar change of 1793 that had tried to end the convention of drawing upon ecclesiastical denomination.

**130**   Anon., "Projet d'embellissements rationnels de la ville de Paris," p. 179.

**131**   Ibid., p. 178.

**132**   Ibid.

**133**   Theses 177–178, in Debord, *La société du spectacle.*

**134**   Ivain [Chtcheglov], "Formulary for a New Urbanism," p. 3. De Chirico became an architectural exemplar again in the work of Aldo Rossi. Had the situationists emphasized the *timelessness* of the city, rather than subversively stressing its "timefullness"—its propensity to *change* through time—they might have anticipated Rossi's hugely influential "postmodern" quest, launched in his 1966 book *The Architecture of the City*, for architectures and places that embody the collective memory of the city in ways that "naive functionalism" never could (see Rossi, *L'architettura della città*, passim, cited in Ockman and Eigen, *Architecture Culture,* p. 392).

**135**   Khatib, "Essai de description psychogéographique des Halles," p. 16; anon., "On détruit la rue Sauvage."

**136**   Debord, "Introduction à une critique de la géographie urbaine," trans. Thomas Y. Levin, as quoted in Sussman, *On the Passage of a Few People,* p. 139, footnote 3.

**137**   Debord, "Introduction to a Critique of Urban Geography," p. 7.

**138**   Khatib, "Essai de description psychogéographique des Halles," p. 17.

### Chapter 3

**1**   Guy-Ernest Debord, "Rapport sur la construction des situations et sur les conditions de l'organisation et de l'action de la tendance situationniste internationale," preparatory text for the Cosio d'Arroscia conference, July 1957, reprinted in Gerard Berreby, ed., *Documents relatifs à la fondation de l'Internationale situationniste: 1948–1957* (Paris: Editions Allia, 1985), pp. 607–619, and trans. as "Report on the Construction of Situations and on the International Situationist Tendency's Conditions of Organization and Action" (excerpts), in Ken Knabb, ed., *Situationist International Anthology* (Berkeley: Bureau of Public Secrets, 1981), pp. 17–25.

**2**   See Henri Lefebvre, *La proclamation de la Commune* (Paris: Gallimard, 1965).

**3**   Note that the architectural term "plan de situation" is routinely used on French building plans.

**4**   See Internationale lettriste, ". . . Une idée neuve en Europe," *Potlatch,* no. 7 (Paris, August 1954), and "La ligne générale," *Potlatch,* no. 14 (Paris, November 1954), both reprinted in *Potlatch 1954–1957* (Paris: Editions Gérard

Lebovici, 1985), pp. 45–46, 76–77; and anon., "Problèmes préliminaires à la construction d'une situation," *Internationale situationniste,* no. 1 (Paris, June 1958), pp. 11–13, trans. as "Preliminary Problems in Constructing a Situation," in Knabb, *Anthology,* pp. 43–45.

**5**   Debord, "Rapport sur la construction des situations."

**6**   Debord, "Report on the Construction of Situations," p. 25.

**7**   Cited in Rose-Lee Goldberg, *Performance Art* (London: Thames and Hudson, 1992), p. 16.

**8**   Anon., "Preliminary Problems in Constructing a Situation," p. 44; Guy-Ernest Debord and Gil J. Wolman, "Pourquoi le lettrisme?," *Potlatch,* no. 22 (Paris, September 1955), reprinted in *Potlatch 1954–1957,* pp. 152–163.

**9**   William Shakespeare, *As You Like It,* II.vii.139; Internationale lettriste, ". . . Une idée neuve en Europe."

**10**   Debord, "Report on the Construction of Situations," p. 25. Note, however, that the situationists struggled to reconcile their avant-garde role with their avowedly anti- avant-garde stance. "If we imagine a particular situation project in which, for example, a research team has arranged an emotionally moving gathering . . . we would no doubt have to distinguish: a director or producer responsible for co-ordinating the basic elements necessary. . . . This relation between the director and the 'livers' of the situation must naturally never become a permanent specialization" (anon., "Preliminary Problems in Constructing a Situation," p. 44).

**11**   Anon., "L'avant-garde de la présence," *Internationale situationniste,* no. 8 (Paris, January 1963), pp. 14–22, trans. as "The Avant-Garde of Presence" (excerpts), in Knabb, *Anthology,* pp. 109–110. The SI's attitude belied the fact that precedents and parallels for the constructed situation had existed in the United States since the activities at Black Mountain College; while in Britain from 1954, the artist John Latham was concerned with the "Eventstructure," i.e., "the structuring of events in time rather than the making of objects." See "Eventstructure," in John A. Walker, *Glossary of Art, Architecture and Design since 1945* (London: Clive Bingley, 1973), p. 88.

**12**   Internationale lettriste, "Réponse à une enquête du groupe surréaliste belge," *Potlatch,* no. 5 (Paris, July 1954), reprinted in *Potlatch 1954–1957,* pp. 37–38. In subsequent editions of *Potlatch* (nos. 6, 14, 25) and *Internationale situationniste* this "fundamentalist" position—that art was to be lived rather than made—was reiterated, even as the divisive theoretical and artistic problems of the constructed situation took hold.

**13**   The party was suggested in the first edition of *Potlatch* as the focus for "the psychogeographic game of the week," and again in Debord's "Report on the Construction of Situations." Readers were asked to relate the results of their situation-party to the editors of *Potlatch.* See anon., "Le jeu psychogéographique de la semaine," *Potlatch,* no. 1 (Paris, June 1954), reprinted in *Potlatch 1954–1957,* p. 14; and Debord, "Report on the Construction of Situations."

**14**   Guy-Ernest Debord, "Introduction à une critique de la géographie urbaine," *Les lèvres nues,* no. 6 (Brussels, 1955), reprinted in Berreby, *Documents,* pp. 287–292, trans. as "Introduction to a Critique of Urban Geography," in Knabb, *Anthology,* pp. 5–8.

**15**   See Mark Francis, "It's All Over: The Material (and Anti-Material) Evidence," in Elisabeth Sussman, ed., *On the Passage of a Few People through a Rather Brief Moment in Time: The Situationist International, 1957–1972* (Cambridge, Mass.: MIT Press/Institute of Contemporary Arts, Boston, 1989), pp. 16–19.

**16**   Constant, "Demain la poésie logera la vie" (1956), reprinted in Berreby, *Documents,* pp. 595–596.

**17**   Debord, "Report on the Construction of Situations," p. 23.

**18**   Anon., "Rédaction de nuit," *Potlatch,* no. 20 (Paris, July 1955), reprinted in *Potlatch 1954–1957,* p. 137.

**19**   Guy Debord and Asger Jorn, *Mémoires* (Copenhagen: Permild and Rosengreen, 1959), unpaginated. The suggestion was repeated by Raoul Vaneigem in "Commentaires contre l'urbanisme," *Internationale situationniste*, no. 6 (Paris, August 1961), pp. 33–37.

**20** Anon., "Prochaine planète," *Potlatch,* no. 4 (Paris, July 1954), reprinted in *Potlatch 1954–1957*, p. 30; Debord and Jorn, *Mémoires.*

**21** Louis Carrogis (Carmontelle), prospectus to the Jardin de Monceau, p. 2, cited in Diana Ketcham, *Le Désert de Retz: A Late Eighteenth-Century French Folly Garden, the Artful Landscape of Monsieur de Monville* (Cambridge, Mass.: MIT Press, 1994), p. 1.

**22** Guy Debord and Gil J. Wolman, "Mode d'emploi du détournement," *Les lèvres nues,* no. 8 (Brussels, 1956), reprinted in Berreby, *Documents,* pp. 302–309, trans. as "Methods of Détournement," in Knabb, *Anthology,* pp. 8–14.

**23** Ibid.

**24** Gilles Ivain [pseudonym of Ivan Chtcheglov], "Formulaire pour un urbanisme nouveau" (1953), reprinted in *Internationale situationniste*, no. 1 (Paris, June 1958), pp. 15–20, trans. as "Formulary for a New Urbanism," in Knabb, *Anthology,* pp. 1–4.

**25** André Breton, "Sur certaines possibilités d'embellissement irrationnel d'une ville," *Le surréalisme au service de la révolution,* no. 6 (Paris, May 1933), p. 18, cited in Greil Marcus, *Lipstick Traces: A Secret History of the Twentieth Century* (London: Secker and Warburg, 1989), p. 410.

**26** Anon., "Projet d'embellissements rationnels de la ville de Paris," *Potlatch,* no. 23 (Paris, October 1955), reprinted in *Potlatch 1954–1957*, pp. 177–180, part translated by Adam Crawford in Marcus, *Lipstick Traces,* pp. 410–411.

**27** Ibid.

**28** Debord and Wolman, "Methods of Détournement," p. 13.

**29** Anon., "Prochaine planète." This was, apparently, the first publication of the LI's concept of *détournement.*

**30** See Sussman, *On the Passage of a Few People,* footnote 2, p. 175, and Troels Andersen, "Asger Jorn and the Situationist International," in ibid., pp. 62–66. Cf. André Breton, *Les vases communicants* (Paris: Gallimard, 1955), p. 163.

**31** Guy-Ernest Debord, "De l'architecture sauvage," in Asger Jorn, *Le jardin d'Albisola* (Turin: Pozzo, 1974), trans. Thomas Y. Levin as "On Wild Architecture," in Sussman, *On the Passage of a Few People,* pp. 174–175.

**32** Ibid.

**33** Guy-Ernest Debord, "L'architecture et le jeu," *Potlatch,* no. 20 (Paris, May 1955), reprinted in *Potlatch 1954–1957,* pp. 137–140.

**34** Michael Petzet, "Ludwig and the Arts," in Wilfred Blunt, *The Dream King* (London: Hamilton, 1970), p. 234.

**35** Anon., "Prochaine planète."

**36** Ivain [Chtcheglov], "Formulary for a New Urbanism," p. 2. Gil J. Wolman also referred to the idea of a baroque intermediary stage in the development of situationist architecture: see "Intervention de Wolman, délégué de l'Internationale lettriste, au congrès d'Alba en septembre 1956," reprinted in Berreby, *Documents,* pp. 596–598, trans. Sabine Wolf.

**37** Constant may have been inspired as well by Maria Elena Vieira da Silva's depictions of infinite space. My thanks to Frank Clark for drawing my attention to Vieira da Silva's work, an example of which Constant would have been able to view at the Musée Nationale d'Art Moderne. The literary heritage of sublime meditation was important, too, from De Quincey to Jorge Luis Borges, whose *Labyrinths* was translated into French in 1951.

**38** Anon., "Décoration," *Potlatch,* no. 24 (Paris, November 1955), reprinted in *Potlatch 1954–1957*, pp. 183–184.

**39** Ivain [Chtcheglov], "Formulary for a New Urbanism," pp. 1–2.

**40** Ibid., p. 4. Chtcheglov's concerns were comparable to those of Michel Colle writing in *Cobra* a few years earlier. See Michel Colle, "Vers une architecture symbolique," *Cobra,* no 1 (Brussels, 1948), pp. 21–23.

**41** See Jacques Fillon, "Tout ordre neuf," *Potlatch,* no. 17 (Paris, February 1955), reprinted in *Potlatch 1954–1957,* pp. 103–105. Such experiments were in fact classed as *métagraphie* (a proposed unification of all forms of signification), a type of *détournement.*

**42** Anon., "Le détournement comme négation et comme prélude," *Internationale situationniste,* no. 3 (Paris, December 1959), pp. 10–11, trans. as "Détournement as Negation and Prelude," in Knabb, *Anthology,* pp. 55–56.

**43** Cf. Marcel Duchamp's obstructive use of twine at the 1942 surrealist exhibition in New York.

**44** Anon., "Die Welt als Labyrinth," in *Internationale situationniste,* no. 4 (Paris, June 1960), pp. 5–7. The Stedelijk labyrinth was designed by the Dutch section of the SI, most likely by Constant in particular (who, although "assisted on some points by Debord, Jorn, Wyckaert and Zimmer," was rapidly becoming a rather lonely protagonist of situationist architecture). Wyckaert's *pallisades détournées* might be related to Raymond Hains's *La palissade des emplacements réservés,* among the *nouveau réaliste* works that created a sensation at the 1959 Paris Biennale. See Alfred Pacquement, "The Nouveaux Réalistes," in Marco Livingstone, ed., *Pop Art* (London: Royal Academy of Arts/Weidenfeld and Nicolson, 1991), pp. 214–218.

**45** Anon., "Die Welt als Labyrinth."

**46** Ibid., p. 6.

**47** Ibid., pp. 6–7.

**48** Ibid., p. 7.

**49** Constant, Debord, and Jorn for the SI, letter to Willem Sandberg, Director of the Stedelijk Museum, Amsterdam, 7 March 1960, in the archives of the Stedelijk Museum, Amsterdam.

**50** Anon., "Die Welt als Labyrinth," p. 7.

**51** See, for instance, the LI's struggles with Georges-Maries Dutilleul in early 1955 (exhaustively reported by *Potlatch*) and with the Milan Triennale in 1957. With the space reserved by the Stedelijk now vacant, Pinot-Gallizio leapt at the chance to show his own paintings, for which he was promptly expelled from the SI's ranks.

**52** Following the claims made in *Internationale situationniste,* no. 4, Sandberg took issue with Jorn over the reasons for the cancellation of the Stedelijk exhibition. It was enough, Sandberg felt, that he was prepared to put the resources of the museum at the disposal of the Situationist International; to further meet the group's demand for 15,000 Dutch guilders (approximately 69,000 guilders, or 13,000 U.S. dollars/22,000 pounds sterling, in today's money) toward the construction of the installation was out of the question. See Willem Sandberg's letter to Asger Jorn, 29 July 1960, Situationist file, Stedelijk Museum Archive. Pressure to cancel the exhibition seems mainly to have come from Debord. My thanks to Paul Kempers at the Stedelijk Museum for archival research, and to Rein Kroes at the Centraal Bureau voor de Statistiek for statistical research.

**53** Anon., "Urbanisme unitaire à la fin des années 50," *Internationale situationniste,* no. 3 (December 1959), pp. 11–16, trans. Thomas Y. Levin as "Unitary Urbanism at the End of the 1950s," in Sussman, *On the Passage of a Few People,* pp. 143–147.

**54** Ivain [Chtcheglov], "Formulary for a New Urbanism," p. 1.

**55** Internationale lettriste, "Manifestate a favore dell'urbanismo unitario" (1956), reprinted in Mirella Bandini, ed., *L'estetico il politico: da Cobra all'Internazionale situazionista, 1948–57* (Rome: Officina Edizioni, 1977), p. 275.

**56** Introduction to the German Democratic Republic's "Sixteen Principles for the Restructuring of Cities," 1950, in Joan Ockman and Edward Eigen, eds., *Architecture Culture 1943–1968: A Documentary Anthology* (New York: Columbia Books of Architecture/Rizzoli, 1993), pp. 125–126.

**57** See Reyner Banham, "City as Scrambled Egg," *Cambridge Opinion,* no. 17, "Living With the 60s" issue (Cambridge, 1959), pp. 18–23.

**58**   Ockman and Eigen, introduction to "Sixteen Principles for the Restructuring of Cities."

**59**   See Hanno-Walter Kruft, *A History of Architectural Theory, from Vitruvius to the Present* (London: Zwemmer/Princeton Architectural Press, 1994), p. 286; and Roberto Ohrt, *Phantom Avantgarde: eine Geschichte der Situationistischen International und der modernen Kunst* (Hamburg: Editions Nautilus/Galerie van der Loo, 1990).

**60**   Walter Benjamin, *Charles Baudelaire: A Lyric Poet in the Era of High Capitalism*, trans. Harry Zohn (London: New Left Books, 1973, reprinted London: Verso, 1983), p. 160.

**61**   Debord, "Report on the Construction of Situations," p. 23.

**62**   In "Vers une architecture symbolique," COBRA's Michel Colle had asserted the need for a "unitary" quality in city design. Colle worried that because art is "carved out in slices, perceptions are thus made in a more and more analytical way." He went on, "The edifice itself is not moreover an 'art object' in a 'city museum,' it must compose itself with others, integrate itself in the landscape in order to form the synthesis of 'city.'" Cf. the findings of CIAM 8 at Hoddesdon, England, 1951, summarized in E. N. Rogers, J. L. Sert, and J. Tyrwhitt, eds., *The Heart of the City: Towards the Humanisation of Urban Life* (New York: Pelligrini and Cudahy, 1952).

**63**   Debord, "Report on the Construction of Situations," pp. 22–23.

**64**   Ibid.

**65**   Asger Jorn, in *Helhesten*, no. 2, cited by Jean-Clarence Lambert, *COBRA* (New York: Abbeville Press, 1985), pp. 36–37.

**66**   Ivain [Chtcheglov], "Formulary for a New Urbanism," p. 1.

**67**   For more on the impact of fragments upon the architectural imagination, see Anthony Vidler, *The Architectural Uncanny: Essays on the Modern Unhomely* (Cambridge, Mass.: MIT Press, 1992).

**68**   "Whoever knows how to design a park well will have no difficulty in tracing the plan for the building of a city according to its given area and situation. . . . There must be regularity and fantasy, relationships and oppositions, and casual, unexpected elements that vary the scene; great order in the details, confusion, uproar, and tumult in the whole." M. A. Laugier, *Observations sur l'architecture* (The Hague, 1765), pp. 312–313, quoted in Manfredo Tafuri, *Architecture and Utopia: Design and Capitalist Development* (Cambridge, Mass.: MIT Press, 1976), p. 4.

**69**   Debord, "Report on the Construction of Situations," p. 23.

**70**   Ivain [Chtcheglov], "Formulary for a New Urbanism," p. 4.

**71**   Debord, "Unitary Urbanism at the End of the 1950s," p. 144.

**72**   Ivain [Chtcheglov], "Formulary for a New Urbanism," p. 1; see Constant, "Demain la poésie logera la vie."

**73**   Debord, "Report on the Construction of Situations," p. 23.

**74**   Constant and Guy-Ernest Debord, "La Déclaration d'Amsterdam," *Internationale situationniste,* no. 2 (Paris, December 1958), pp. 31–32, trans. as "Declaration of Amsterdam," in Ulrich Conrads, ed., *Programmes and Manifestoes on Twentieth Century Architecture* (London: Lund Humphries, 1970), pp. 161–162. The Declaration was the product of a voluminous correspondence between the two authors. See the "Correspondance Constant-Debord" file, Constant archive, Rijksbureau voor Kunsthistorische Documentatie, The Hague.

**75**   Attila Kotányi and Raoul Vaneigem, "Programme élémentaire du bureau d'urbanisme unitaire," in *Internationale situationniste,* no. 6 (Paris, August 1961), pp. 16–19, trans. as "Elementary Program of the Bureau of Unitary Urbanism," in Knabb, *Anthology,* pp. 65–67. See also anon., "Unitary Urbanism at the End of the 1950s," p. 144: "Unitary urbanism is not ideally separated from the current terrain of the cities. It is developed out of the experience of this terrain and is based on existing constructions. As a result it is just as important that we exploit the existing decors—through the affirmation of a playful urban space such as is revealed by the *dérive*—as it is that we construct completely unknown ones. This interpenetration (employment of the present city and construction of the future city) entails the deployment of architectural *détournement*."

**76**  Anon., "Urbanisme unitaire à la fin des années 50."

**77**  Debord, "Report on the Construction of Situations," p. 24; and caption for the illustrations in *Potlatch New Series,* no. 1 (Paris, July 1959).

**78**  Guy-Ernest Debord, Attila Kotányi, and Jørgen Nash, "Critique de l'urbanisme," *Internationale situationniste*, no. 6 (Paris, August 1961), pp. 5–11, trans. in Knabb, *Anthology,* p. 373, note 113.

**79**  See for instance Manfredo Tafuri, "The New Babylon: The 'Yellow Giants' and the Myth of Americanism," in *The Sphere and the Labyrinth: Avant-Gardes and Architecture from Piranesi to the 1970s* (Cambridge, Mass.: MIT Press, 1990). Tafuri shows, for instance, that the project for a system of roof gardens and bridges suspended over the streets in Rockefeller Center "is only a belated result of the widespread identification" of the modern North American city and Babylon.

**80**  See Genesis 11:1–9.

**81**  See Leif Furhammar, *Politics and Film* (London: Studio Vista, 1971), pp. 98ff.

**82**  Guy Debord, Attila Kotányi, and Raoul Vaneigem, "Theses on the Paris Commune" (Paris, March 1962), trans. in Knabb, *Anthology,* pp. 314–317.

**83**  Cited in Hein van Haaren, *Constant* (Amsterdam: Meulenhoff, 1966), trans. Max Schuchart, p. 8.

**84**  *Constant* (Paris: Bibliothèque d'Alexandrie, 1959), unpaginated. Bibliothèque d'Alexandrie was the situationist press.

**85**  See the "Néovision Spatiodynamisme" file, Constant archive, Rijksbureau voor Kunsthistorische Documentatie, The Hague.

**86**  Constant, "New Babylon" (1960), in *Constant— Amsterdam* (Städtische Kunstgalerie Bochum, 1961), trans. in Conrads, *Programmes and Manifestoes,* pp. 177–178.

**87**  See "Notes editoriales," *Internationale situationniste,* no. 3 (Paris, December 1959), pp. 6–7.

**88**  See *Constant* (Bibliothèque d'Alexandrie, 1959).

**89**  By 1974, with the publication of the catalogue accompanying the New Babylon exhibition at the Gemeentemuseum (J. L. Locher, ed., *New Babylon* [The Hague: Gemeentemuseum, 1974]), New Babylon had been fully maneuvered by Constant and others into its theoretical and historical framework. Authorities invoked included Chombart de Lauwe, Choay, Lefebvre, and Arendt, while the project was compared to those of More, Campanella, Fourier, Owen, and Marx.

**90**  Debord and Jorn, *Mémoires,* n.p.

**91**  Reyner Banham was hasty when he suggested, in *Megastructure* (London: Thames and Hudson, 1976), that other megastructural projects had anticipated New Babylon. Frei Otto's Suspended City and Constant's Hanging Sector, for example, were both designed in 1960, and the importance of New Babylon to the experimental scene was illustrated by its inclusion in *L'Architecture d'aujourd'hui*'s 1962 survey of "fantastic architecture." See *Architecture d'aujourd'hui,* no. 102 (June-July 1962), a wonderful special edition that reviewed the history of fantastic architecture from the Tower of Babel to the present day. Printed matter like this ensured a steady exchange of ideas; from 1950 the well-known art and architecture critic Michel Ragon regularly wrote about Constant.

**92**  Reyner Banham (*Megastructure*, p. 217) defined megastructure as "a large frame in which all the functions of a city or part of a city are housed," borrowing the definition from Fumihiko Maki, *Investigations in Collective Form* (St. Louis: Washington University, 1964), pp. 8–13.

**93**  See van Haaren, *Constant,* p. 8, and Constant Nieuwenhuys, "New Babylon/An Urbanism of the Future," *Architectural Design*, June 1964, p. 304.

**94**  The term was popularized by Michel Ragon.

**95**  Constant exhibited with GEAM at the Stichting Nieuw Beelden, Amsterdam, May-June 1962, and attended the accompanying conference at Knoll International, 26 May 1962.

**96** Cited in van Haaren, *Constant,* p. 8.

**97** See, for instance, Le Corbusier's Plan Obus for Algiers, 1930.

**98** Sigfried Giedion, José Luis Sert, and Fernand Léger, "Nine Points on Monumentality" (1943), in Sigfried Giedion, *Architektur und Gemeinschaft* (1956), trans. as *Architecture, You and Me* (Cambridge, Mass.: Harvard University Press, 1958), and reprinted in Ockman and Eigen, *Architecture Culture,* pp. 29–30.

**99** This tension between structure and ephemerality was one of the preoccupations of the design avant-garde, as in the work of the Independent Group or, more open-endedly, of Charles and Ray Eames. See for instance the Eames's "House of Cards" display structure for found images, or their Santa Monica house.

**100** See *Architectural Design*, June 1964. The Moulton had just received an award from the Council for Industrial Design. See also Reyner Banham's celebration of the Moulton Bicycle, "A Grid on Two Farthings," *New Statesman* (London, 29 October 1960), reprinted in Reyner Banham, *Design By Choice*, ed. Penny Sparke (London: Academy Editions, 1981), pp. 119–120.

**101** Anon., "Design Notes," *Architectural Design*, June 1964, p. 308.

**102** Constant, "Une autre ville pour une autre vie," *Internationale situationniste,* no. 3 (Paris, December 1959), pp. 36–38.

**103** Guy-Ernest Debord, "Théorie de la dérive," *Les lèvres nues,* no. 9 (Brussels, 1956), reprinted in *Internationale situationniste*, no. 2 (Paris, December 1958), pp. 14–23, trans. as "Theory of the Dérive," in Knabb, *Anthology,* pp. 50–54. The helicoidal house was presumably based in turn on Bruce Goff's extraordinary Bavinger House, Norman, Oklahoma, 1950–1955. The building combined the baroque, Frank Lloyd Wright-ish form beloved by situationists with a daring suspended structural system of the type adopted by New Babylon's Hanging Sector, amplifying aspects of the work of Buckminster Fuller, such as his Dymaxion House, 1927. De Stijl's elastic architectural visions of the 1920s were another inspiration.

**104** Constant Nieuwenhuys, "New Babylon/An Urbanism of the Future," also cited by Banham, *Megastructure*, p. 83. This Dutch vision of architectural flexibility also developed, parallel with Constant's work, in the activity of N. J. Habraken.

**105** Constant, "Description de la zone jaune," *Internationale situationniste,* no. 4 (Paris, June 1960), pp. 23–25.

**106** As a fellow exhibitor at the 1958 Brussels Expo, Constant was also familiar with the daring open-lattice structures of the Pollak/Waterkeyn Atomium and René Sarger's French Pavilion, beacons of progressive construction.

**107** Jacqueline de Jong, ed., *Situationist Times,* no. 4 (Paris, 1963), p. 180.

**108** "Situation," *Archigram,* no. 3 (1963), reprinted in Archigram, ed., *A Guide to Archigram 1961–74* (London: Academy Editions, 1994), p. 88.

**109** The similarity between Constant's work and that of Archigram was noted by Banham in *Megastructure*, pp. 81, 89, and has been recently discussed by Herbert Lachmayer, "Archigram: The Final Avant-Garde of an Aging Modernism?," in Archigram, *A Guide to Archigram*, pp. 417–447. I am indebted to Barry Curtis for generously discussing with me ideas about Archigram.

**110** Joan Littlewood and Cedric Price, "A Laboratory of Fun," *New Scientist,* no. 14 (London, May 1964), p. 433, cited in James Burch, "Situationist Poise, Space and Architecture," *Transgressions: A Journal of Urban Exploration,* no. 1 (London and Newcastle, Summer 1995), pp. 9–28.

111   See, for instance, the introduction to Yona Friedman, "Program of Mobile Urbanism," in Ockman and Eigen, *Architecture Culture,* p. 273.

112   Constant Nieuwenhuys, "New Babylon/An Urbanism of the Future."

113   See *Provo,* no. 4, New Babylon issue (Amsterdam, 28 October 1965), and *Stant bulletin babylonprogramma* (Amsterdam: Provo, January 1967), preview for the rally "Naar een niew Babylon," Parkkerk (a church near the Vondelpark), 13–20 February 1967. Constant declined to take part in the rally. My thanks to Marcel Hummelink for helping me clarify this matter at short notice.

114   Peter Cook, *Architecture: Action and Plan* (London: Studio Vista/Reinhold, 1967), cited in Kenneth Frampton, *Modern Architecture: A Critical History* (London: Thames and Hudson, 1985), p. 282.

115   See also Burch, "Situationist Poise," p. 19.

116   See Krishan Kumar, *Utopianism* (Buckingham: Open University Press, 1991), passim.

117   Constant Nieuwenhuys, "New Babylon/An Urbanism of the Future."

118   Ivain [Chtcheglov], "Formulary for a New Urbanism," pp. 4, 2. Chtcheglov's word *amusé* is translated here as "fun."

119   Banham, *Megastructure*, p. 80.

120   Constant Nieuwenhuys, "New Babylon/An Urbanism of the Future."

121   Ibid. The editor for Constant's feature was Kenneth Frampton.

122   See Constant, "Description de la zone jaune," and the discussion of flexibility and participation in Banham, *Megastructure*, pp. 81ff.

123   Cited in Blunt, *The Dream King*, p. 151.

124   Ivain [Chtcheglov], "Formulary for a New Urbanism," p. 4.

125   Debord, "Theory of the Dérive," p. 53.

126   Where cities were deemed to have little historic core of any worth, New Babylon carried on to the heart of the city, as in the case of Rotterdam.

127   Frampton, *Modern Architecture*, pp. 275–276. The "open-city" thesis was a development of the urban ideas of Louis Kahn, who was emerging as something of a mentor for younger, experimentally minded architects.

128   Anon., "Unitary Urbanism at the End of the 1950s," p. 144.

129   See Kristin Ross, *The Emergence of Social Space: Rimbaud and the Paris Commune* (Basingstoke: Macmillan, 1988), p. 37. Lateral piercing was discussed, for instance, in the memoirs of the Commune's first delegate of war, Gustave-Paul Cluseret.

130   Reyner Banham found the Theme Pavilions at the '67 Montreal Expo evocative of the hypothetical New Babylon sector, with visitors wandering around the space frame platforms held within a slightly disorientating tetrahedral structure, "so that minor constructed situations would arise as visitors found themselves on an unpredicted balcony over the canal, in the presence of an unexplained exhibit, confronted by the silhouettes of thousands of other visitors in superimposed layers on bridges against the sky, or at the top of an escalator they were sure they had just descended . . . in 'Man the Producer' there were nothing but alternative routes, to be selected at conscious will or simply at random—the Situationists' psychogeographical drift." Banham, *Megastructure*, pp. 116–117.

131   Constant, "Reflex Manifesto," *Reflex* (Amsterdam, 1948), trans. Leonard Bright in Willemijn Stokvis, *Cobra* (New York: Rizzoli, 1988), pp. 29–31.

132   Cited in van Haaren, *Constant,* p. 8.

133   See Victor Considérant, *Considération sociales sur l'architectonique* (Paris, 1834), cited in Thomas A. Markus, *Buildings and Power* (London: Routledge, 1993), pp. 296–297; and Charles Fourier, *Théorie de l'unité universelle* (1822), in Charles Fourier, *Oeuvres complètes*, vols. 2–5

(1841–1842; reprinted Paris: Editions Anthropos, 1966), cited in Hanno-Walter Kruft, *A History of Architectural Theory* (London: Zwemmer/Princeton Architectural Press, 1994), pp. 286–287.

**134** Cited in van Haaren, *Constant,* pp. 12–13. The notion of the "No-Stop City" had intrigued Buckminster Fuller, and it gained considerable currency by the late 1960s. See, for instance, Frampton, *Modern Architecture*, p. 288, and Banham, *Megastructure*, p. 197.

**135** See Constant, "Description de la zone jaune."

**136** For the spectacle of urban transport, cf. Norman Bel Geddes's General Motors exhibit at the 1939 New York World's Fair.

**137** Cited in van Haaren, *Constant,* pp. 12–13.

**138** Ibid.

**139** "Housing: New Look and New Outlook," in Marshall McLuhan, *Understanding Media: The Extensions of Man* (New York: McGraw-Hill, 1964), p. 123. McLuhan was analyzing Joyce's *Ulysses* (1922).

**140** Cited in van Haaren, *Constant,* pp. 12–13.

**141** Superstudio, "Description of the Microevent/Micro-environment," in Emilio Ambasz, ed., *Italy: The New Domestic Landscape* (New York: Museum of Modern Art, 1972), pp. 242–251.

**142** Ivan Chtcheglov, "Lettres de loin," *Internationale situationniste,* no. 9 (Paris, August 1964), pp. 38–40, trans. as "Letters from Afar," in Knabb, *Anthology,* p. 372, note 52.

**143** Constant, "Description de la zone jaune," part trans. in Vidler, *The Architectural Uncanny,* p. 213. Cf. Chtcheglov's "Formulary for a New Urbanism," p. 4: the Sinister Quarter "would be difficult to get into, with a hideous decor (piercing whistles, alarm bells, sirens wailing intermittently, grotesque sculptures) . . . and as poorly lit at night as it is blindingly lit during the day by an intensive use of reflection."

**144** Vidler, *The Architectural Uncanny,* p. 213, provides this comparison with Nietzschean thought.

**145** Tafuri, *Architecture and Utopia*, p. 18. Vidler's criticism (*The Architectural Uncanny,* p. 213) that Constant's mobile architecture was "as prone to panoptical implications as that which it apparently replaced" is difficult to understand.

**146** See Constant's 1973 essay on "Het principe van de desorientatie," in Locher, *New Babylon,* pp. 65–69.

**147** See William Gibson's novel *Neuromancer* (London: HarperCollins, 1984) for the origin of the term *cyberspace*.

**148** David Greene and Michael Webb, *Story of the Thing* (1963), reprinted in Peter Cook et al., eds., *Archigram* (London: Studio Vista, 1972), p. 22.

**149** Situationism rarely chimed with McLuhan's technological euphoria, but this should not obscure the bizarre overlap between them. They shared a preference for sweeping, unsubstantiated, but nonetheless intriguing arguments; and on p. 88 of *The Medium Is the Massage* (New York: McGraw-Hill, 1967), McLuhan made a claim that could serve well as an epithet to the situationist exposure of the "naked city." "The poet, the artist, the sleuth—whoever sharpens our perception tends to be antisocial; rarely 'well-adjusted,' he cannot go along with currents and trends. A strange bond often exists among anti-social types in their power to see environments as they really are. This need to interface, to confront environments with a certain antisocial power, is manifest in the famous story, 'the Emperor's New Clothes.' . . . The 'antisocial' brat . . . clearly saw that the Emperor 'ain't got nothin' on.'" On p. 68 of the same book McLuhan noted that "anti-environments, or countersituations made by artists, provide means of direct attention and enable us to see and understand more clearly." McLuhan even promoted a sort of *détournement*: against the restrictions of copyrighted intellectual property, he suggested that his reader "take any books on any subject and custom-make your own book by simply Xeroxing a chapter from this one, a chapter from that one—instant steal! . . . people are less and less convinced of the importance of self-expression. Teamwork succeeds private effort" (p. 123).

**150**   Cf. the sorts of "arcologies" that had been envisaged by Buckminster Fuller, Frank Lloyd Wright, and Paolo Soleri.

**151**   McLuhan, "Housing: New Look and New Outlook," p. 123.

**152**   Ibid.

**153**   Discourse can nonetheless be updated, as the cybernetic fantasies that intrigued Constant and McLuhan currently enjoy an authority bestowed by their proximity to voguish cyberspace.

**154**   See Norbert Wiener, *Cybernetics, or Control and Communication in the Animal and Machine* (Cambridge, Mass.: MIT Press, 1948); and the "Automatie" file, Constant archive, Rijksbureau voor Kunsthistorische Documentatie, The Hague, containing, for instance, copies of "Technology: The Cybernated Generation," from *Time*, 2 April 1965, pp. 46–50, and "Les machines gouverneront-elles les hommes" (interview with Dr. Norbert Wiener), from *Readers' Digest*, French ed., November, 1964, pp. 6–11. For a synopsis of cybernetics, see Stafford Beer, "Cybernetics," in Alan Bullock, Oliver Stallybrass, and Stephen Trombley, eds., *The Fontana Dictionary of Modern Thought*, 2d ed. (London: Fontana, 1988), p. 197. For brief introductions to the impact of cybernetics upon the arts, see "Cybernetic Art," in Walker, *Glossary of Art, Architecture and Design,* p. 72, and "The Computer—or Information Processing Technology," in Jonathan Benthall, *Science and Technology in Art Today* (London: Thames and Hudson, 1972), pp. 41–84.

**155**   Abdelhafid Khatib, "Essai de description psychogéographique des Halles," *Internationale situationniste,* no. 2 (Paris, December 1958), pp. 13–17. Khatib ascribes the definition to Asger Jorn.

**156**   Constant, "Description de la zone jaune."

**157**   McLuhan, "Housing: New Look and New Outlook," p. 130.

**158**   See Locher, *New Babylon,* p. 58.

**159**   See "Experiment Studio Rotterdam," in ibid., p. 67.

**160**   Cf. Debord and Wolman, "Mode d'emploi du détournement."

**161**   Arguing that the human subject requires some material resistance against which to test her or his freedom, the historian Richard Sennett believes that Revolutionary Festivals in Paris in the 1790s failed precisely because of the excess of empty space in the city's places of assembly. See Richard Sennett, "Citizenship and the Body: David's Revolutionary Festivals," paper delivered at the Association of Art Historians' 19th Annual Conference, London, 1993. Deliberate material resistance to the body in New Babylon harked back to a principle of Sartrian existentialism, revived by Gaston Bachelard, who dubbed such resistance "the coefficient of adversity"; the resistance of objects to our bodies helps to define our bodies. For a discussion of the relevance of such ideas to architecture, see Vidler, *The Architectural Uncanny,* pp. 80–82.

**162**   Vidler, *The Architectural Uncanny,* p. 213.

**163**   Perhaps this is not surprising, since 1980s and 1990s rave culture consciously revived the countercultural spirit of twenty years earlier; as the New Babylon project expanded into the later 1960s it inevitably became implicated with the so-called counterculture, itself anticipated and informed by 1950s situationism.

**164**   Anon., "La frontière situationniste," *Internationale situationniste,* no. 5 (Paris, December 1960), pp. 7–9. Although the article and the issue (edited by Debord, Jorn, Kotányi, Nash, Sturm, and Wyckaert) were hostile to Constant and his sympathizers, the quotation confirms a continuity of thought within situationism regarding the intimacy of environment and body.

**165**   McLuhan, "Housing: New Look and New Outlook," p. 128.

**166**   Herbert Marcuse, *Eros and Civilisation* (London, 1969), p. 19, cited in David Mellor, "Bodies and Gender—Heroines and Heroes: 1958–67," *The Sixties Art Scene in London* (London: Barbican Art Gallery/Phaidon, 1993), which features a wider discussion of tendencies toward the liberation of the body.

**167**   Ivain [Chtcheglov], "Formulary for a New Urbanism," pp. 1–4.

**168**   Cited in van Haaren, *Constant,* p. 11. For a discussion of relevant utopian tendencies, see Kumar, *Utopianism,* p. 40.

**169**   See Constant, "Demain la poésie logera la vie."

**170**   Debord, dir., *Sur le passage de quelques personnes à travers une assez courte unité de temps* (1959), reprinted in *Oeuvres cinématographiques complètes, 1952–1978* (Paris: Editions Champ Libre, 1978), trans. as "On the Passage of a Few Persons through a Rather Brief Period of Time," in Knabb, *Anthology,* p. 30.

**171**   Constant, "Sur nos moyens et nos perspectives," *Internationale situationniste,* no. 2 (Paris, December 1958), pp. 23–26. The article was constituted from "notes on a debate opened by Constant in the Situationist International."

**172**   Giuseppe Pinot-Gallizio, "Discours sur la peinture Industrielle et sur un art unitaire applicable," *Internationale situationniste,* no. 3 (Paris, December 1959), pp. 31–35.

**173**   Asger Jorn, "Notes sur la formation d'un Bauhaus Imaginiste" (1957), from "Contre le fonctionalisme," reprinted in *Pour la forme* (Paris: Internationale situationniste, 1958), and in Berreby, *Documents,* pp. 428–429, trans. as "Notes on the Formation of an Imaginist Bauhaus," in Knabb, *Anthology,* pp. 16–17. See also Asger Jorn, "Les situationnistes et l'automation," *Internationale situationniste,* no. 1 (Paris, June 1958), pp. 22–25, trans. as "The Situationists and Automation" (excerpts), in Knabb, *Anthology,* pp. 46–47. I derive the term "situationist frontier" from anon., "La frontière situationniste," *Internationale situationniste,* no. 5 (Paris, December 1960), pp. 7–9.

**174**   Constant Nieuwenhuys, "New Babylon/An Urbanism of the Future," p. 304.

**175**   Anon., "Unitary Urbanism at the End of the 1950s," p. 143, and cited in Debord, Kotányi, and Nash, "Critique de l'urbanisme," p. 5.

**176**   See Kumar, *Utopianism,* passim.

**177**   Anon., "L'opération contre-situationniste dans divers pays," *Internationale situationniste,* no. 8 (Paris, January 1963), pp. 23–26, trans. as "The Counter-Situationist Campaign in Various Countries," in Knabb, *Anthology,* pp. 111–114. See also anon., "Maintenant, l'I.S.," *Internationale situationniste,* no. 9 (Paris, August 1964), pp. 3–5, trans. as "Now, the S.I.," in Knabb, *Anthology,* pp. 135–138.

**178**   Anon., "The Counter-Situationist Campaign in Various Countries," p. 113.

**179**   Anon., "La frontière situationniste." Although the article is unattributed, it bears the hallmarks of Debord and his supporters (including Jorn and Kotányi).

**180**   Constant to Sean Wellesley-Miller, 8 August 1966, pp. 1–2, "Correspondance 1966–1969" file, Constant archive, Rijksbureau voor Kunsthistorische Documentatie, The Hague. Wellesley-Miller became a founder of the Eventstructure Research Group the following year: see "Eventstructure," in Walker, *Glossary of Art, Architecture and Design,* p. 88.

**181**   Pierre Restany to Constant, 10 May 1967, "Correspondance 1966–1969" file, Constant archive, Rijksbureau voor Kunsthistorische Documentatie, The Hague.

**182**   See "Architectures fantastiques," special edition of *L'architecture d'aujourd'hui,* no. 102 (June-July 1962).

**183**   Anon., "Now, the S.I.," p. 113.

**184**   Anon, "L'avant-garde de la présence," p. 17.

**185**   The "Anti-Public Relations Service" was advertised in *Internationale situationniste,* no. 8 (Paris, January 1963); Debord, Kotányi, and Nash, "Critique de l'urbanisme," trans. in Knabb, *Anthology,* p. 373, note 113. Debord could nonetheless be found writing the catalogue for an exhibition of Constant's work at the Galerie van de Loo, Essen, as late as 1960.

**186**   Reyner Banham, *Megastructure*, p. 83.

**187**   Ivain [Chtcheglov], "Formulary for a New Urbanism," p. 3; and see Constant, "Une autre ville pour une autre vie."

Vidler (*The Architectural Uncanny,* p. 213) has gone so far as to suggest that the Archigram group was effectively Constant's architectural heir.

**188**   Peter Cook, "It's All Happening," in "Some Notes on the Archigram Syndrome," *Perspecta,* supplement no. 11 (New Haven, 1967), reprinted in Archigram, *A Guide to Archigram,* pp. 20–34. For discussion and partial reprint of Christopher Alexander's essay, see Ockman and Eigen, *Architecture Culture,* pp. 379–388.

## Conclusions

**1**   See Charles Jencks, *Modern Movements in Architecture* (Harmondsworth: Penguin, 1973), p. 372.

**2**   See "Définitions," *Internationale situationniste,* no. 1 (Paris, June 1958), p. 13–14, trans. as "Definitions" in Ken Knabb, ed., *Situationist International Anthology* (Berkeley: Bureau of Public Secrets, 1981), pp. 45–46.

**3**   Most of the early expulsions were of situationists who regarded the group as a forum for relaxed, Imaginist Bauhaus–style experimentation. Jacques Fillon and Gil J. Wolman were excluded just prior to the foundation of the SI in July 1957 (see *Potlatch,* no. 28 [Paris, May 1957], unpaginated). Ralph Rumney was expelled in 1957, and Walter Korun, a situationist activist who had presented the first COBRA retrospective and who had worked with Debord on a psychogeographic exhibition in Brussels in 1957, was expelled in 1958. See Stewart Home, *The Assault on Culture: Utopian Currents from Lettrisme to Class War* (London: Aporia Press and Unpopular Books, 1988), p. 33. Pinot-Gallizio was expelled for accepting the space vacated by the withdrawal of the SI exhibition at the Stedelijk in March 1960. In April 1960 Constant resigned under pressure from situationist fun-

damentalists. The supposedly historic split between pro-art and non-art factions, officially marked by the secession in 1962 of the German situationists and then of the Second Situationist International under Jørgen Nash, was in fact rather a crude representation of the difficulties that had been inherent in situationism. Mere coexistence with establishment society was objectionable enough, the Paris-based situationist fundamentalists argued, without accepting "offers to sponsor 'creations' on the conventional avant-garde artistic plane" as well. Hard-line situationists at least accepted that the German section genuinely wished to strike an oppositional stance and fight culture from within, "to find a satisfactory field of activity in the here and now," but it was felt in Paris that this would "recuperate" the SI, bringing it "back into the old classification of artistic praxis" (anon., "L'opération contre-situationniste dans divers pays," *Internationale situationniste,* no. 8 [Paris, January 1963], pp. 23–26, trans. as "The Counter-Situationist Campaign in Various Countries," in Knabb, *Anthology,* pp. 111–114). There was now a question of who could legitimately claim to be "situationist." Paris retained the title of "l'Internationale situationniste," as if to confirm an essential continuity in its version of situationism, and Prositus and historians alike have since tended to look toward this group as the source of situationism proper, but in his history Stewart Home refers to the Parisian group as the "Specto-SI," thus refusing it any more situationist legitimacy than the Situationist Bauhaus. The latter-day London Psychogeographic Association likewise invokes Scandinavian and German situationism.

**4**   Anon., "Contradictions de l'activité Lettriste-Internationaliste," *Potlatch,* no. 25 (Paris, January 1956), reprinted in *Potlatch 1954–1957* (Paris: Editions Gérard Lebovici, 1985), pp. 197–199.

**5**   Guy-Ernest Debord, "Un pas en arrière," *Potlatch,* no. 28 (Paris, May 1957), reprinted in *Potlatch 1954–1957,* pp. 227–230.

**6**   The creation of architectural ambiance is a problem that still intrigues architects and theorists. See, for instance,

Anthony Vidler's consideration of the meaning of the "haunted house" in *The Architectural Uncanny: Essays on the Modern Unhomely* (Cambridge, Mass.: MIT Press, 1992), pp. 11–12.

**7**   The only "situationist" productions of Jorn were some exercises in "détourned" painting.

**8**   The determinedly nonanalytic, absent-minded nature of this tradition was illustrated in Walter Benjamin's *Charles Baudelaire: A Lyric Poet in the Era of High Capitalism* (London: New Left Books, 1973, reprinted London: Verso, 1983), pp. 69–70. "The revealing presentations of the big city . . . are the work of those who have traversed the city absently, lost in thought or in worry. . . . In his book on Dickens, Chesterton has masterfully captured the man who roams about the big city lost in thought. . . . 'Whenever he had done drudging, he had no other resource but drifting, and he drifted over half London. . . . He did not go in for "observation," a priggish habit; he did not look at Charing Cross to improve his mind or count the lamp-posts in Holborn to practice his arithmetic. . . . Dickens did not stamp these places on his mind; he stamped his mind on these places.'" (Also quoted in Home, *Assault on Culture,* p. 21.)

**9**   Anon., "Prochaine planète," *Potlatch,* no. 4 (Paris, July 1954), reprinted in *Potlatch 1954–1957*, pp. 30–31.

**10** Jens-Jørgen Thorsen, "The Communication State in Art," in Carl Magnus, Jørgen Nash, Heimrad Prem, Hardy Strid, and Jens-Jørgen Thorsen, *Situationister i konsten* (Örkelljunga: Bauhaus situationiste, 1966), quoted in Simon Ford, *The Realization and Suppression of the Situationist International: An Annotated Bibliography 1972–1992* (Edinburgh and San Francisco: AK Press, 1995), p. 49. (Quotation modified.)

**11** Anon., "The Counter-Situationist Campaign in Various Countries," in Knabb, *Anthology,* p. 113. See also "Maintenant, l'I.S.," *Internationale situationniste,* no. 9 (Paris, August 1964), pp. 3–5, trans. as "Now, the S.I.," in Knabb, *Anthology,* pp. 135–138.

**12** Quoted in Krishan Kumar, *Utopianism* (Buckingham: Open University Press, 1991), p. 32.

**13** Attila Kotányi and Raoul Vaneigem, "Programme élémentaire du bureau de l'urbanisme unitaire," *Internationale situationniste,* no. 6 (1961), pp. 16–19, trans. as "Elementary Program of the Bureau of Unitary Urbanism," in Knabb, *Anthology,* pp. 65–67.

**14** Home, *Assault on Culture,* p. 21.

**15** Peter Fuller, *Left High and Dry* (London: Claridge, 1990), p. 28.

**16** Kumar, *Utopianism,* p. 87.

**17** Anon., "L'avant-garde de la présence," *Internationale situationniste,* no. 8 (Paris, January 1963), pp. 14–22, trans. as "The Avant-Garde of Presence" (excerpts), in Knabb, *Anthology,* pp. 109–110.

**18** See, for instance, the introduction to T. J. Clark, *The Painting of Modern Life: Paris in the Art of Manet and his Followers* (London: Thames and Hudson, 1985), pp. 3–22. For more on situationist-style activities at the AA, see Rick Poynor, *Nigel Coates: The City in Motion* (London: Blueprint, 1989). Tschumi even seemed to adopt attitudes similar to the situationist hard line: "Architecture is the adaptation of space to the existing social structures. No spatial organisation ever changes the socio-economic structure of reactionary society." Bernard Tschumi, "The Environmental Trigger," in James Gowan, ed., *A Continuing Experiment: Learning and Teaching at the Architectural Association* (London: The Architectural Press, 1975), p. 93, quoted in James Burch, "Situationist Poise, Space and Architecture," *Transgressions: A Journal of Urban Exploration,* no. 1 (London and Newcastle, Summer 1995), pp. 9–28, note 69.

**19** Anon., "36 rue des Morillons," *Potlatch,* no. 8 (Paris, August 1954), reprinted in *Potlatch 1954–1957*, p. 54.

# BIBLIOGRAPHY

Aarhus Kunstmuseum. *Constant: det Ny Babylon*. Aarhus: Kunstmuseum, 1976.

Allen, Stan, and Kyong Park, eds. *Sites and Stations: Provisional Utopias, Architecture and Utopia in the Contemporary City*. Lusitania no. 7. New York: Lusitania Press, 1996.

Ambasz, Emilio, ed. *Italy: The New Domestic Landscape*. New York: Museum of Modern Art, 1972.

Appleyard, Bryan. *Richard Rogers—a Biography*. London: Faber and Faber, 1986.

Aragon, Louis. *Paris Peasant*. Trans. Simon Watson-Taylor. London: Pan, 1978.

Archigram, ed. *A Guide to Archigram 1961–74*. London: Academy Editions, 1994.

*Architectural Design*. "Les Halles" issue. Nos. 9–10 (1980).

*Architecture d'aujourd'hui*. "Architectures fantastiques" issue. No. 102 (June-July 1962).

*ARK: The Journal of the Royal College of Art*. No. 24 (London, 1958).

Atkins, Guy. *Asger Jorn: The Crucial Years*. London: Lund Humphries, 1977.

Atkins, Guy. *Asger Jorn: The Final Years*. London: Lund Humphries, 1980.

Ball, Edward. "The Great Sideshow of the Situationist International." *Yale French Studies*, no. 73 (1987), pp. 21–37.

Bandini, Mirella. *L'estetico il politico: da Cobra all'Internazionale situazionista, 1948–57*. Rome: Officina Edizioni, 1977.

Banham, Reyner. *Design by Choice*. Ed. Penny Sparke. London: Academy Editions, 1981.

Banham, Reyner. *Megastructure*. London: Thames and Hudson, 1976.

Banham, Reyner. *The New Brutalism: Ethic or Aesthetic?* London: Architectural Press, 1966.

Benjamin, Walter. *Charles Baudelaire: A Lyric Poet in the Era of High Capitalism*. Trans. Harry Zohn. London: New Left Books, 1973, reprinted London: Verso, 1983.

Benthall, Jonathan. *Science and Technology in Art Today*. London: Thames and Hudson, 1972.

Berreby, Gérard, ed. *Documents relatifs à la fondation de l'Internationale situationniste: 1948–1957*. Paris: Editions Allia, 1985.

Birtwistle, Graham. "Old Gotland, New Babylon: Peoples and Places in the Work of Jorn and Constant." *Kunstlich* 11, no. 4 (Amsterdam, 1990). Reprinted in *Transgressions: A Journal of Urban Exploration*, no. 2/3 (London and Newcastle, August 1996), pp. 55–67.

Blazwick, Iwona, ed. *An Endless Adventure, an Endless Passion, an Endless Banquet: A Situationist Scrapbook*. London: Institute of Contemporary Arts/Verso, 1989.

Blunt, Wilfred. *The Dream King*. London: Hamilton, 1970.

Bonnett, Alastair. "Art, Ideology and Everyday Space: Subversive Tendencies from Dada to Postmodernism." *Environment and Planning D: Society and Space*, no. 10 (1992).

Bonnett, Alastair. "Situationism, Geography and Poststructuralism." *Environment and Planning D: Society and Space*, no. 7 (1989).

Borden, Iain, Joe Kerr, Alicia Pivaro, and Jane Rendell, eds. *Strangely Familiar: Narratives of Architecture in the City*. London: Routledge, 1996.

*Bouw*. 29 October 1966, pp. 1727–1731, and 27 February 1971, pp. 350–357.

Branzi, Andrea. *The Hot House: Italian New Wave Design*. London: Thames and Hudson, 1984.

Breton, André. *Nadja*. Paris: Editions Gallimard, 1928. Trans. New York: Grove Press, 1960.

Bullock, Alan, Oliver Stallybrass, and Stephen Trombley, eds. *The Fontana Dictionary of Modern Thought*. 2d ed. London: Fontana, 1988.

Burch, James. "Situationist Poise, Space and Architecture." *Transgressions: A Journal of Urban Exploration,* no. 1 (London and Newcastle, Summer 1995), pp. 9–28.

Burney, Jan. *Ettore Sottsass*. London: HarperCollins, 1991.

Calder, Angus. *Britain by Mass Observation*. London: Cresset, 1986.

*Cambridge Opinion*. "Living with the 60s" issue. No. 17 (Cambridge, 1959).

Cantsin, Monty, ed. *Smile 11*. London, n.d.

Centre Pompidou. *Cartes et figures de la terre*. Paris: Editions du Centre Pompidou, 1980.

Centre Pompidou. *La ville: art et architecture en Europe, 1870–1993*. Paris: Editions du Centre Pompidou, 1994.

Certeau, Michel de. *The Practice of Everyday Life*. Trans. Steven Rendell. Berkeley: University of California Press, 1984.

Chevalier, Louis. *L'assassinat de Paris*. Paris, 1977. Trans. David P. Jordan as *The Assassination of Paris*. Chicago: University of Chicago Press, 1994.

Chombart de Lauwe, Paul-Henri. *La découverte aérienne du monde*. Paris: Horizons de France, 1948.

Chombart de Lauwe, Paul-Henri. *Paris et l'agglomération parisienne*. Paris: Presses Universitaires de France, 1952.

Clark, Timothy J. *The Painting of Modern Life: Paris in the Art of Manet and His Followers*. London: Thames and Hudson, 1985.

*Cobra 1948–1951: bulletin pour la coordination des investigations artistiques*. Reprinted in facsimile in one volume. Amsterdam: Van Gennep, 1980.

Conrads, Ulrich. *Programmes and Manifestoes on Twentieth Century Architecture*. London: Lund Humphries, 1970.

Constant [Nieuwenhuys]. "Art et habitat." Unpublished manuscript, n.d.

Constant [Nieuwenhuys]. *Constant*. The Hague: Gemeentemuseum, 1965.

Constant [Nieuwenhuys]. "Copenhagen Lecture" for the Danish Royal Academy. Unpublished manuscript, 1964.

Constant [Nieuwenhuys]. "Manifeste spatiodynamique." Various unpublished manuscripts, 1954.

Constant [Nieuwenhuys]. "New Babylon/An Urbanism of the Future." *Architectural Design*, no. 34 (June 1964), pp. 304–305.

Constant [Nieuwenhuys]. *New Babylon Bulletin*, no. 1. Amsterdam: New Babylon Informatief, c. 1963.

Constant [Nieuwenhuys] and Simon Vinkenoog. *New Babylon*. Amsterdam: Galerie d'Eendt, 1963.

*Constant*. Paris: Bibliothèque d'Alexandrie, 1959.

Cook, Peter. *Architecture: Action and Plan*. London: Studio Vista/Reinhold, 1967.

Cook, Peter. *Experimental Architecture*. London: Studio Vista, 1970.

Cook, Peter, et al., eds. *Archigram*. London: Studio Vista, 1972.

Couperie, Pierre. *Paris au fil de temps*. Paris: Joël Cuénot, 1968. Trans. as *Paris through the Ages: An Illustrated*

*Historical Atlas of Urbanism and Architecture*. London: Barrie and Jenkins, 1970.

Crary, Jonathan. "Spectacle, Attention, Counter-memory." *October,* no. 50 (Fall 1989), pp. 97–107.

Crosby, Theo, ed. *Uppercase 3*. London: Whitefriars Press, 1960.

Debord, Guy-Ernest. *Contre le cinéma*. Aarhus: Institut Scandinave de vandalisme comparé, 1964.

Debord, Guy-Ernest. *Oeuvres cinématographiques complètes: 1952–1978*. Paris: Editions Champ Libre, 1978.

Debord, Guy-Ernest. "Premières maquettes pour l'urbanisme nouveau." Unpublished manuscript for the Stedelijk Museum, 1959.

Debord, Guy-Ernest. *La société du spectacle*. Paris, 1967. Trans. as *The Society of the Spectacle*. London: Rebel Press and Aim Publications, 1987.

Debord, Guy, and Asger Jorn. *Mémoires*. Copenhagen: Permild and Rosengreen, 1959.

De Quincey, Thomas. *Confessions of an English Opium-Eater* (1821). Ed. Grevel Lindop. Oxford: Oxford University Press, 1985.

Dickens, Charles. *The Uncommercial Traveller*. Ed. Peter Ackroyd. London: Mandarin, 1991.

Dufrenne, Mikel. *Main Trends in Aesthetics and the Sciences of Art*. New York: Holmes and Meier, 1979.

Dunford, Martin, and Jack Holland. *Amsterdam: The Rough Guide*. London: Rough Guides, 1994.

Edwards, Phil. "Guy Debord." Manuscript in preparation for publication.

Elsken, Ed van der. *Love on the Left Bank*. London: André Deutsch, 1957.

Evenson, Norma. *Paris: A Century of Change*. New Haven and London: Yale University Press, 1979.

Faulkner, Simon. "The Aestheticisation of Politics in the English SI and King Mob." Unpublished paper for the Association of Art Historians Conference, Newcastle, 1996.

Fiedler, Jeannine, ed. *Social Utopias of the Twenties: Bauhaus, Kibbutz and the Dream of the New Man*. Wuppertal: Müller and Busmann Press, 1995.

Ford, Simon. *The Realization and Suppression of the Situationist International: An Annotated Bibliography 1972–1992*. Edinburgh and San Francisco: AK Press, 1995.

Forsyth, Lucy. "The Sup(e)r(s)ession of Art." Unpublished paper for the Manchester University conference "The Hacienda Must Be Built: On the Legacy of the Situationist Revolt." Manchester, January 1996.

*Forum* (magazine of the Congrès internationaux d'architecture moderne). No. 3 (Amsterdam, 1953).

Frampton, Kenneth. *Modern Architecture: A Critical History*. London: Thames and Hudson, 1985.

Frascina, Francis, and Charles Harrison, eds. *Modern Art and Modernism: A Critical Anthology*. London: Harper and Row, 1982.

Fuller, Peter. *Left High and Dry*. London: Claridge, 1990.

Furhammar, Leif. *Politics and Film*. London: Studio Vista, 1971.

Gibson, William. *Neuromancer*. London: HarperCollins, 1984.

Giedion, Sigfried. *Architecture, You and Me*. Cambridge, Mass.: Harvard University Press, 1958.

Giedion, Sigfried. *CIAM: A Decade of Contemporary Architecture*. Zurich: Girsberger, 1954.

Goldberg, Rose-Lee. *Performance Art*. London: Thames and Hudson, 1992.

Gray, Christopher. *Leaving the Twentieth Century: The Incomplete Work of the Situationist International*. London: Free Fall, 1974.

Gruppe Spur. *Spur,* no. 5, "Spezialnummer über den unitären Urbanismus." Munich: Gruppe Spur, June 1961.

Haaren, Hein van. *Constant*. Trans. Max Schuchart. Amsterdam: Meulenhoff, 1966.

Hall, Tim. "The Use of Urban Spectacle in the Regeneration of Blighted Urban Areas. Preliminary Considerations." Unpublished paper for the Urban Morphology Research Group, Birmingham University, 1990.

Harrison, Charles, and Paul Wood, eds. *Art in Theory 1900–1990: An Anthology of Changing Ideas*. Oxford: Blackwell, 1992.

Henri, Adrian. *Environments and Happenings*. London: Thames and Hudson, 1974.

*Here and Now Guy Debord Supplement*. Issued with *Here and Now*, no. 16/17 (Glasgow and Leeds, Winter 1995/1996).

Heskett, John. *Industrial Design*. London: Thames and Hudson, 1980.

Hewison, Robert. *Too Much: Art and Society in the Sixties*. London: Methuen, 1988.

Highmore, Ben. "Lefebvre's Dialectics of Everyday Life." Ph.D. dissertation in preparation, University of the West of England.

Hill, Anthony, ed. *DATA*. London: Faber, 1968.

Hirsh, Arthur. *The French Left: A History and Overview*. Montreal: Black Rose Books, 1982.

Hitchcock, Henry-Russell, and Philip Johnson. *The International Style: Architecture since 1922*. New York: Museum of Modern Art, 1932, reprinted New York: Norton, 1966.

Hollier, Denis. *Against Architecture: The Writings of Georges Bataille*. Cambridge, Mass.: MIT Press, 1989.

Home, Stewart. *The Assault on Culture: Utopian Currents from Lettrisme to Class War*. London: Aporia Press and Unpopular Books, 1988.

Huizinga, Johan. *Homo Ludens* (1944). Trans. 1949, reprinted London: Paladin, 1970.

*Internationale situationniste*. Nos. 1–12. Paris: Internationale situationniste, 1958–1969.

Jacobs, Jane. *The Death and Life of Great American Cities*. New York: Random House, 1961.

Jameson, Fredric. *Postmodernism, or, the Cultural Logic of Late Capitalism*. London: Verso, 1991.

Jencks, Charles. *Modern Movements in Architecture*. Harmondsworth: Penguin, 1973.

Jong, Jacqueline de, ed. *The Situationist Times*. Various issues. Copenhagen and Paris, 1963–1967.

Jorn, Asger. *Pour la forme: ébauche d'une méthodologie des arts*. Paris: Internationale situationniste, 1958.

Jorn, Asger, and Guy Debord. *Fin de Copenhague*. Copenhagen: Permild and Rosengreen, 1957.

Jorn, Asger, and Guy Debord. *Le jardin d'Albisola*. Turin: Pozzo, 1974.

Ketcham, Diana. *Le Désert de Retz: A Late Eighteenth-Century French Folly Garden, the Artful Landscape of Monsieur de Monville*. Cambridge, Mass.: MIT Press, 1994.

King, Rex. *The Arts, and Other Social Diseases*. Rev. ed. Edinburgh and San Francisco: AK/Pentagon, 1993.

Knabb, Ken, ed. and trans. *Situationist International Anthology*. Berkeley: Bureau of Public Secrets, 1981.

Kruft, Hanno-Walter. *A History of Architectural Theory, from Vitruvius to the Present*. London: Zwemmer/Princeton Architectural Press, 1994.

Kumar, Krishan. *Utopianism*. Buckingham: Open University Press, 1991.

Lambert, Jean-Clarence. *COBRA*. New York: Abbeville Press, 1985.

Le Corbusier. *Le modulor*. Paris, 1948. Trans. as *The Modulor*. London: Faber and Faber, 1954.

Le Corbusier. *Vers une architecture*. Paris, 1923. Trans. Frederick Etchells as *Towards a New Architecture*. London, 1927, reprinted London: Butterworth, 1987.

Lefebvre, Henri. *La production de l'espace*. Paris, 1974. Trans. Donald Nicholson-Smith as *The Production of Space*. Oxford: Blackwell, 1991.

Lefebvre, Henri. *Writings on Cities*. Ed. and trans. Eleonore Kofman and Elizabeth Lebas. Oxford: Blackwell, 1996.

LeGates, Richard T., and Frederic Stout, eds. *The City Reader*. London: Routledge, 1996.

*Les lèvres nues*. Various issues. Brussels, 1955–1956.

Livingstone, Marco, ed. *Pop Art*. London: Royal Academy of Arts/Weidenfeld and Nicolson, 1991.

Locher, J. L., ed. *New Babylon*. The Hague: Gemeentemuseum, 1974.

London Psychogeographical Association. *Newsletter*. Various issues. London, 1993–.

Lucan, Jacques. *Eau et gaz à tous les étages. Paris, 100 ans de logement*. Paris: Pavillon de l'Arsenal/Picard Editeur, 1992.

Lynch, Kevin. *The Image of the City*. Cambridge, Mass.: MIT Press, 1960.

Magnago Lampugnani, Vittorio, ed. *The Thames and Hudson Encyclopaedia of 20th-Century Architecture*. London: Thames and Hudson, 1986.

Marcus, Greil. *Lipstick Traces: A Secret History of the Twentieth Century*. London: Secker and Warburg, 1989.

Markus, Thomas A. *Buildings and Power*. London: Routledge, 1993.

Markus, Thomas A. *Visions of Perfection*. Glasgow: Third Eye Gallery, 1985.

Martos, Jean-François. *Histoire de l'Internationale situationniste*. Paris: Editions Gérard Lebovici, 1989.

McDonough, Thomas F. "Situationist Space." *October,* no. 67 (Winter 1994), pp. 58–77.

McLuhan, Marshall. *The Medium Is the Massage*. New York: McGraw-Hill, 1967.

McLuhan, Marshall. *Understanding Media: The Extensions of Man*. New York: McGraw-Hill, 1964.

Mellor, David. *The Sixties Art Scene in London*. London: Barbican Art Gallery/Phaidon, 1993.

Ministère de Construction. *Construction et urbanisme dans la Région parisienne*. Paris: Ministère de Construction, 1958.

Mumford, Lewis. *The City in History: Its Origins, Its Transformation, and Its Propsects*. London: Secker and Warburg, 1961.

Nairn, Ian. *Outrage*. London: Architectural Press, 1956.

*New Babylon Informatief*. Various issues. Amsterdam, 1965–1966.

Ockman, Joan, and Edward Eigen, eds. *Architecture Culture 1943–1968: A Documentary Anthology*. New York: Columbia Books of Architecture/Rizzoli, 1993.

Ohrt, Roberto. *Phantom Avantgarde: eine Geschichte der Situationistischen International und der modernen Kunst*. Hamburg: Editions Nautilus/Galerie van der Loo, 1990.

*Opus International*. No. 27 (Paris, September 1971).

Pindar, David. "Subverting Cartography: The Situationists and Maps of the City." *Environment and Planning A* 28 (March 1996), pp. 405–427.

Pinot-Gallizio, Giuseppe. *Pinot-Gallizio: le situationnisme et la peinture*. Paris: Galerie 1900–2000, 1989.

Plant, Sadie. *The Most Radical Gesture: The Situationist International in a Postmodern Age*. London: Routledge, 1992.

*Le port-folio situationniste*. 2 vols. Paris: Editions Le lundi au soleil, 1993.

*Potlatch 1954–1957*. Reprinted in one volume. Paris: Editions Gérard Lebovici, 1985.

Poynor, Rick. *Nigel Coates: The City in Motion*. London: Blueprint, 1989.

*Provo*. "New Babylon" issue and "Nieuw urbanisme" issue. Nos. 4, 5 (Amsterdam, 28 October 1965 and 12 May 1966).

Ragon, Michel. "New Babylon." *Urbanisme,* no. 133 (Paris, 1972).

*Rassegna.* "Architecture in the Avant-Garde Magazines" issue. No. 12 (Milan, 1982).

Ravetz, Alison. *The Government of Space.* London: Faber and Faber, 1986.

Rigby, Brian. *Popular Culture in Modern France: A Study of Cultural Discourse.* London: Routledge, 1991.

Robbins, David, ed. *The Independent Group: Postwar Britain and the Aesthetics of Plenty.* Cambridge, Mass.: MIT Press, 1990.

Rogers, E. N., J. L. Sert, and J. Tyrwhitt, eds. *The Heart of the City: Towards the Humanisation of Urban Life.* New York: Pelligrini and Cudahy, 1952.

Roose-Evans, James. *Experimental Theatre.* London: Routledge, 1989.

Ross, Kristin. *The Emergence of Social Space: Rimbaud and the Paris Commune.* Basingstoke: Macmillan, 1988.

Ross, Kristin. *Fast Cars, Clean Bodies: Decolonization and the Reordering of French Culture.* Cambridge, Mass.: MIT Press, 1995.

Rowe, Colin, and Fred Koetter. *Collage City.* Cambridge, Mass.: MIT Press, 1978.

Rubel, Maximilien, and John Crump, eds. *Non-Market Socialism in the Nineteenth and Twentieth Centuries.* Basingstoke: Macmillan, 1987.

Sadler, Simon. "The Beautiful Village." Unpublished paper for the Association of Art Historians Conference. Newcastle-upon-Tyne, 1996.

Sadler, Simon. "'Situationism' and Architecture." M.A. dissertation, University of Central England, 1993.

Sadler, Simon. "The Situationist City." Unpublished paper for the Association of Art Historians Conference. Birmingham, 1994.

Sam Fogg Rare Books and Manuscripts. *Documents of the Avant-Garde 1945–1990.* London: Sam Fogg Rare Books and Manuscripts, 1990.

Seale, Patrick, and Maureen McConville. *French Revolution 1968.* Harmondsworth: Penguin, 1968.

Sennett, Richard. *The Conscience of the Eye: The Design and Social Life of Cities.* London: Faber and Faber, 1990.

Sharp, Dennis. *20th Century Architecture: A Visual History.* London: Lund Humphries, 1991.

Smithson, Alison, ed. *Team 10 Primer.* London: Studio Vista, 1968.

Soja, Edward W. *Postmodern Geographies: The Reassertion of Space in Critical Social Theory.* London: Verso, 1989.

Sparke, Penny. *Ettore Sottsass Jnr.* London: Design Council, 1982.

*Stant bulletin babylonprogramma.* Amsterdam: Provo, January 1967.

Stokvis, Willemijn. *Cobra.* New York: Rizzoli, 1988.

Strauven, Francis. *Aldo van Eyck relativiteit en verbeelding.* Amsterdam: Meulenhoff, 1994.

Sussman, Elisabeth, ed. *On the Passage of a Few People through a Rather Brief Moment in Time: The Situationist International, 1957–1972.* Cambridge, Mass.: MIT Press/Institute of Contemporary Arts, Boston, 1989.

Sutcliffe, Anthony. *Paris: An Architectural History.* New Haven: Yale University Press, 1993.

Tafuri, Manfredo. *Architecture and Utopia: Design and Capitalist Development.* Cambridge, Mass.: MIT Press, 1976.

Tafuri, Manfredo. *The Sphere and the Labyrinth: Avant-Gardes and Architecture from Piranesi to the 1970s.* Cambridge, Mass.: MIT Press, 1990.

Timms, Edward, and David Kelley. *Unreal City: Urban Experience in Modern European Literature and Art.* Manchester: Manchester University Press, 1985.

Trocchi, Alexander. *Sigma Portfolio*. Various issues. London, 1964.

Vague, Tom, ed. *Vague,* no. 22 (London, 1989).

Vaneigem, Raoul, *Traité de savoir-faire à l'usage des jeunes générations*. Paris, 1967. Trans. Donald Nicholson-Smith as *The Revolution of Everyday Life*. London: Rebel Press, 1983.

Vidler, Anthony. *The Architectural Uncanny: Essays on the Modern Unhomely*. Cambridge, Mass.: MIT Press, 1992.

Walker, John A. *Glossary of Art, Architecture and Design since 1945*. London: Clive Bingley, 1973.

Walker, N. "Aldo van Eyck." P.G. Dip. thesis in architecture. Birmingham Polytechnic, 1989.

Whitney Museum of American Art. *The Power of the City, the City of Power*. New York: Whitney Museum of American Art, 1992.

Wilde, E. de, and Fanny Kelk. *Constant, schilderijen 1969–77*. Amsterdam: Stedelijk Museum, 1978.

*XS,* no. 1. Coventry: Excess, 1968.

Yates, Frances A. *The Art of Memory*. London: Routledge, 1966.

Young, Michael, and Peter Willmott. *Family and Kinship in East London*. London, 1957, reprinted Harmondsworth: Penguin, 1962.

McDonough, Thomas F., ed. "Guy Debord and the *Internationale situationniste*." Special issue of *October*, no. 79 (Winter 1997).

\*   \*   \*

Since this book went to press several important additions to the literature have been published:

Andreotti, Libero, and Xavier Costa, eds. *Situacionistas: arte, política, urbanismo / Situationists: Art, Politics, Urbanism*. Barcelona: Museu d'Art Contemporani de Barcelona / Actar, 1996.

Andreotti, Libero, and Xavier Costa, eds. *Theory of the Dérive and Other Situationist Writings on the City*. Barcelona: Museu d'Art Contemporani de Barcelona / Actar, 1996.

# ILLUSTRATION CREDITS

The author has made every reasonable effort within his limited means to trace, clear, and acknowledge the copyrights of the pictures used in this book. It is nonetheless possible that some attributions or ownerships have been omitted or are incorrect, in which case the author will add credits if required in any subsequent editions.

© 1997 ADAGP, Paris, and DACS, London: figs. 1.8, 1.20, 2.13, 3.4

Bayerische Verwaltung der staatlichen Schlösser, Gärten und Seen, Munich: fig. 3.2

Tim Benton: figs. 0.5, 1.7

Bibliothèque Nationale, Paris: fig. 2.17

© Blondel la Rougery, Rosny-sur-Bois, 1956: fig. 2.16

Brazilian Embassy, London: figs. 1.18, 1.19

Constant: figs. 0.2, 1.12, 1.15, 1.25, 1.26, 1.27, 3.3, 3.7, 3.9, 3.12, 3.13, 3.16, 3.22, 3.23, 3.24, 3.25, 3.26, 3.28, 3.30, 3.31, 3.32

Peter Cook: fig. 3.18

© 1997 DACS, London: fig. 2.26

François Dallegret: fig. 1.16

Aldo van Eyck: fig. 1.11

Yona Friedman: fig. 3.14

Haags Gemeentemuseum, c/o Beeldrecht, Amsterdam: figs. 1.12, 3.25, 3.32

Richard Hamilton: fig. 1.3

KLM: fig. 1.11

Alex Moulton: fig. 3.15

Musée du Louvre/Réunion des Musées Nationaux: figs. 2.6, 2.7

Roberto Ohrt: fig. 2.21

Olivetti U.K.: fig. 1.17

Pavillon de l'Arsenal, Paris: figs. 1.30, 1.31

Presses Universitaires de France: figs. 2.18, 2.23

Cedric Price: fig. 3.19

Rijksbureau voor Kunsthistorische Documentatie, The Hague: frontispiece, figs. 1.5, 1.32, 3.24

Ralph Rumney: fig. 2.14

Peter Smithson: figs. 1.4, 1.6, 3.5

Judith Wachsmann/Huntington Museum, San Marino: fig. 3.17

Michael Webb: figs. 3.20, 3.21

Witt Library, Courtauld Institute, London: fig. 3.27

# *INDEX*

Gypsies, 37. *See also* Nomadism; Vagrancy and vagabondage

Habraken, Nicolaas, 193(n.104)
Halles, Paris. *See* Paris: Les Halles
Hamilton, Richard, 19, 33
    *Just What Is It That Makes Today's Homes So Different,*
        *So Appealing . . . ?,* 17; fig. 1.3
Happenings, 64–65, 106, 112, 163
Harvey, David, 45, 47
Haussmann, Georges. *See* Paris: Haussmannization;
        Planning; Urbanism
Hegel, Georg Wilhelm Friedrich, and Hegelianism, 44, 108
Hejduk, John, 185(n.89)
Henderson, Nigel, 20, 170(n.17); fig. 1.4
Hierarchy
    of culture, 40, 69, 99, 108
    of design, 34
    social, 16, 34, 38, 52
    of space, 30
    of value, 27
High-rise buildings and tower blocks, 13, 22, 58, 62; fig.
    1.29
High-tech, fig. 3.32
History, 92, 94, 98, 100, 145, 153, 160. *See also* Time
    and the historic, 62, 138; figs. 3.24, 3.28
    memory and mnemonics, 99–100
    practice of, 1
    relationship between past, present, and future, 8, 77,
        109, 118; fig. 3.5
Hitchcock, Henry-Russell
    *The International Style* (with Johnson), 8
Hochschule für Gestaltung, Ulm, 8, 168(n.26)
Hoddesdon. *See* Congrès Internationaux d'Architecture
    Moderne
Holland, 8, 26, 35, 42, 134. *See also* Amsterdam; Rotterdam
Home, Stewart, 163, 198(n.3)
Housing, 24, 49, 52, 57–58, 63, 70, 130, 152
    estates and programs, 13, 16, 22, 43, 155

*grands ensembles,* 49, 52, 59–60; fig. 1.23
    Pruitt-Igoe, St. Louis, Missouri, 157
Howard, Ebenezer, 9. *See also* Garden cities
Howell, Gill and Bill, 27
Huizinga, Johan, 34–36, 44, 134
    *Homo Ludens,* 34
Hungary, 41
Hygiene and sanitation, 32, 60, 62

ICA. *See* Institute of Contemporary Arts
Ideology, 19, 27, 32, 41, 73, 96, 116, 134, 138, 148
Imaginist Bauhaus. *See* International Movement for an
    Imaginist Bauhaus
Immigrants and immigration, 26, 52, 60. *See also*
    Colonialism and imperialism; Ethnic minorities
Impressionism, 16
Independent Group, 9, 17, 20, 33, 35–36, 40–44, 148,
    174(n.78), 193(n.99)
    and architecture, 10, 27, 29
    and mass culture, 15, 17, 19, 29, 33–36, 40, 43; fig. 1.3
    and the Situationist International, 9–10, 15, 19, 41
India, 49, 108
Individualism, 7, 30, 92, 97, 122, 132, 135, 145, 151.
    *See also* Collectivism
Indochina, 52, 100
Indonesia, 42
Industrial design, 11, 34, 36, 40, 65, 172(nn.54,55); fig.
    0.3
Industrial painting, 37, 115, 160, 173(n.66); fig. 1.14
    *Cavern of Anti-Matter,* 37, 115; fig. 1.14
Industrial Revolution, 35
Infinity. *See* Sublime and infinite
Informality, 10, 168(n.33); figs. 1.17, 2.22. *See also*
    Architecture autre; Art autre; New brutalism
Information technology. *See* Technology
Information theory. *See* Communication
Institute of Contemporary Arts (ICA), London, 3, 9–10, 41,
    43, 132–133, 163, 173(n.75), 181(n.31)